MALTESE ISLANDS

DIVING GUIDE

This book is dedicated to the memory of Marc Moody (1937 - 1995). The man who taught me to dive, my dearest friend and probably the finest diver I ever met.

MILLER

Miller Distributors Limited

MALTESE ISLANDS

DIVING GUIDE

Texts and photographs
Ned Middleton

Editorial production
Valeria Manferto De Fabianis
Viviana Valmacco

Graphic design
Patrizia Balocco Lovisetti
Andrea Russo

Illustrations of the dives
Cristina Franco

Biological files
Texts
Angelo Mojetta

Illustrations
Alessandra Arnoletti
Monica Falcone
Sabrina Moscatelli
Patrizia Pavanello

Translation of biological files
Studio Traduzioni Vecchia, Milan

Contents

This edition published by Miller Distributors Limited
Miller House, Tarxien Road, Airport Way, Luqa Malta,
tel. (00356+) 66 44 88, fax (00356+) 67 67 99
P.O.Box 25, Malta International Airport, LQA 05

ISBN 88-8095-271-4

Printed in Italy by Milanostampa (Cuneo)in June 1997
Colour separation by Cliché Offset (Milano)

1 Underwater cavities are an important feature of the seabeds of the Maltese islands: they contain the fauna typical of Mediterranean underwater caves.

2-3 An intricate interlacing of plants and invertebrates covers a rock in the open water: the gaudy colours of the orange and yellow sponges predominate. Feeding on them is a dense group of long-spined sea urchins (Centrostephanus longispinus).

CHANNEL
26
28
COMINOTTO
Blue Lagoon
COMINO
27
SOUTH COMINO CHANNEL
4
3
1
2
Marfa Ridge
Mellieha Bay
5
St. Paul's Bay
12
MEDITERRANEAN
SEA
Golden Bay
Gnejna Bay
MALTA
Marsamxett Harbour
7
VALLETTA
6
Grand Harbour
RABAT
ZURRIEQ
8
Delimara
Marsaxlokk Bay
9
11
10

A

A - The contrasting colours are one of the most pleasant sights that the archipelago of Malta offers its visitors.

B - Malta from the air. The tongues of sea that creep in among the rocks are an enticing invitation to dive in.

B

INTRODUCTION

C - Numerous groups of saddled seabreams gather outside the caves of Comino, in search of hand-outs from divers.

D - The presence of numerous sponges indicates the passage of currents transporting organic material which is intercepted by the intricate network of channels that run through the bodies of these primitive invertebrates.

As a country, Malta comprises the islands - Malta, Gozo and Comino - plus the smaller islands such as Cominotto and Filfla. They are made of yellow limestone and, needless to say, this forms the main building material throughout the country. At the end of a clear and beautiful day when the sun is setting and the horizon becomes a deep red colour, the buildings that face the sunset suddenly begin to shine like buildings of gold.

Within these pages I have compiled what many people consider to be the most outstanding dive sites to be found in this beautiful Mediterranean country. I soon realised, however, that it became very confusing every time I used the word "Malta" - was it a reference to the country or to the single and largest island of Malta itself? To avoid such confusion I decided to call this book *Maltese Islands - Diving Guide* and any reference to Malta is, therefore, a reference to the largest of the islands mentioned.

Being centrally placed in the Mediterranean Sea, this country was always regarded as strategically important - both from trading and military viewpoints. This was especially so during World War II when the battle for Malta - one of the epic struggles of the entire war - was won by the bravery and determination of the Maltese people themselves.

This bravery was immediately recognised by King George VI to the extent that he bestowed Britain's highest civilian award for bravery on the people of Malta: the George Cross, which can be seen today on the Maltese flag.

From a military viewpoint, however, modern technology soon rendered Malta - just like the famous Rock of Gibraltar - as obsolete. Consequently, the only invaders today are tourists and almost all of these come to enjoy the Marine Environment in one way or another. Whether their pleasures stem from above or below the surface, they are never disappointed with what they find. Any country that is entirely surrounded by the sea cannot help but have evolved from rich maritime traditions and history -

C

D

none more so than the Maltese Islands where, many thousands of years ago, the very first settlers had to cross the Mediterranean Sea and discover the islands before making them their home. The islands historical connections with Great Britain have resulted in English being officially regarded as Malta's second language but other European languages are widely spoken.

A BRIEF HISTORY OF MALTA

The Maltese Archipelago comprises the islands of Malta, Gozo, Comino, Cominotto and Filfla. As with any country surrounded by the sea, Malta is steeped in maritime history and every single facet of that history could prove to be of great interest to the visiting diver. The first people to settle on Malta probably came from Sicily about 5000 BC and many prehistoric sites dating from that time still exist today including the magnificent temples of Tarxien which lay buried for thousands of years until discovered in 1913.
By 900 BC, the Phoenicians had established a large trading empire which dominated the entire region and Malta's strategic location was recognised and coveted.
The many battles for her possession would now last for several centuries. As soon as the Roman Empire began to expand southwards, a clash with the Phoenicians was inevitable. These were the Punic Wars during which the Phoenicians were defeated and Malta invaded in 218 BC.
In AD 60 St. Paul and St. Luke were shipwrecked in the area known today as St. Paul's Bay. St. Paul remained in Malta and continued his holy work and the miracles he was supposed to have performed became so popular that even the Roman Governor became converted to Christianity and later went on to become Malta's first Bishop. Malta has steadfastly remained a Christian country from that day.
As the Roman Empire began to decline, Arabs became the new rulers in AD 870 and many Maltese were sold into slavery, two centuries of Arab rule inevitably left an indelible impression and none more so than the country's official language - called Malti, which is more like Arabic than any other. Eventually the Arabs generally lost interest and a nobleman called Count Roger, who owned

A

B

C

D

A - Seabeds teeming with life can be glimpsed in these crystal clear waters.

B - The surprising landscape of the Maltese coast, a series of inlets, caves and crevices, frames the crystalline sea crossed by ships and boats of all sizes.

C - The Blue Lagoon separates the west coast of Comino, the small island between Malta and Gozo, from Cominotto, its tiny appendage. This Mediterranean paradise is usually a point of transit, although you can stay here as well.

D - Gozo, the second largest island after Malta, is mostly rocks plunging steeply into the blue waters.

E - The most beautiful sandy area on the coast of Gozo is Ramla Beach, on the northeast side of the island.

F - The west coast of Gozo is home to the so-called Azure Window, a natural rock arch that joins a large rock to the mainland.

G - It is not uncommon to see structures like this one, perched on the rocky shores of the Maltese archipelago.

E

F

G

large tracts of Southern Italy, decided to increase his strategic position by controlling Malta.
In 1090 Malta duly became part of the Kingdom of Sicily.
The Christian Church was now encouraged and began to flourish and Malta became a key staging post for the Crusades.
There now followed a succession of feudal lords interested in Malta only as a source of revenue since they imposed exorbitant tax demands on the population.
During the 15th Century Spain had taken a special interest in Malta but by the 16th Century, however, they had become preoccupied with the vast riches available in the New World.
In the 10th and 11th centuries certain brotherhoods of monks chose an order of life in order to live by various codes. Several created their own orders of Knights to defend their particular faith and many of these fought together in the Crusades - in defence of the Christian Religion.
In the 11th century, a hospice was set up in Jerusalem for Christian pilgrims and *The Order of the Hospital of St. John of Jerusalem* was founded.
The calling of the brothers was principally to care for the sick - but this was later extended to include military duties in order to protect themselves, and those in their care.
In 1187 they were driven from the Holy Land and, over the Centuries, were also driven from Acre, Cyprus, and Rhodes in 1522. They went first to Sicily and then to Italy seeking refuge, but Southern Europe's loyalties at this time were divided between different warring factions.
Eventually, in 1530, they reluctantly agreed to take over Malta in exchange for a payment of one "falcon" per year. Then, as now, falcons were much prized sporting birds and this gesture coined the term "The Maltese Falcon" - though the film of the same name has no connection whatsoever. Soon after their arrival, the Turks decided to renew their own attacks on the islands. The North African

A

Barbary Pirates under command of Dragut also plundered the country. In 1546 they completly devastated Gozo and in 1551 took thousands of Gozitans as slaves. Eventually Dragut joined forces with the Turks and the future of the Maltese Islands was very bleak indeed.

The Grand Master at this time was called de la Valette and word reached him of a Turkish armada en route to Malta. The combined Turkish pirate fleet of 138 galleys and 38,000 men landed at Marsaxlokk on 19 May, 1565 and the Great Siege of Malta began. With only 600 Knights and 9,000 other troops, de la Valette conducted one of the most valiant

B

D

C

defences in history. Whilst Christian Europe awaited the outcome with baited breath, none responded to Malta's many cries for help!

Every citizen of Malta fought alongside the Knights in a fiercely defiant gesture and, despite their superiority in manpower and ammunition, the Turks were slowly worn down. At one critical point, even de la Valette - at the age of 72 - threw himself into the fray and fought hand to hand with the enemy. On 7 Sep 1565, help finally arrived from Sicily. Fooled into believing the fresh troops to be far more numerous than they actually were, the remnants of the Turkish forces sailed away never

A - Senglea faces Grand Harbour, right across from Valletta. The urban conglomerate of Cospicua, Vittoriosa and Senglea is known as the Three Cities.

B - An aerial view of Valletta shows the cupola of the church of Our Lady of Mount Carmel and the pointed bell tower of the Anglican St. Paul's cathedral.

C - Typical Maltese houses show off their characteristic Arabic-style bow windows, often completed with brightly coloured shutters.

D - The sumptuous interior of St. John's Co-Cathedral, built between 1573 and 1577, is the result of the express wish of the Grand Masters of the Order of St. John.

to return - over two thirds of the enemy forces had been lost.
The reconstruction of the islands' fortifications and defences now became critical and several European governments decided to be far more generous in terms of cash than they had been when manpower was required. Even the Pope's own architect was appointed to oversee the entire rebuilding programme which included plans for a brand new city to be sited between the two long harbours on the Sceberras peninsula and thus Valletta (using the Italian spelling of his name) was born .
The Knights continued to rule Malta for over two hundred years during which time trade prospered. The building boom started in 1565, continued for many years with the Maltese architect Gerolamo Cassar being responsible for much of Valletta as it is today. By the 18th century, however, things began to change.
Larger ships and new trading routes meant that many Mediterranean merchants were looking to far off lands in order to establish richer trading links. That, coupled with the downfall of the aristocracy in France as a result of the French Revolution quickly deprived Malta of much of its support and revenue.
In 1798, Napoleon Bonaparte secretly fitted out a large force of troops and a mighty Armada of ships with the intention of crossing the Mediterranean Sea, invading Egypt and marching into India at the head of his *Army of the Orient*. By coincidence, on May 2nd of that year, the newly promoted Rear Admiral, Sir Horatio Nelson, was ordered *"to proceed with three battleships and five small craft to Toulon to report on the preparations and destination of a powerful French fleet."* Nelson relished this opportunity and immediately sailed. This was his first independent command and he was about to be pitted against the most brilliant military genius of

G

H

E

F

E - The Palace of the Grand Masters in Valletta is only a little older than the co-cathedral. Inside are rooms, corridors, and courtyards and like this one, known as the Prince of Wales corridor.

F - Upon the death of its knights, the Order took possession of their weapons and armor, which were made available to anyone who needed them.

G - Vittoriosa extends into Grand Harbour, between Dockyard Creek and Kalkara Creek. The city, located in a strategic position that has affected its development, is of Phoenician origin.

H - The sturdy bastions that surround Vittoriosa were put to a harsh test during the Turkish siege of 1565.

his age - Napoleon Bonaparte. After several weeks of fruitlessly searching the Mediterranean - during which time he was given much inaccurate information - Nelson was informed that the French had successfully captured Malta - which they had - but that they had already sailed eastwards which was not true. Nelson duly set course for Alexandria but when he arrived the French were still at Malta.
By now the Knights had grown used to a lavish life-style and decided against armed resistance. They surrendered to Napoleon who promptly took possession of *"the strongest place in Europe"* without hardly a shot being fired.

B

A

C

He then helped himself to the accumulated wealth of seven centuries of riches comprising the "Principal Treasures of the Knights of Malta", part of which included 12 life-size, solid silver statues of the Apostles - much needed as a financial base for his *Army of the Orient.*
Napoleon then sailed for Alexandria on June 19th, and in so doing created the most curious situation. Nelson was chasing the French and the French were following him. The two fleets even passed close to each other at night - the French lumbering slowly towards Crete and the British racing for Alexandria. This became one of the most decisive moments of world history.
Had Nelson been aware of the whereabouts of the enemy fleet, he would have turned to face them, and the result of such an encounter in the open sea would have been certain. Though superior on paper, the French sailor had little or no training in gunnery or manoeuvre. Napoleon and his army would have found a watery grave and there would have been no Waterloo seventeen years later!
When Nelson arrived, the seas were empty but, still believing the French to be ahead of him, he immediately set off seeking out every possible landing site. As for the inhabitants of Alexandria - they could hardly believe their eyes. As British sails disappeared over the eastern horizon, French sails appeared from the west. Napoleon, still unaware of Nelson's presence, wasted no time in disembarking and preparing for battle. By July 5th, he had stormed Alexandria and two weeks later he routed the main Egyptian Army and added Egypt to his long list of conquests.
In the meantime, Nelson conducted a long, thorough but and fruitless search and eventually returned to Sicily and for much needed supplies before departing for Alexandria once again. On August 1st, the French

A - Marsaxlokk, or "port of the warm wind," is a picturesque fishing village on the southeast coast of Malta. In the past, it was the preferred route for invaders of the island, but today it is a tranquil place popular with both foreign and local tourists.

B - Catholicism is the officially aknowledged religion in Malta and is widespread all aver the islands which are rich in beautiful churches and cathedrals.

C - The coasts are scattered with sunny seaside villages. Despite the fact that Malta is an island, fishing is not one of its primary economic activities.

D - In addition to its Neolithic and Bronze Age remains, Birzebbuga also has a massive fortress.

E - Hagar Quim is one of the most important prehistoric sanctuaries on the Maltese archipelago. It is actually three unrelated temples dating back to about 3000 BC.

F - In this aerial image of Mdina, the long walls that gave the city its Arabic name are clearly visible.

G - In the centre of Mgarr, a small village in northwest Malta, there is a modern church with cupola.

fleet were sighted in Aboukir Bay just fifteen miles east of Alexandria. Sixteen French ships were at anchor in a defensive straight line. Thirteen were ships of the line - bigger and more heavily gunned than anything the British had and three frigates. Admiral Brueys' giant flagship *L'Orient* was in the centre but he was confident there would be no battle that day - it was too late in the afternoon. Many of the French seamen were ashore and the decks of their ships were encumbered with stores and booty. Brueys was relying on the inferior British force not knowing of these problems and putting off battle until at least the morrow. Nelson, however, did not even pause. He immediately saw the strength and weaknesses of Brueys' defensive positioning and realised that if there was sufficient room for each enemy ship to swing at anchor, then there was sufficient depth to allow him to attack the enemy from both sides at once - a tactic that would stretch the depleted French crews even further.
It was the bloodiest of battles during which the British never lost the initiative. By 9 pm, the *Orient* was on fire and the flames spread quickly. Nelson, although injured in the battle, gave the order to rescue survivors. At 9:45 pm, the *Orient* blew up with a terrifying explosion that lifted her from the water. Shock waves were felt a full 10 miles away! This single event demoralised the French and took the momentum out of the battle.
At first light, the magnitude of the victory became apparent. The French had been truly routed and the British had lost not a single vessel. Two enemy battleships were sunk, six had struck their colours (surrendered) and three others were at the mercy of the British. Captain Villeneuve and his frigates were totally unscathed although one of these then ran aground and was fired. Only two capital ships, the *Guillaume Tell* and *Généreux* were able to escape and they were quickly joined by the frigates.

D

E

F

G

A - Massive Arabic style buildings, particularly walls and fortresses such as this, pearl the coasts and the inland of the Maltese archipelago.

B - The sanctuary of Ta' Pinu on the island of Gozo is the most popular place of pilgrimage on the archipelago. The neo-Romanesque limestone structure is dedicated to the cult of the Virgin.

C - The cathedral of Victoria is a simple baroque structure which Gafà built on the foundations of a Roman temple and a medieval church.

D - In the past it was believed that a giantess built the two megalithic temples near Xaghra. This is reflected in the name of Gozo's main attraction: Ggantija.

A

B

The *Guillaume Tell* was later captured off Malta, refitted and renamed *HMS Malta*. Villeneuve went on to command the Joint French Spanish Fleet at the Battle of Trafalgar in 1805.
Most importantly, as far as Malta is concerned, however, was that the Principal Treasures of the Knights of Malta had been stored on board the *Orient* and were now at the bottom of sea in a remote place called Aboukir Bay - the target for many treasure hunting expeditions. Some insist that the twelve life-size solid silver statues of the Apostles could not have totally disintegrated in spite of the terrible force of the explosion that blew apart *L'Orient*. Maybe so, but there is now considerable doubt as to whether the Treasures were still on board when the ship met her end. Perhaps they are still at the bottom of the bay, perhaps they were broken into small pieces and had already been taken ashore, perhaps they were shipped back to France, perhaps they lie hidden in Egypt.

One thing is certain, should they ever be found, in whole or in part, there is only one rightful owner - the people of Malta from whom they were taken.
Napoleon succeeded where many others had failed and ousted the Knights of St. John after a 268-year reign in Malta. They never returned. Six days later, Napoleon also departed but the French continued to rule Malta for the next two years.
The Order of St. John of Jerusalem is now based in Rome, undertaking mainly charitable work - a much different role from the present day Roman Catholic "Sovereign Military Order of Malta" - which still retains similar robes and insignia. The ideals of the hospitallers, however, still flourish in many European countries in the form of The St. John's Ambulance Brigade.
At midnight, on 10th June 1940, Italy declared war and entered World War II on the side of Germany. At this point, the entire Mediterranean coastline was either allied or neutral with British and French fleets unchallenged. On the 11th June, Admiral Cunningham's reaction to Italy was to take his battle fleet to sea and sweep the central Mediterranean - an initiative that was never surrendered throughout the war.
In these pre-jet engine and pre-

C

D

guided missile days of warfare, Malta occupied a vitally strategic position right in the centre of the Mediterranean. With battles raging - on land and in the air all around, her position was never more important. Consequently, the German Fliegerkorps repeatedly bombed the island destroying dockyards ships and submarines,

airfields, aircraft and runways, and anything else found in their sights - thus severely reducing the island's offensive capabilities. Malta's heroic response to this period of conflict is a matter of historical record but in the early days of the war things were very bleak, indeed. Resources were scarce on every front and, although Malta was given the means to defend herself, there were simply never enough aircraft, ships or submarines - or even anti-aircraft guns. Force K - the Mediterranean striking force of cruisers and destroyers - was based in Malta. A submarine base was established at Manoel Island and small numbers of Spitfires and Hurricane aircraft were periodically flown in from Aircraft Carriers to replace losses. Wellington bombers were also based in Malta for a time but, with their long range capabilities much needed elsewhere, were eventually replaced by the smaller Blenheim bombers.
Altogether, these meagre resources brought about successes wholly disproportionate to their size. During the first months of 1941, Fleet Air Arm Swordfish sank three ships totalling 16,000 tons, Wellington bombers attacked enemy ports and further bombing raids hammered Tripoli in a series of night attacks. In December 1941, HMS *Maori* (now a very popular dive site) was one of four destroyers responsible for sinking two enemy cruisers without loss. Even the Malta Flotilla of small "S" class submarines sank a cruiser and a submarine before creating havoc with Rommel's supply lines.
The response of the Axis Powers was an attempt to bomb Malta into submission and in that aim alone they were defeated by the proud and defiant people of Malta themselves who simply continued to fight back with every means at their disposal. These people stood, almost alone, against the most concentrated bombing in the history of warfare. The Axis powers repeatedly tried to break their spirit to the admiration of enemy and foe alike. On 15th April, 1942, a very proud King George VI bestowed on the people of Malta the George Cross - his country's highest civilian award for bravery.

G

E

F

E - A lovely image of the Blue Lagoon shows the contrast between the shallow turquoise water and the nearly bare land that surrounds it.

F - This photo shows a stretch of the rocky coast around Comino, an ideal place for a pleasant boat excursion.

G - The Tower of Santa Marija, or Fort St. Mary, is located southwest of Comino, although it no longer plays the defensive role it once did, when the entire archipelago was under constant Turkish attack.

The post war years have seen improvements in Malta's economic and social well being. Following Independence from Britain in 1964, Malta became a Republic in 1979 and for the first time in its thousands of years chequered history became truly in charge of its own destiny. Malta is a neutral state, not forming part of any military block with a declared policy of maintaining and improving relations with its neighbours. The Malta Labour Party under the leadership of Dr.A.Sant was returned to government in October 1996 with a mandate of strenghtening relations with the E.U. but stopping short of membership.

DIVING THE MALTESE ISLANDS

There are many more dive sites in addition to those detailed within this book. So much so that the country's reputation for outstanding diving has made it one of the Mediterranean's most popular destinations for Scuba Divers. In fact there is now such an abundance of dive operators that visitors - many of whom never even considered diving prior to their arrival - suddenly decide to take up the sport. Others use the opportunity to gain further qualifications although the majority simply wish to enjoy the first class diving to be found. I am often asked *"What precisely has this country to offer the diver?"* and my response is always the same - *"Malta has something for everyone - whatever their experience or grade!"* Overall, it is a country of spectacular coastline which comprises steep, vertical cliffs within which are some of the most fantastic arches, caves, tunnels and other spectacular rock formations. Many of these stretch down well below the surface of the sea and are, therefore, only visited by divers. Whether deep or relatively shallow, they add phenomenal excitement to the diving.

Add to this the natural characteristics of the Mediterranean Sea - warm climate, clear blue waters - with virtually no tides or currents, and a prolific marine life plus the further ingredients of all dives being easily accessible and a total absence of the run-off created by excessive rainfall on green vegetation and fertilisers (which, in other countries, creates poor visibility and does much harm to the underwater environment) and you have clean, clear waters with underwater visibility of 50 metres at a depth of 20-30 metres.

As far as scuba diving is concerned, the Maltese Government have considered the safety of all divers and certain rules have been imposed to offer what protection is possible. Permission to use scuba equipment must be obtained from the Department of Health and the diver must be in possession of a valid, in-date medical certificate and a photograph - all of which is easily arranged through any of the dive centres - although you should bring your own medical certificate if you possess one.

Before being permitted to take charge of and lead a dive, however, a Maltese Instructor's "C Card" must be obtained.

The Government also seek to protect the marine environment

A

B

C

A - A group of ornate wrasses swims on the summit of a rock. This is a species similar to tropical fish and is one of the most colourful inhabitants of the Mediterranean.

B - A diver enters a dark cave. Caves are generally stable environments, and in deeper areas the only light is often that brought in by divers.

C - A Greek bathing sponge (Spongia officianalis) *grows on the summit of a rock. Its globular appearance and the absolute absence of movement make it hard to believe that it's an animal.*

D - Cave walls are almost always completely bare. The lack of light and low hydrodynamics make it almost impossible for plants and invertebrates to colonize them.

E - Cave diving requires special safety measures and should only be done in an area where the light from the entry is always visible.

F - The bearded fire worm (Hermodice carunculata) *is a worm typical of the southern Mediterranean.*

which is an important source of food and employment. Spearfishing is, therefore, tightly controlled and absolutely forbidden without a license - but then, real divers never use spear guns! Finally, any finds of an historic or cultural nature are also protected by law and, although even the visiting diver has a duty to record and report any such finds, the local diving instructor is always available to assist with such matters. To get the most out of diving in Malta, the use of a local guide is essential - you will not see the best without being pointed in the right direction. Diving is generally available all year round although some of the dive centres are only seasonal - so check prior to leaving!

D

Equipment is available for hire with packages provided for the experienced diver and novice alike.

Climate: Hottest: July/August - Sea 24-26ºC. Air 26-30 degrees C. Coolest: January/February - Sea 13-18 degrees C. Air 15-25 degrees C.
Chart Nos: 2537, 2538, 974 & 195.
Currency: Maltese Lira (often called Pound)-
Electricity: 240 volts.
Time: GMT + 1 Hr (Summer time is GMT + 2 hrs)

E

F

WRECK DIVING

There are a limited number of wrecks in Malta - including ships, submarine and aircraft and some of these are detailed within this book. For example, the 40 metres harbour tug *Rozi* is probably one of the most photogenic wrecks to be found anywhere in the world as it sits proudly upright and intact at a depth of 36 metres. Others include casualties of WW2 - *HMS Maori*, the *Carolita Barge* and a *Blenheim Bomber*.
There are plans to deliberately add more wrecks in the very near future (very soon indeed) with a large vehicle ferry to be sunk off the south west corner of Gozo in order to suit divers. There are people who strongly disagree with this policy, without considering that these ships have an important impact on the marine environment. Throughout the world, similar sites are attracting species of fish not previously seen for many years - and any improvement in this area has to be a good thing!
In addition, there are ancient wrecks and, whether already discovered or not, they are all protected by law - thus avoiding the tragic mistake of so many countries that have failed to protect their underwater treasures from those visiting divers who believe a personal trophy cabinet full of ancient and historical artefacts is far more important than allowing a country to place another small piece of knowledge and learning into the complex jigsaw of its maritime traditions and history.
Within recent years Gozo has developed as an all-year-round diving destination - even in January the climate is similar to an English summer.
In addition, underwater visibility

A

B

C

remains constantly very good - and there is nowhere in Gozo more than 20 minutes from a suitable access point into the sea. Gozo itself is an island of immense charm largely unspoilt by the ravages of mass tourism. Only 30 minutes by ferry from Cirkewwa, there is a marked contrast with the slightly faster pace of Malta.
Here the people of Gozo (Gozitans) are very proud of their separate identity and individual heritage - some would even claim to be independent altogether!
The difference between the two islands is part of the overall magnetic attraction of the entire country.

E

D

F

A - Here, a diver examines the propeller of a Blenheim *bomber sunk near Malta.*

B - Quite often it takes several dives in order to get a clear picture of a wreck.

C - When wrecks are almost completely intact, like the tugboat Rozi, *they become even stranger and more intriguing.*

D - Here, picarels and bogues swim above a sunken hull.

E - An exploration of sunken hulls requires precautions: it is important to always stay in contact with the exit.

F - Fine sediments are deposited within these wrecks and can rapidly cloud the water. Special techniques and training are recommended for anyone

G - A shy conger eel peeps out from behind the hull of a wreck.

G

FLORA AND FAUNA

A - Golden zoanthids (Parazoanthus axinellae) *form vast carpets on shaded rocks exposed to the currents.*

B - The saddled seabream (Oblada melanura) *is a typical gregarious fish. It can be distinguished from other seabreams by its elongated body and the unmistakable "eye" on the caudal peduncle.*

C - Combers (Serranus cabrilla), *which live among the rocks on the sea floor, are quite territorial. Combers are one of the few species of Mediterranean fish that can develop both male and female sex organs at the same time.*

As for the largest creatures, very few sharks are seen in and around Malta. On one dive we did see what we thought was a shark but its features were not clear due to it being right on the very edge of our limit of visibility. It was certainly a fairly large fish but was not behaving like any shark I have ever seen - it was in too much of a hurry! On reflection, I am certain that we saw a swordfish which, although common, is rarely seen by divers.
Encounters with dolphins, however, though still not too common, are more frequent.
In recent years, two bottlenose dolphins were actually rescued and placed in the Inland Sea - a small inlet not far from the Azure Window, that is only accessible through a cave-like entrance in the surrounding rock face. Here, they were regularly fed until such time as they were ready to return to the open sea.
Mediterranean groupers can be seen on most dives and vary in size from minute to quite large.
A species of parrotfish, that appears to be a refugee from the Red Sea, has become particularly well established, and outside the entrance to Comino Caves, the diver will encounter thousands of saddled seabream expecting to be hand-fed.
A similar phenomena with damselfish occurs on top of the Rozi's funnel - in sufficient number to obscure the diver completely from view.
My own experience has been to witness a significant increase in the numbers of fish throughout much of the Mediterranean in recent years. This may be partly due to a wider understanding of conservation, but credit must also be given to local diving industries who seek to protect the smaller species in order to

C

D

A

B

D - A hermit crab (Dardanus arrosor) *carries along its cargo of sea anemones* (Calliactis parasitica). *The quantity of sea anemones is important is sexual competition, and the hermit crab with the most sea anemones on its shell has the most probability of finding a mate.*

E - The shift from light to shadow causes great changes on the sea floor: a meadow of Neptune grass borders a shady area covered with encrusting sponges.

provide additional interest for visiting divers. The result is that the numbers of fish - be they of solitary or of a shoaling nature, are certainly increasing.
There is very little coral to be found throughout the Mediterranean Sea but that found in Malta, both hard and soft, is also on the increase. The brightly coloured *Astroides calycularis* can now be found in the shade of many arches, reefs and caves where Virgin lace and other harder corals are also found.
In the open sea, however, the rocks are covered with a mat of different types of plant-life, sponges and tunicates - all of which combine to provide perfect cover for those creatures that like to sit and wait for their prey to pass by. Here are the octopus and scorpionfish - but they are only seen by those divers who dive with their eyes open!
By comparison, on the sandy seabeds of the valleys and gullies that stretch a short distance inland, the diver can find the more exciting and even rarer species. At Il-Kantra we encountered Mediterranean plaice, John Dory, star-gazer, cuttlefish and a splendid example of flying gurnard.

E

F

G

F - A large rock rises from the meadow of Neptune grass; its upper portion is covered by brown algae, while orange patches of encrusting sponges grow on its shaded sides.

G - During the night the small Ilia nucleus crab moves along the rocks, while by day it lives buried in the sediments or hidden in cracks.

ENVIRONMENTAL HAZARDS

Diving in and around the Maltese Islands is trouble free for divers of all levels of experience. During a time of full moon the diver may encounter currents. Although relatively rare, such currents impose such hard finning as to become "out of breath." With so much to see - quite often at depths more than 30 metres, it is also quite easy to stay down for too long with all the resultant problems of air consumption and decompression. Keep your diving instructor in sight at all times - and stay with him!
I have already mentioned the importance of becoming familiar with a site during the day before contemplating a night dive. With all the underwater arches, caves and swim-throughs it is very easy to become disorientated at night time and enter a cave or swim-through and become lost.

A - A dive in a cave always requires a reliable flashlight, and you should never lose sight of the exit.

B - When diving in caves, it is always wise to employ special safety measures and use an expert guide who knows the zone.

C - When swimming under vaults, the air released by your tank may remain trapped and damage the organisms attached to the rock. Often it only requires a bit of care to avoid this.

C

A

B

DANGEROUS CREATURES

Throughout my own extensive experience of diving the length and breadth of the Mediterranean I have never seen a shark of any species in that sea, but I do feel that these dangerous creatures should be included, simply because they do exist. Should the diver encounter a shark, all that is required is to respect the master in his own home. By all means watch, observe - even take a few photographs. Any attempt to suddenly surface will put the diver - not the shark - at a disadvantage. Of course no respectable diver will have been spear-fishing but, if you have, the catch must be jettisoned immediately and you must get away from it as quickly as possible. The creatures which are really potentially dangerous are: scorpionfish, bristleworms (or fireworms), long-spined sea urchins and stingrays. None of these will actually attack a diver and any injury is received, therefore, either through accident or ignorance.
The scorpionfish is very common -

D - The red scorpionfish (Scorpaena scrofa) *is quite mimetic in ambient light. The spines of its dorsal fin and the operculum exude a poisonous substance that causes swelling and great pain.*

E - The bearded fire worm has a body covered by very fine stinging bristles. The best way to avoid it is by keeping a neutral position and staying off the sea floor.

F - Swimming at the water's surface in a neutral position is the best way to enjoy your dive. You'll save on air and avoid contact with organisms attached to the sea floor.

though often not seen. Its method of hunting is to settle down and blend with the back-ground. Here it will remain motionless until the prey swims close enough to be caught.
If approached by a diver, however, the fish will wait until the last possible moment before moving away but, should contact occur, the spines of this fish pump poison into the offending object - which could be a human hand!
The bristleworm is so often overlooked as a dangerous creature. On both sides of the entire length of the body are white bristles that are in fact stinging cells. If left alone, this creature presents no harm to the diver and is easily photographed. It should not, however, be handled - not even when wearing gloves - otherwise the stinging cells can detach and become embedded within the glove only to sting the owner at a later time. The result of any personal contact with these creatures should be regarded as serious but not life-threatening.
The long-spined sea urchin, however, presents a different problem that is usually confined to inexperienced divers. Descending a little too hard onto the seabed, divers have been known to land feet first onto sea urchins and get a number of spines embedded in the heel. More commonly, however, divers do tend to grasp rocks without checking behind them and then get spines in the hand.
The stingray poses the least problem of all, simply because it normally swims away whenever it sees a diver. The fish selects a suitable site on the seabed and digs itself into the sand until only its eyes protrude. The so-called "sting" is actually a sharp blade right at the end of its tail. Generally speaking, the only harm to human beings has been when the smaller stingrays have been inadvertently stepped on by people wading in shallow water. Stingrays are not to be found amongst either the wrecks or the rocks of the Maltese Islands.

D

E

F

THE TUGBOAT ROZI

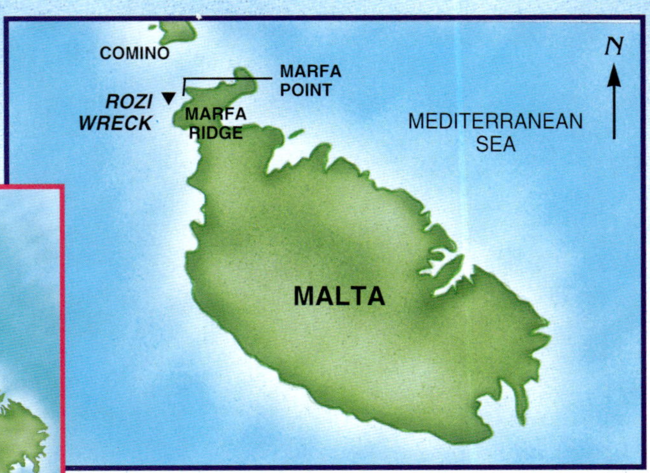

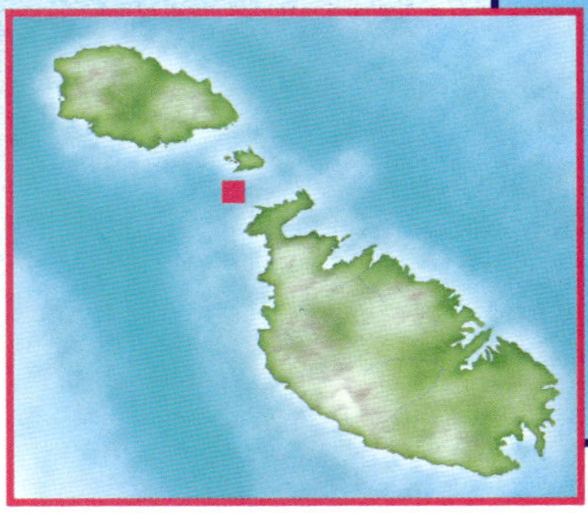

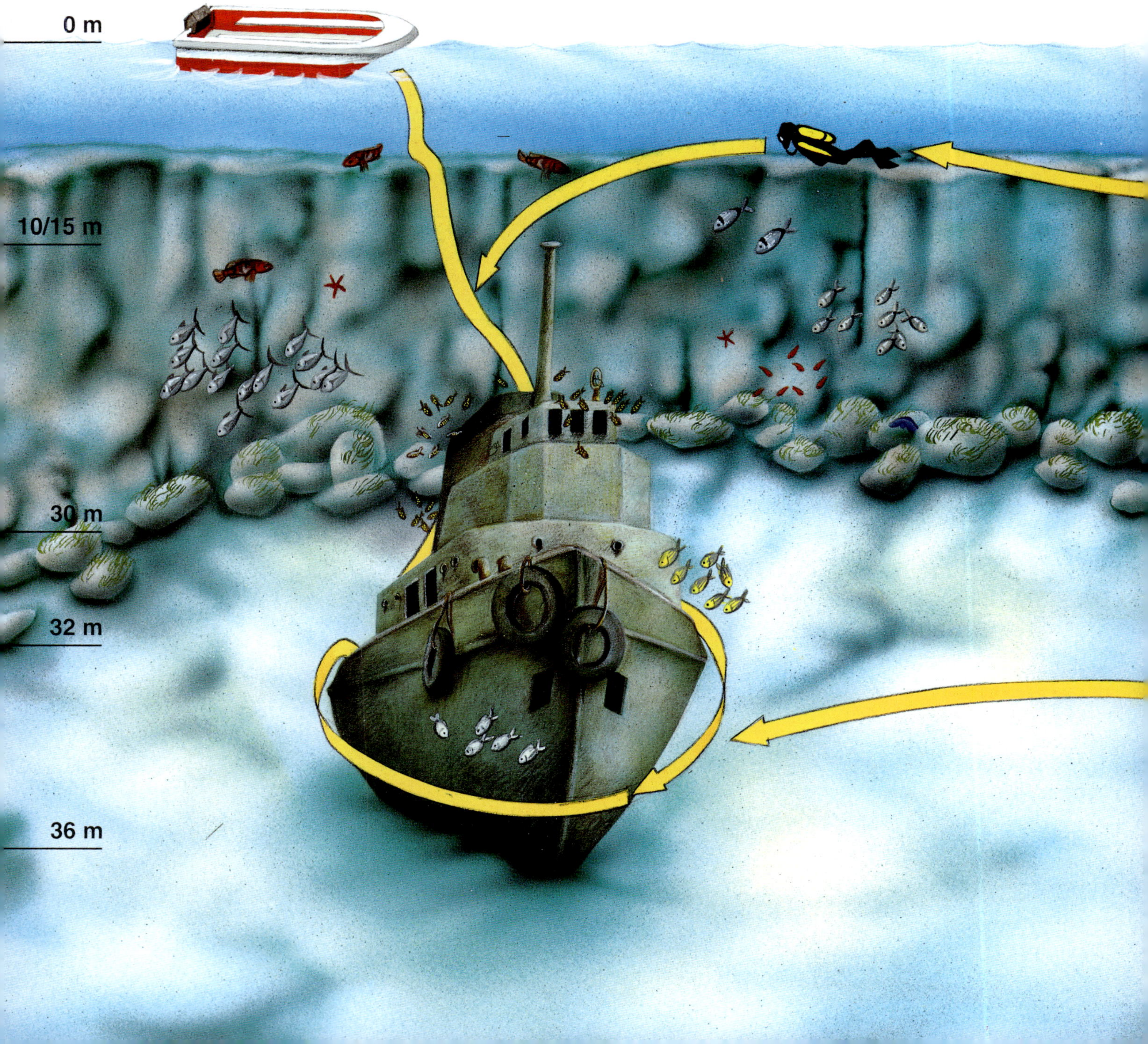

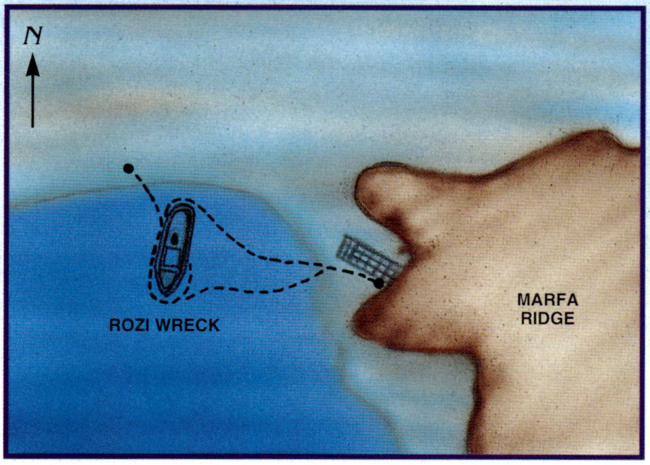
N
ROZI WRECK
MARFA
RIDGE

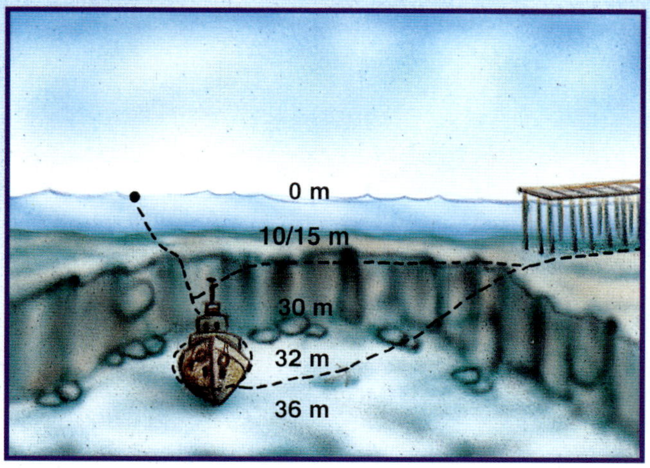
0 m
10/15 m
30 m
32 m
36 m

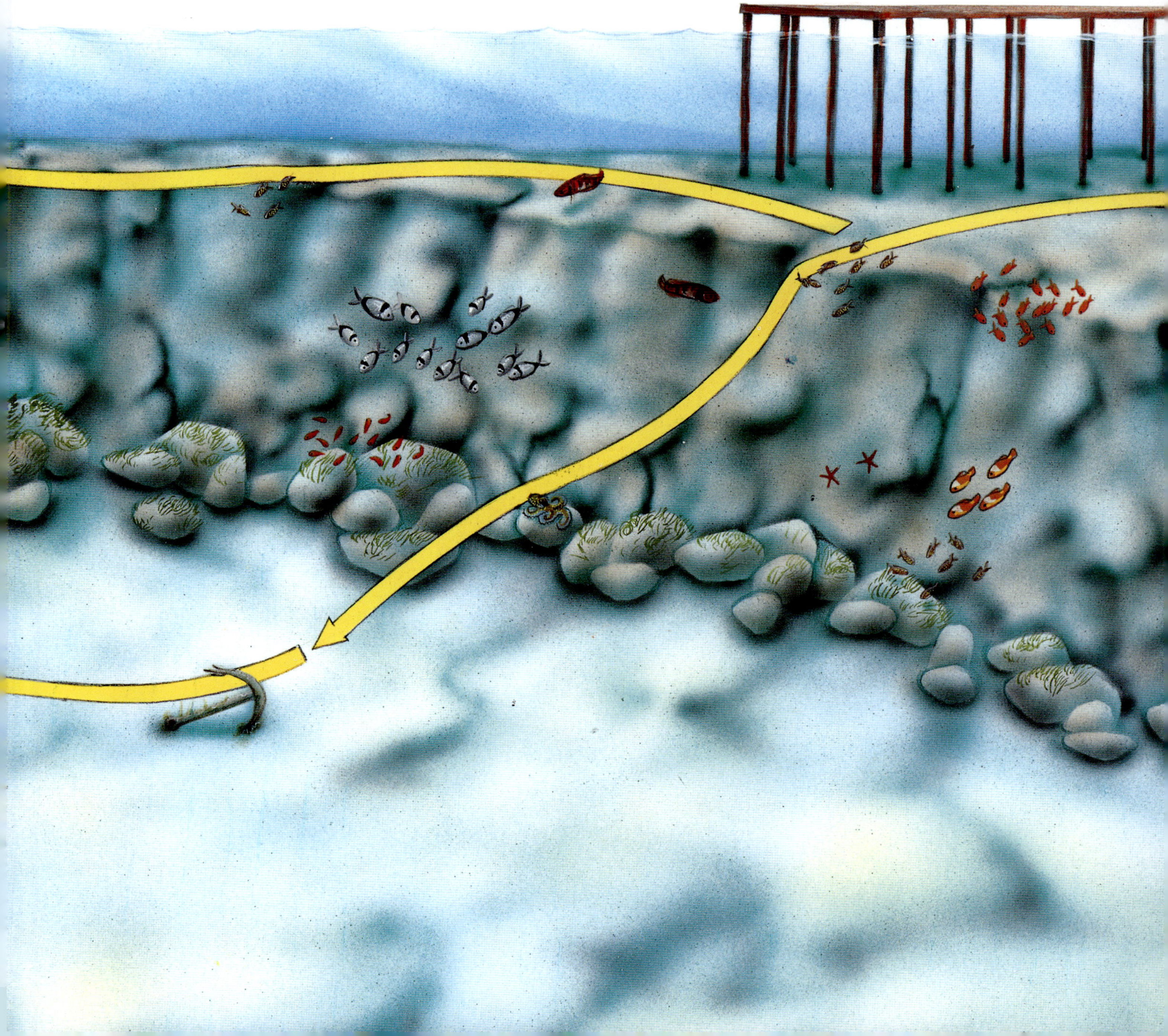

LOCATION

Just north of Marfa Point on the north-west corner of the island of Malta, at the opposite side of the headland to where the Malta-Gozo ferries dock, is an old metal jetty. Approximately 120-150 metres from the end of this jetty, on a bearing of 280 degrees Magnetic, lies the tugboat *Rozi*. This is such a popular dive that many visitors regard a visit to the *Rozi* as the high point of their stay.
At varying distances of 80-120 metres from the wreck, there is a steep sided cliff 10-15 metres deep at the top and 36 metres deep at its base. Dive boats generally prefer the secure anchorage provided above this ledge, leaving the diver with a short swim south towards the wreck. The wreck is also easily found from the shore.
The relevant depths are 30 metres to the top of the wreck, 32 metres at deck level and 36 metres to the seabed. This dive site is ideal for divers of all levels of experience.

B

C

A - The bow of the Rozi *is still protected by large tires. The hull, in sailing position, can be visited in its entirety.*

B - The interior of the hull is in perfect condition, and you can enter from various openings, from which the doors have been removed for safety reasons.

C - The crew's bathrooms can be seen inside the wreck.

A

THE DIVE

The *Rozi* was a 40-metre harbour tug deliberately sunk in 1991 as an extra attraction for the operators of a glass-bottomed boat. Apart from the engines and propeller - which were removed prior to sinking - the *Rozi* is completely intact and sits upright on the seabed with all other fittings still in place. This is a fabulous dive site which has quickly become one of the most popular within the Maltese Islands - and it is easy to understand why.
Assuming the divers have arrived by boat, they should gather and proceed in a southerly direction until they reach the steep edge of the cliff. From here the stern of the *Rozi* is easily seen.
Many divers choose to cross over to the vessel in mid-water and deliberately avoid the deeper waters of the seabed in order to spend a greater time inspecting the superstructure where there is much to see and explore.
The bows are quite dramatic with large lorry tyres - once used as fenders - still in place. Beyond a short area of forward deck space they will then discover the wheelhouse. Here the doors have been removed so that it can be easily and safely entered.
Immediately astern of the wheelhouse is a narrow gap before the diver encounters the funnel. Here the damselfish (*Chromis chromis*) gather in their thousands and are often fed by divers who temporarily become lost to view as they feed them.
Below the wheelhouse and funnel are various doorways which once gave the crew access to the inside of the vessel. Today these are visited by divers who will even discover the heads (toilets) still in place. Further to the stern there is a large open deck space which was once the centre of all the hard work that is an essential part of all such vessels. A little to the west of the wreck, the diver is usually able to see the entire vessel.
The nearby reef contains an abundance of marine life but, understandably, this is so often overlooked with the divers being so intent on getting to the wreck. At the base of the cliff are large boulders providing adequate accommodation for groupers and even the occasional conger and moray eel. Above these are

plenty of octopus, seabreams, wrasses and damselfish.
Because the wreck is still relatively new, marine life is still in its infancy, but this will continue to increase as the vessel ages. Even so, there is still plenty to see and any diver standing on the funnel with a few bread crumbs will soon be lost to view as he is surrounded by damselfish. Other inhabitants include, two-banded seabreams, cardinal fish, rainbow wrasses, scorpionfish and the occasional angler fish is sometimes seen on the sand alongside.
Because the doors and hatches were removed prior to sinking, there is little chance of anyone becoming lost within the wreck, so very few difficulties can arise. It should always be remembered that this is a very exciting dive - especially for the first time visitor. In addition, one cannot inspect the entire wreck in a single dive. For these reasons some divers are, therefore, inclined to stay a little too long and this can lead to problems of decompression and/or a lack of sufficient air to complete the dive.

PHOTOGRAPHY

This small ocean- going tugboat sits upright and intact on the seabed and can only be described as an archetypal wreck - precisely what one would expect to see in a cartoon film about diving. To photograph the various fittings and details above and below the decks a 50mm lens is ideal. To capture the divers in and around the wreck a wider angle of around 24mm is required. As for the vessel itself, a 20mm lens - or even a wider "fisheye" is essential - though the latter may produce distorted images.
The *Rozi* is a wreck that requires many different visits before all the photographs have been taken.
A 20mm wide angle lens allows the photographer to get close to the subject and, at the same time, get all of the subject in the frame.
On a good day the photographer will be able to see the entire wreck but, because this cannot be fully lit, it should be used as a back-drop with a well-lit diver in the foreground. Whenever divers are in front of or alongside any wreck, they give the photograph that added dimension of scale.

D

E

F

D - The wreck of the Rozi *is one of the most popular diving sites in Malta. It is a 40 foot long tugboat which sank in 1991 on a seabed about 36 metres deep. The highest parts of the wreck come to 30 metres from the surface.*

E - The non-excessive depth makes it possible to take the time for a careful exploration. At the same time, the wreck is far enough away from the surface so that it is not exposed to the destructive effects of the tides.

F - Although the Rozi *sank only a few years ago, many marine organisms have colonized the wreck, and seabreams, scorpionfish, rainbow wrasses and cardinal fish swim about.*

MARFA POINT

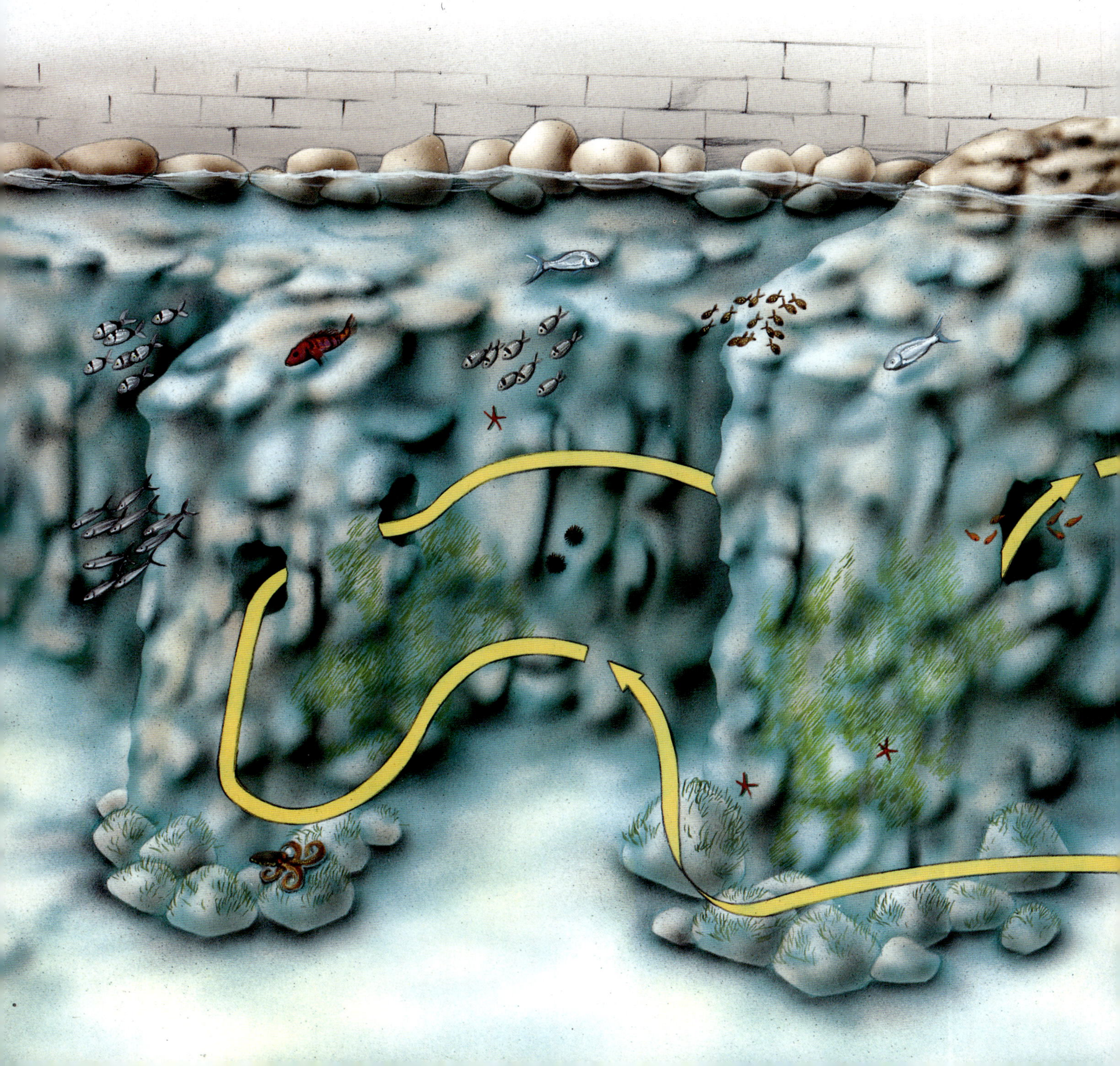

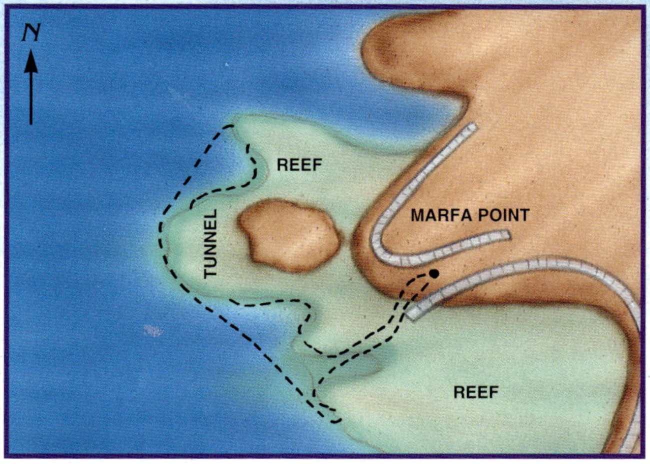
N
REEF
TUNNEL
MARFA POINT
REEF

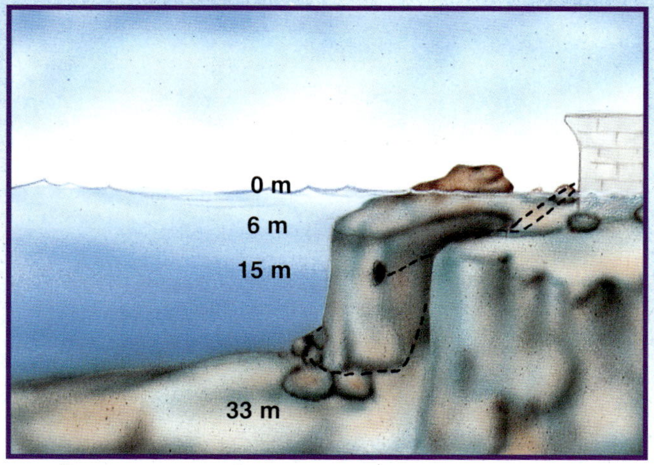
0 m
6 m
15 m
33 m

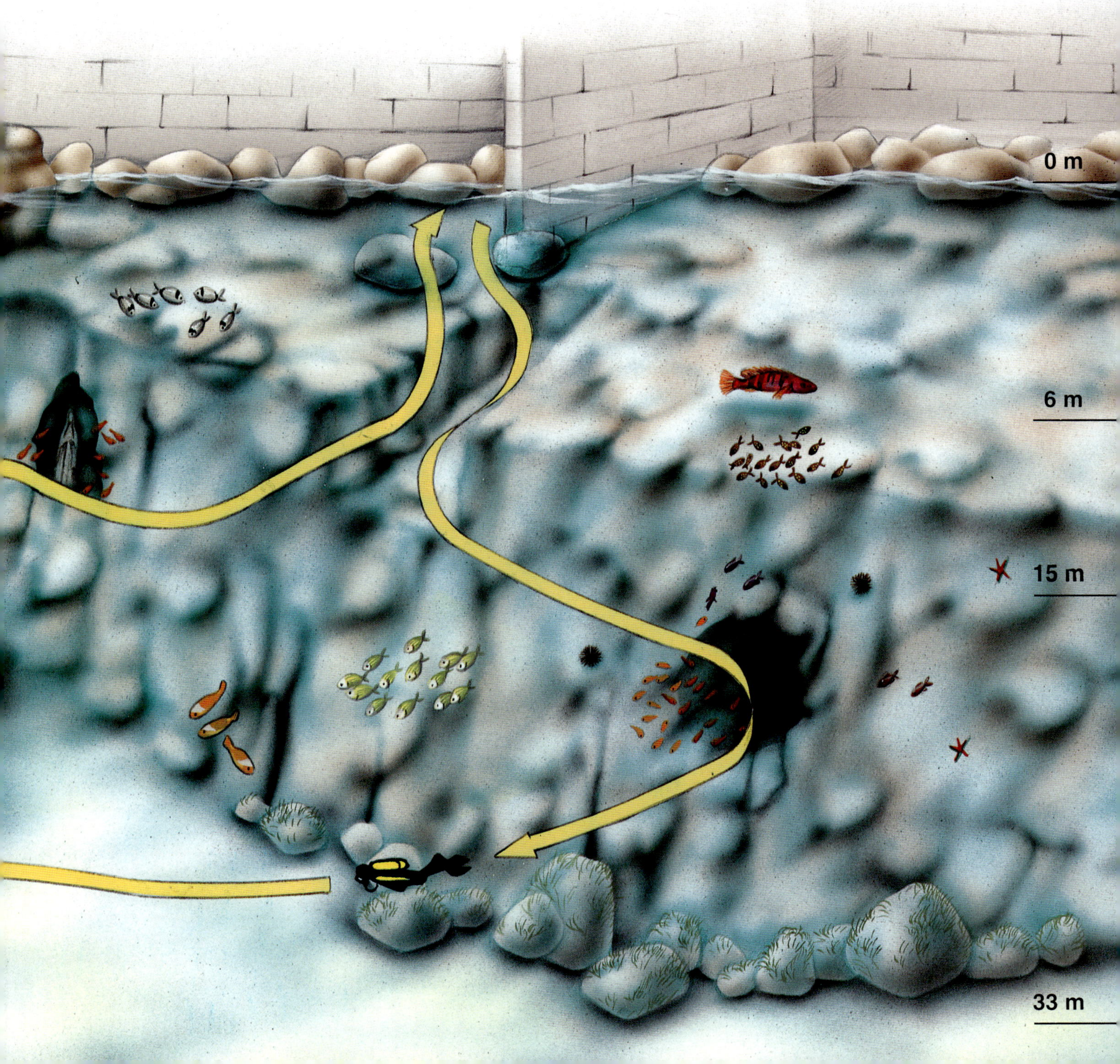
0 m
6 m
15 m
33 m

LOCATION

The very busy Malta-Gozo car ferry operates between Mgarr in Gozo and the narrow spit of land on the north-west corner of Malta known as Cirkewwa, where, immediately opposite the docking facilities, the diver will find a gap through the sea defences with a path leading down to the waters edge. It is here that the dive commences. After a short swim through some shallow water, the diver heads in a westerly direction to a prominent break through the rocks which acts like a gateway to the dive. From here the diver follows the natural underwater contours.

A

THE DIVE

There is so much to see and so many possibilities on this dive that two dives here are no exactly the same. I have, therefore, selected a route which will include the major features of this dive which always begins in very shallow water as you head towards a wider area known as the valley. This is an oblong shute which leads directly to the reef wall and is an ideal area for decompression after the dive.
On reaching the drop-off, there is a cave just below to the left which may be visited now or at the end of the dive. On leaving the cave, the diver drops to the bottom of the reef wall and turns right heading in

B

C

D

a generally northerly direction but weaving in and out as the underwater contours are followed. Following the base of the reef, the divers will skirt around a very large rocky promontory where there are some very large boulders providing both home and refuge for countless creatures. It is always exciting when you see something underwater for the very first time and it was here that I saw my first flying gurnard. Further to the north there is another smaller, rocky "headland" and this marks the turning point of the dive. From here the divers ascend from 33 metres to 15 metres where they will discover a narrow tunnel (in the shape of a letter "L" lying on its side) leading right through the rock.

You cannot see the exit of this tunnel until you are inside and have gone round the corner, so it is not quite so appealing to many divers - it is also a very tight squeeze - best left alone by anyone who is not completely happy with swimming in confined spaces.
Further to the south, as the divers head back to the start point, they will find another tunnel right through the rock. This is also a bit of a squeeze but is so short that even the most novice of divers are quite happy to swim through. A short distance further on, a very small cave containing an almost life-size statue of the Madonna is located. There is an inscription at the base of the statue describing when it was placed there and by whom. From here, it is only a short distance to the "valley" which is a very distinctive, almost square, shape cut into the top of the reef wall.

PHOTOGRAPHY

There is so much to see and enjoy at Marfa Point that it is not possible to include everything with a single camera and lens. Beginning with the 20mm and 24mm lenses, I found the reef wall to be ideal for photographs of divers - either singly or in groups with the small tunnels and caves providing excellent backdrops for framing these subjects.
Some divers actually swim out towards the anchor (featured in the Rozi dive!) during this particular dive on the grounds that they have more time for this marvellous feature than they ever have during a dive on the Rozi.
As for the 55mm lens, this was put to good use when we often encountered some really good sized fish such as the greater amberjack and even groupers amongst the rocks at the bottom of the reef wall.
Of course, the ever-present smaller species of fish are found almost everywhere making macro photography possibly the best choice for this site.

E

F

G

H

A - A large admiralty anchor resting on the sand is one of the attractions of the dive at Marfa Point.

B - The dive at Marfa Point begins from land, from an opening in the pier of Cirkewwa, where a path leads to the entrance point.

C - The final portion of the most classical route leads to a small cavity in which a nearly life-size statue of the Virgin stands. A plaque indicates who placed it there and when.

D - A diver offers food to saddled seabreams, who immediately gather in large, confident numbers.

E - The central portion of the dive follows two relatively narrow tunnels which cross the rock at a depth of 15 metres.

F - The painted comber (Serranus scriba) *is quite common. During the mating season its colours become gaudy, and its blue belly and orange fins stand out.*

G - This image shows the delicate structure of a spiny starfish.

H - Transparent tentacles oscillate softly with the rhythmical movement of the current.

CIRKEWWA ARCH

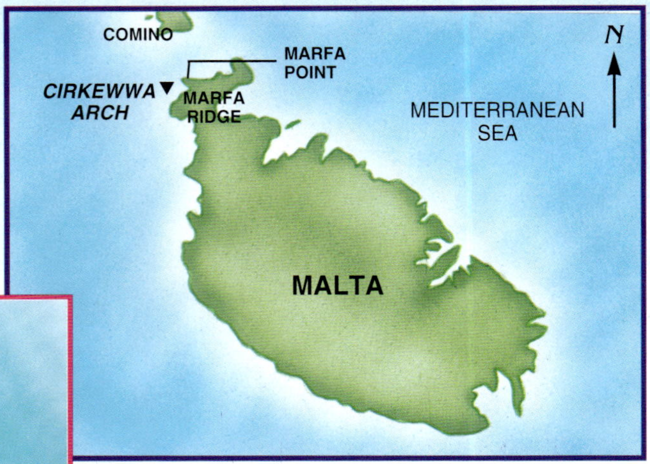

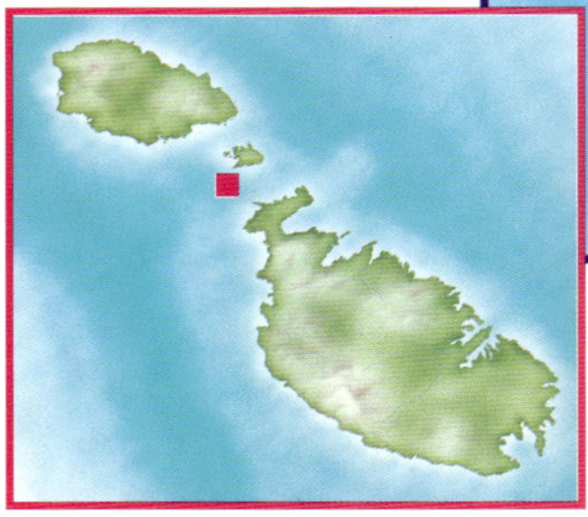

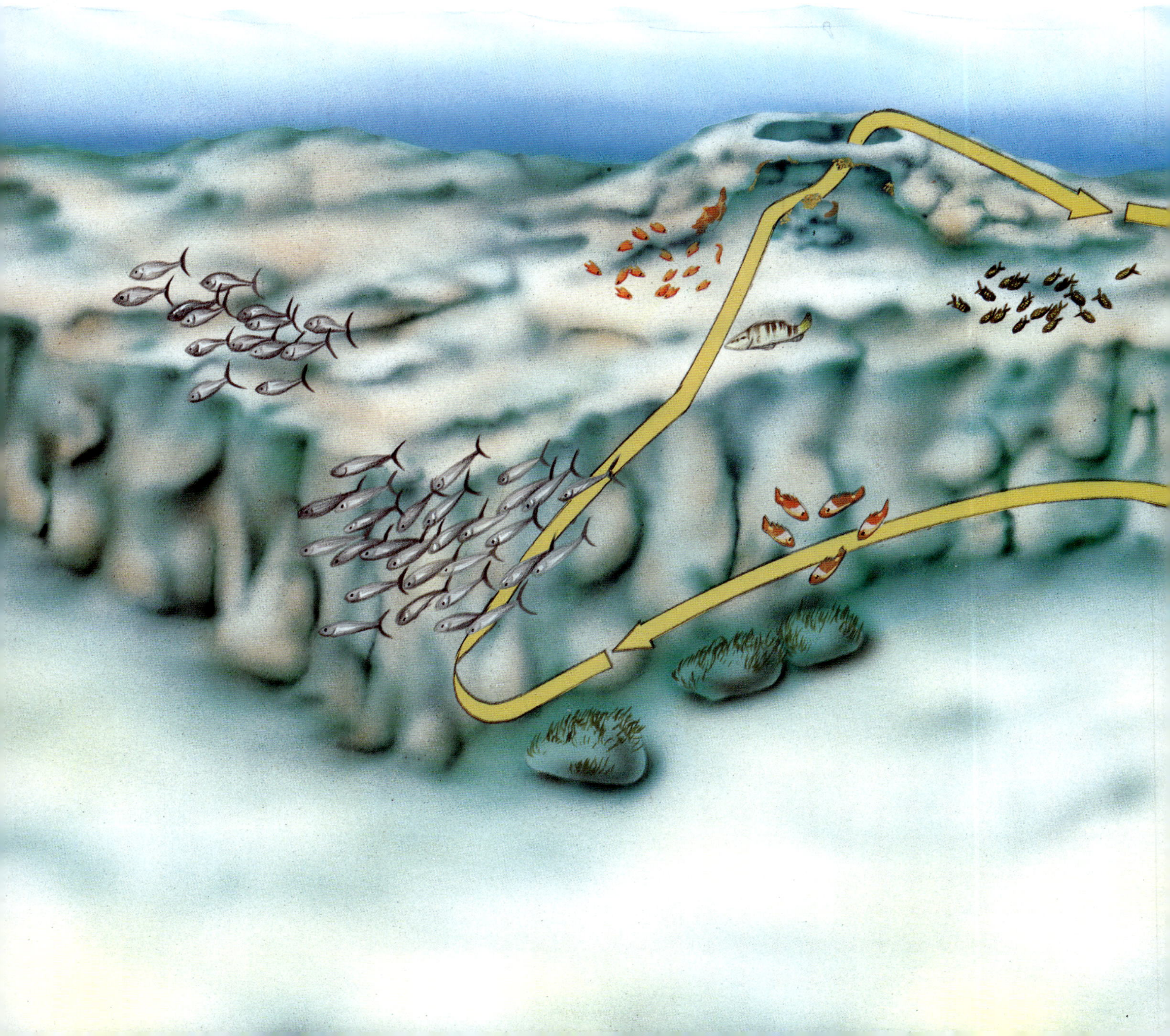

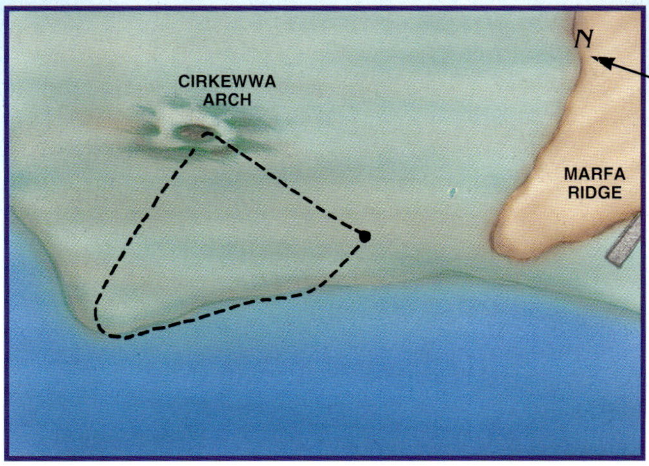
N
CIRKEWWA
ARCH
MARFA
RIDGE

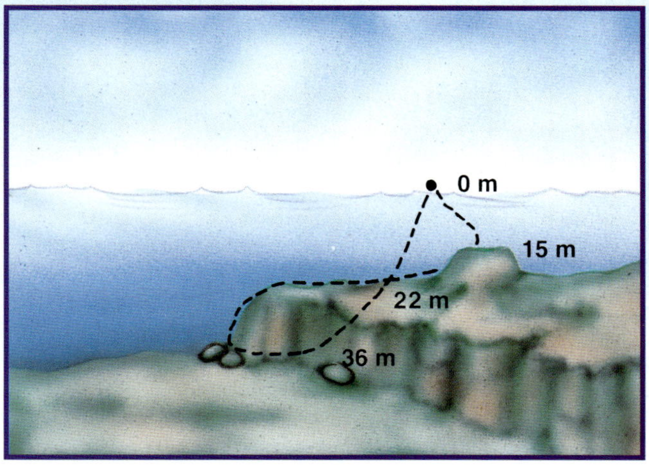
0 m
15 m
22 m
36 m

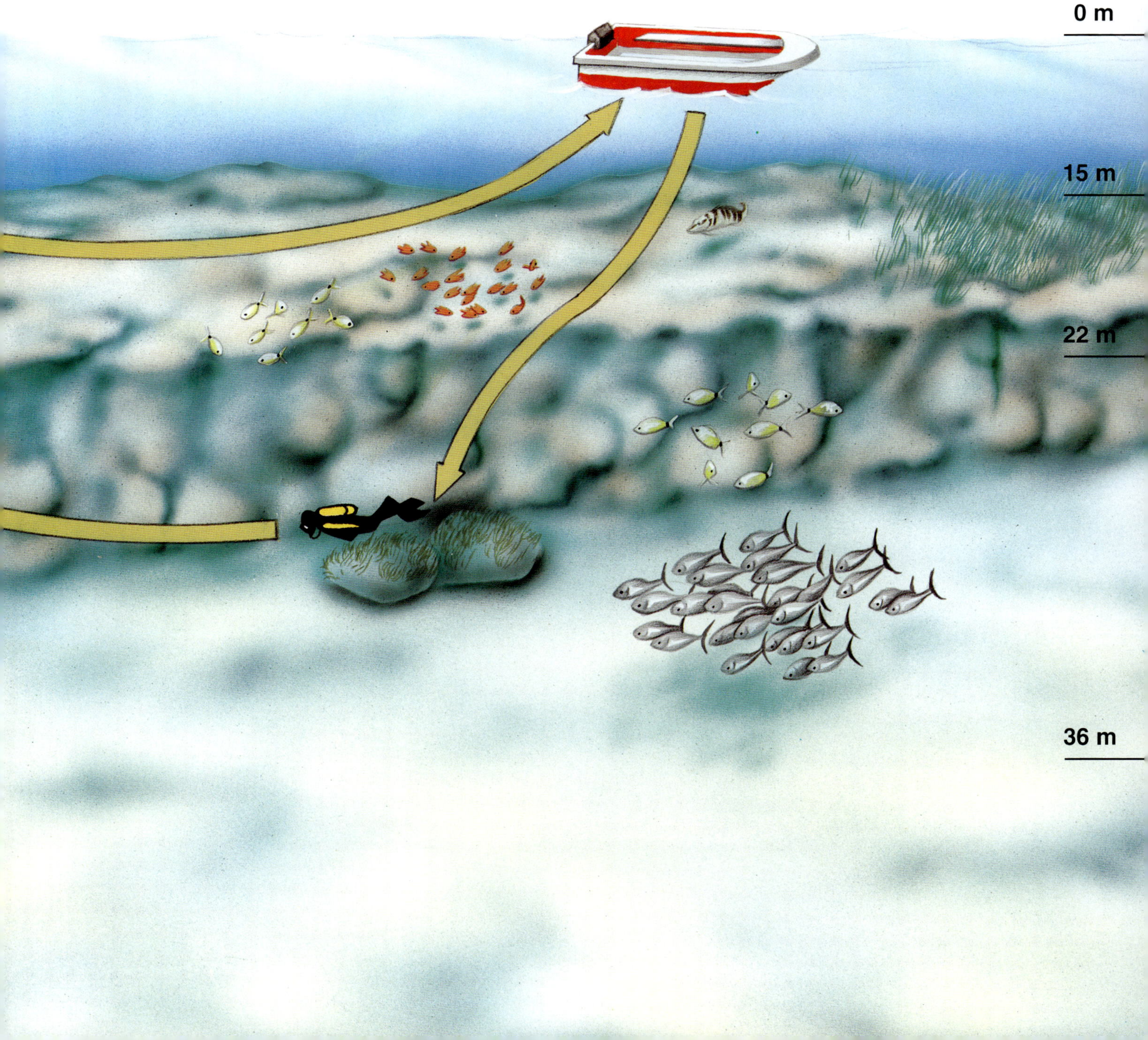
0 m
15 m
22 m
36 m

A - At the beginning of the dive the route follows a gully through the rocks, with the sea floor covered with a dense meadow of Neptune grass.

B - The arch is the main attraction of the dive. It can be reached through a long underwater route. The vaults of the arch are covered with Astroides corals and red sponges.

C - Hermit crabs (Dardanus arrosor) *are common in the less illuminated areas of the arch, and some are quite large.*

D - The shadowy areas are covered with carpets of orange corals (Astroides calycularis). *These corals have a calcareous skeleton covered with the soft tissues of its body, and form characteristic cushion-shaped formations.*

E - An octopus seeks refuge in a crevice. It relies on its mimetic abilities to defend itself from predators.

F - An encrusting sponge (probably Spirastrella cunctatrix) *covers the rock, showing off the intricate maze of channels that criss-cross its body.*

G - The bearded fire worm is an annelid worm typical of temperate waters and is common in the southern Mediterranean. It is one of the most colourful worms, but also one of the most dangerous, due to the painful stings it can inflict with its bristles.

H - A small hermit crab carries its shell through the algae on the sea floor. The pink colour of the shell is due to a layer of encrusting red algae.

A

B

C

D

LOCATION

Approximately 200 metres north of the entry point described for Marfa Point, the diver will find a very narrow gap through a much taller sea wall. On the far side is a path leading right down to the water edge and Cirkewwa Arch is located some 200 metres north-north-west of this ideal entry and exit point. Normally a shore dive, it is also a boat dive and ideal for all levels of experience.

The Arch is located inside one of several ridges amongst a very uneven seabed and is best described as a large semi-circular curve cut back into the rock with a bridge of rock connecting both top leading edges of that curve. Or, to put it another way, it is a cave with no roof whatsoever, but with the entrance still intact!

THE DIVE

On entering the water there is a clear route through a small valley of rock on the far side of which is a relatively shallow (10-15 metres) rocky seabed covered with seagrass. Keeping the shoreline to your left, you will soon encounter the edge of this rocky seabed which then forms a reef as it drops to 36 metres. Staying above this reef, proceed in a north-west direction until you can see the stern of a wreck to your left - but if you turn right, away from the Rozi and after a short swim, the ridge you are seeking will appear in the distance. As it comes into focus, the Arch stands out as a very prominent feature.

By now the divers will have already covered something like 250 metres in distance, so they will always welcome the rest that comes with, inspecting this magnificent feature at close range. Below the Arch, the diver will find bright yellow soft corals and deep red sponges brought alive by artificial torch-light. Amongst the little gullies and cracks there are also numerous cardinalfish and even some very large hermit crabs. At the same time, all around are seabreams, painted comber and many of the species so common in these waters.

PHOTOGRAPHY

It is a long swim out to Cirkewwa Arch and, along the way, the diver will encounter many different species of fish with every chance of discovering a sea horse in the seagrass - which is very prolific in this area. For this a macro lens is ideal but the main objective, however, would be to reach the Arch and photograph this rather large structure. To include a diver within such a photograph always adds scale and dimension to such a picture. A wide angle lens is, therefore, essential.

F

E

G

H

L-AHRAX POINT

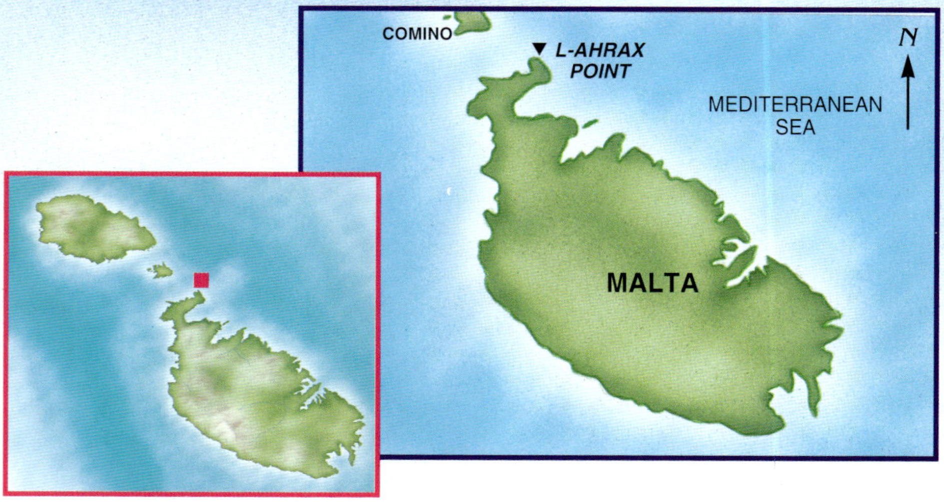

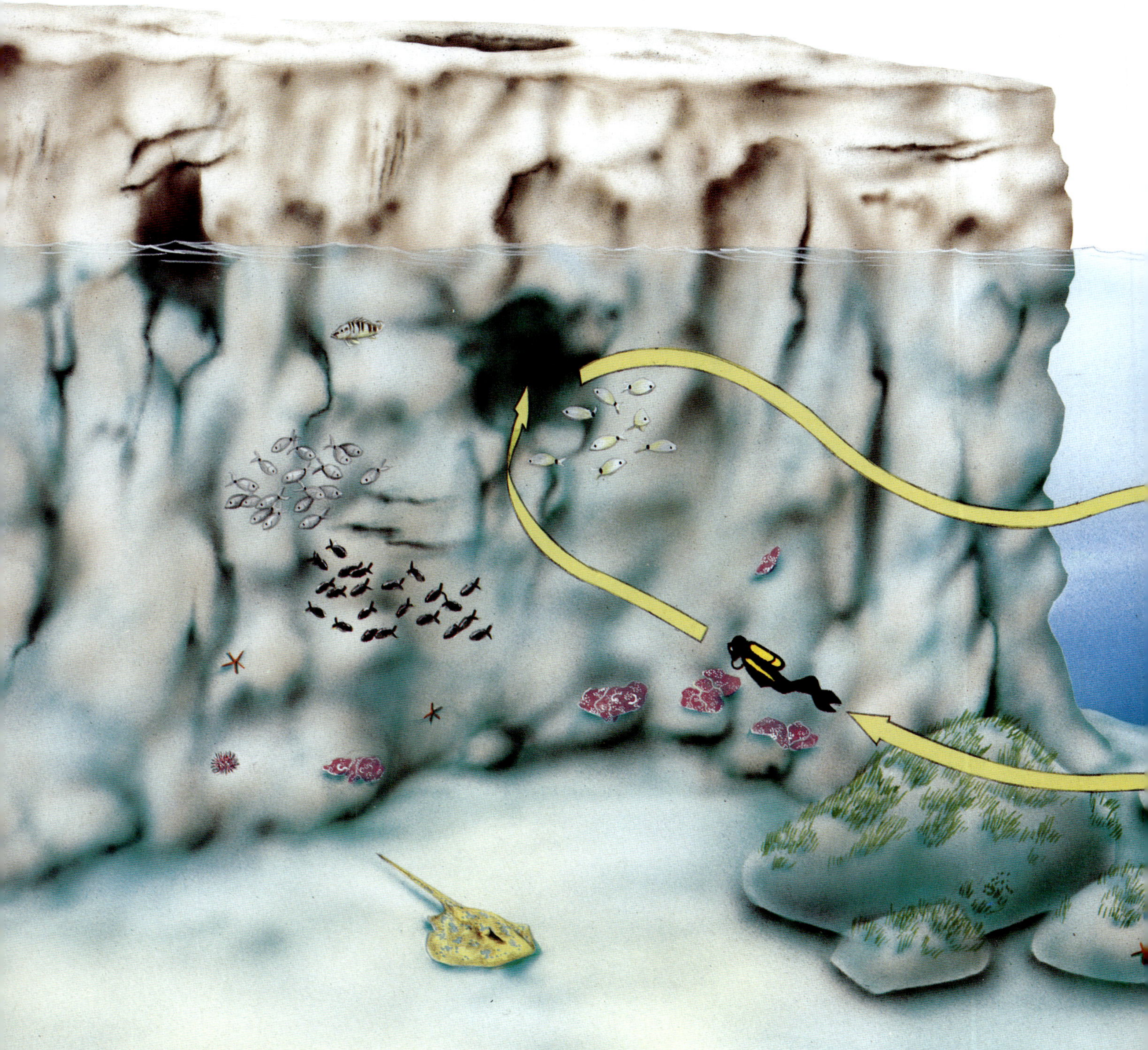

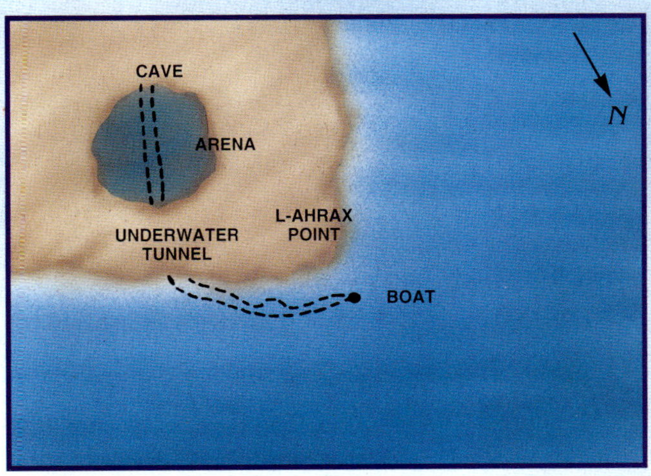
CAVE
ARENA
L-AHRAX POINT
UNDERWATER TUNNEL
BOAT
N

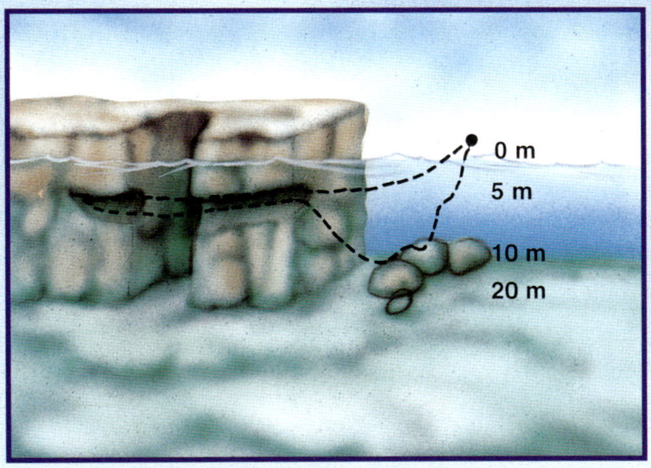
0 m
5 m
10 m
20 m

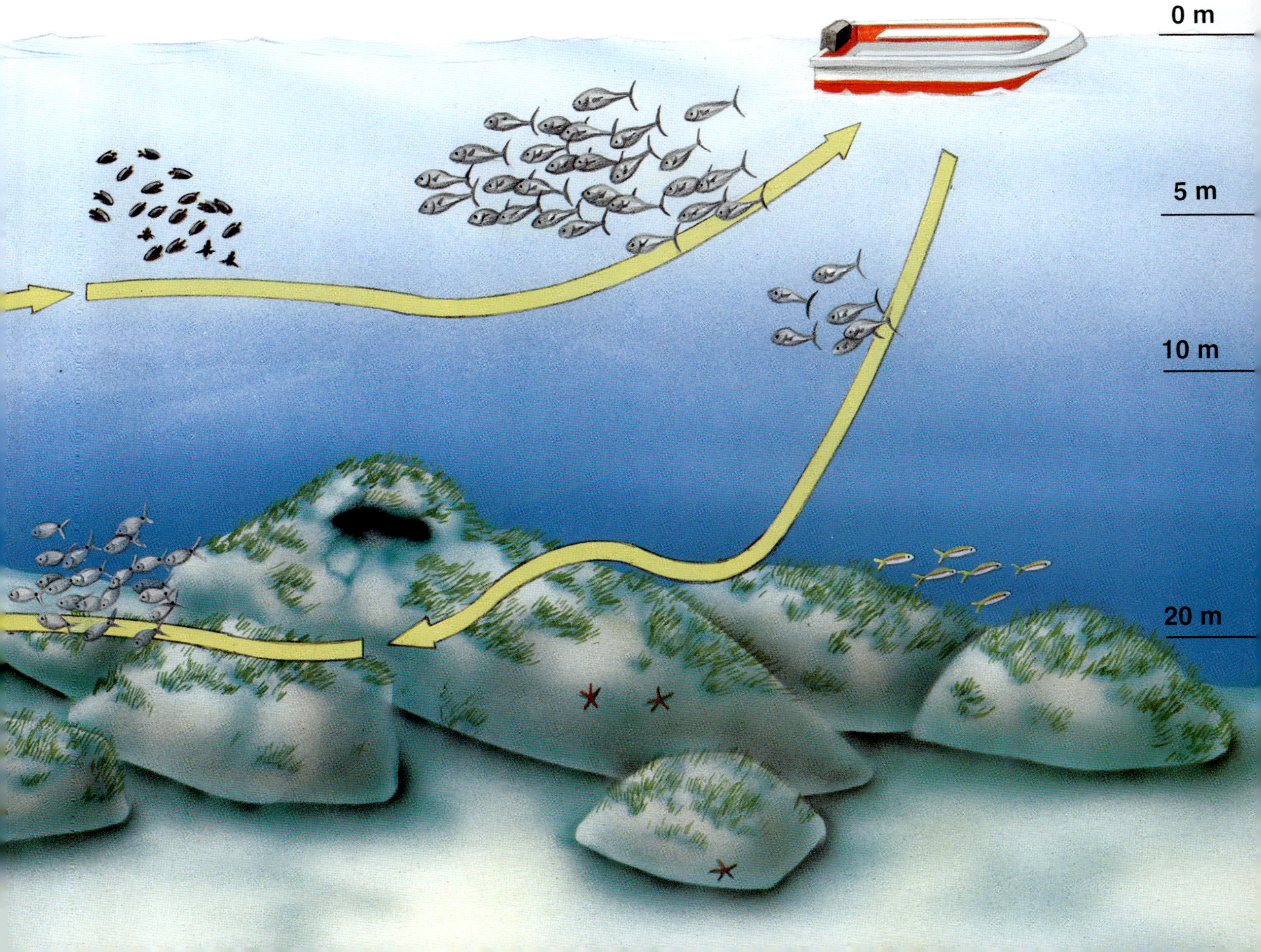
0 m
5 m
10 m
20 m

A - The north coast of Malta is vertical, and the L-Ahrax area is dotted with numerous cavities in and out of the water. This is the northernmost diving area on the island.

B - One of the many cavities during the dive runs through the final portion of the route and leads to the amphitheatre. You should use this passageway only when visibility is good.

C - Piles of rocks form tunnels, passageways and openings that make the dive varied and entertaining. The most characteristic passageway leads to a shallow amphitheatre in which you can surface.

D - The tompot blenny is a classic resident of dark crevices. Blennies are always in contact with the sea floor and will swim in the open water only rarely and for extremely short distances.

LOCATION

L-Ahrax Point is the most northerly point on the island of Malta. When approached from the sea, the diver will notice a number of caves at the surface - inside several of which, further tunnels (and caves leading from them) are easily identified. Underwater is no different. One cave in particular, however, is the entrance to a rather unique experience - even by Maltese standards.
This is normally a boat dive but on one occasion, as we were coming to the end of our dive, we passed another pair of divers on their way into the cave.
On leaving the water, we were very surprised to find that they were in fact conducting a shore dive - having scrambled down the rocks with all their equipment. The terrain is such that I cannot recommend this dive be undertaken from the shore - after all, you do have to get out again - safely!

THE DIVE

Although this dive is relatively shallow, it is no less spectacular for that. It is also a very curious dive. Like most boat dives, it commences with the divers following the anchor line down to the seabed where they will encounter numerous large boulders at a depth of 20 metres. These boulders provide many creatures with a home and refuge from would-be predators, so they are always worthy of closer examination. In addition, many of these rocks have fallen against each other in such a way as to create some very interesting "tunnels" and swim-throughs, thus providing the diver with considerable harmless sport. There are also a few interesting rock windows.
Eventually, however, the divers approach the outer tunnel for which this dive is so well known. Here the diver will find those iridescent cardinalfish - always enjoying life in the shade.
The entrance is fairly shallow

A

B

C

D

and gets even shallower before it opens into what I can only describe as an underwater outdoor arena. Here the divers will normally surface in order to establish exactly what they have entered. It is a large, circular area - open to the sky and not unlike some ancient amphitheatre - except that it contains water. All the diver can see is a tall circular cliff face stretching all around. In the far corner, however, - on the opposite side from the tunnel - there is the unmistakable entrance to a cave and the diver will now submerge and head in that direction. Here the diver must swim very carefully. A lot of weed and other detritus is washed into the arena and invariably ends up in this cave. The underwater visibility, therefore, can quickly be reduced to zero! Assuming that is not allowed to happen, the divers are able to swim the complete length of the cave and slowly work their way to the surface right at the back. Yet again, there are plenty of cardinalfish, bright yellow soft corals and red sponges to fill the divers torchlight with a rich taste of colour. In short, this single dive site allows the diver to enjoy all the features that Malta is famous for as a destination for scuba divers.

G

H

E - A tiny, brightly coloured fish seeks, in vain, to camouflage itself against the detrital seabed.

F - A little goby peeps out from among the rocks. Gobies live in constant contact with the seabed and prey mostly on small crustaceans, which they capture with quick darting movements.

E

F

PHOTOGRAPHY

This is quite difficult. Within the first tunnel, the open arena and the final cave there is little or no scope for macro photography and yet, poor underwater visibility can quickly remove the possibility of anything else. Assuming, however, that the photographer is blessed with some very careful diving partners, both are possible. When using a wide angle lens, the photographer should ideally get ahead of his fellow divers in order to photograph them as they enter before they are able to reduce the underwater visibility and leave fish portraiture or macro photography to those areas outside the cave at the beginning and end of this dive.

G - Colonies of hydrozoans (probably Eudendrium) *grow vertically at the openings to the cavities, where currents are created that bring in nourishment.*

H - In the dark areas near cave entrances, the rock is covered by encrusting red algae and velvety cushions of a green algae, Palmophyllum crassum.

ST. PAUL'S ISLANDS

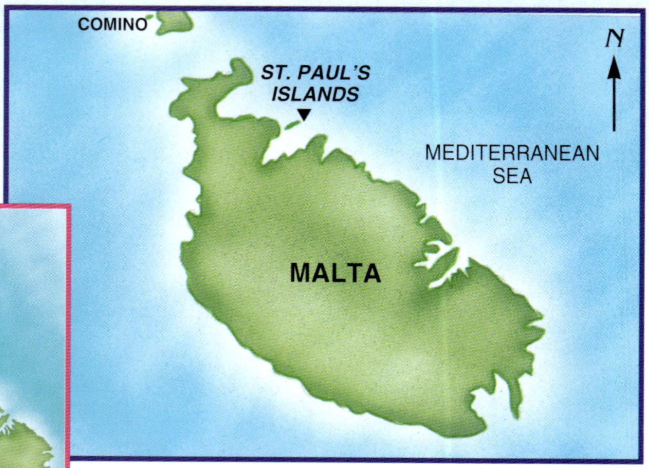

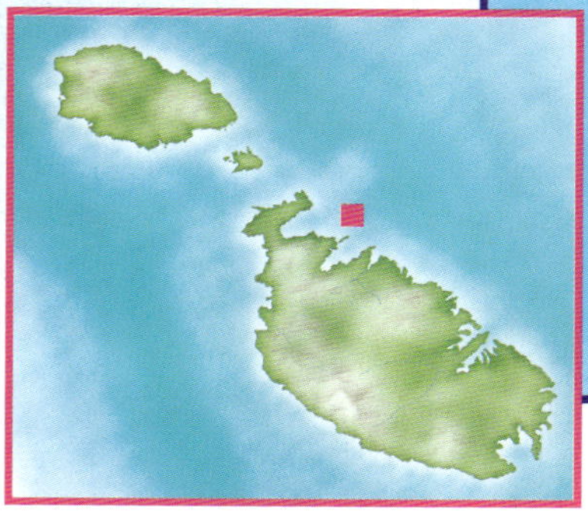

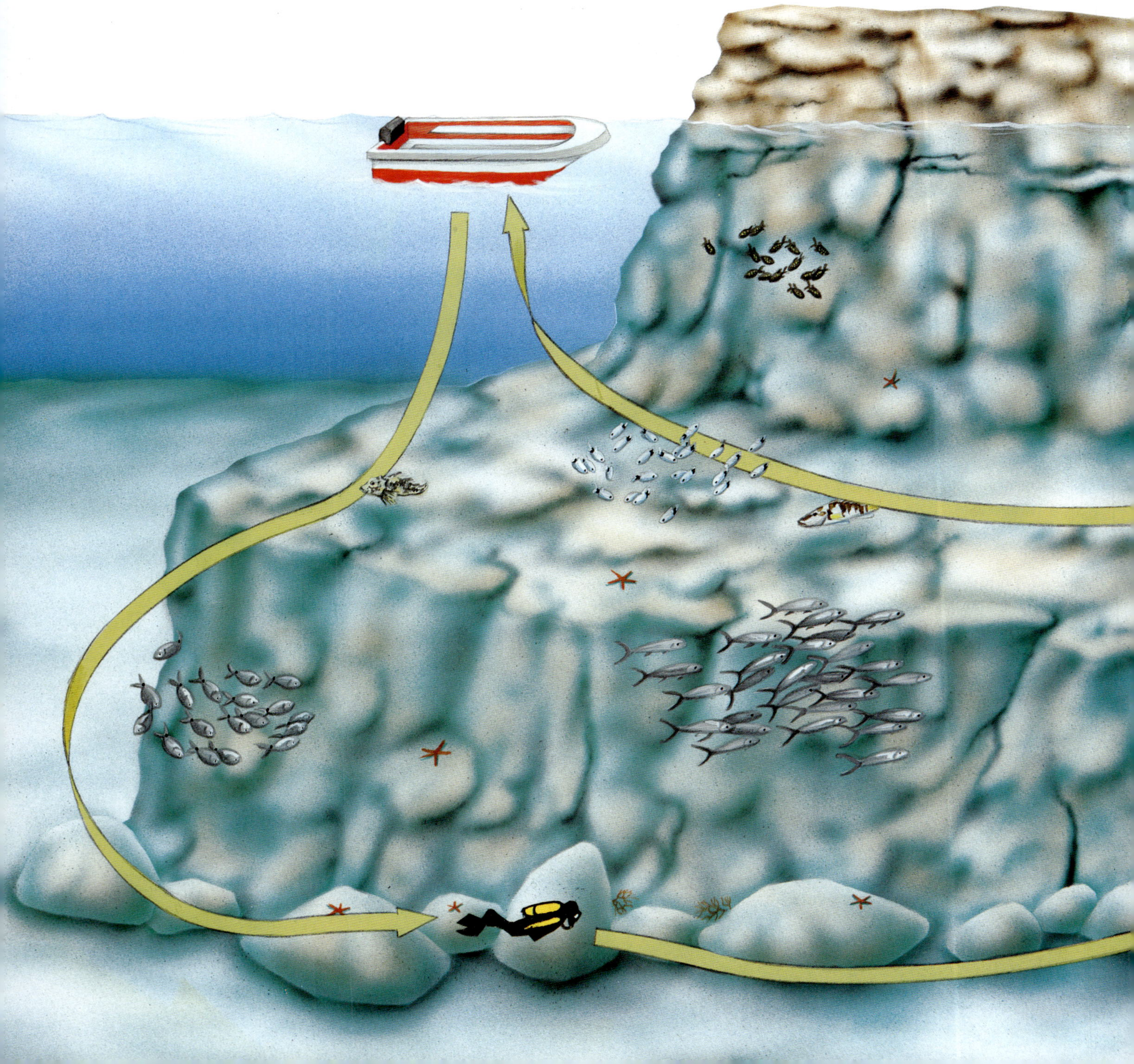

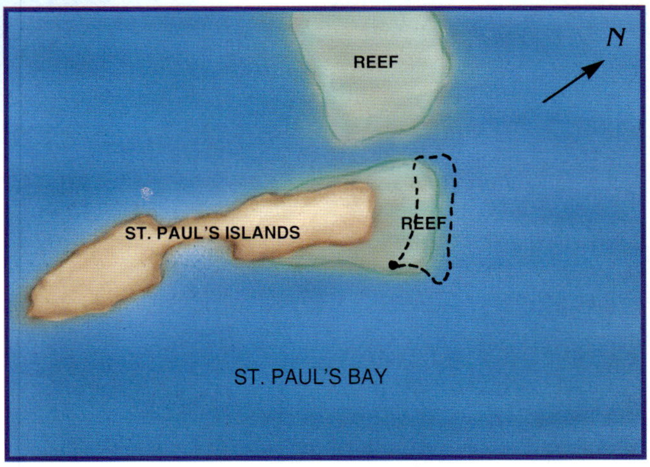
REEF
N
ST. PAUL'S ISLANDS
REEF
ST. PAUL'S BAY

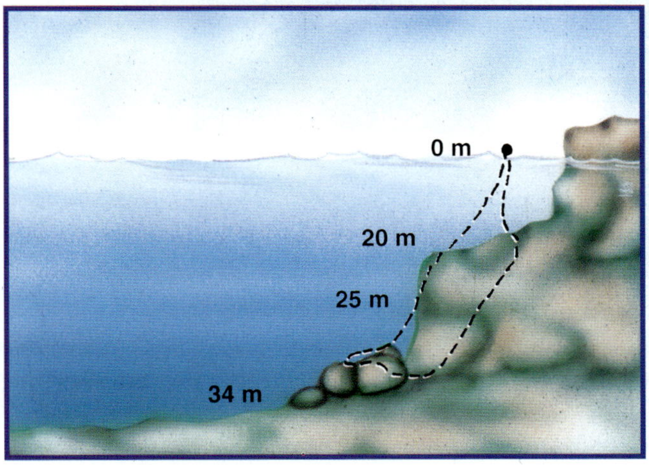
0 m
20 m
25 m
34 m

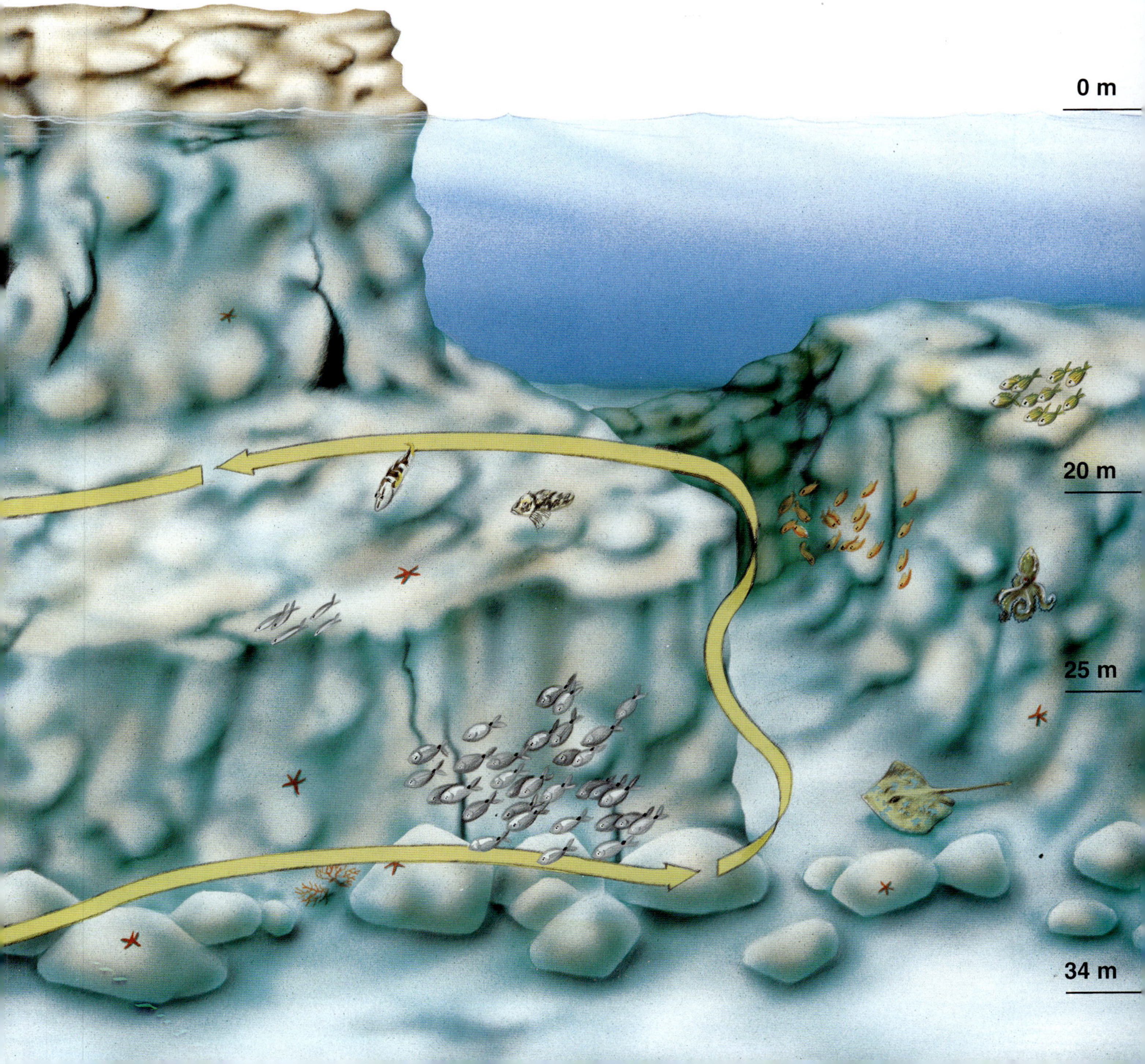
0 m
20 m
25 m
34 m

A - Cavities are quite common during dives around Malta. The light from the surface diminishes to the deep darkness of the caves.

B - A group of wrasses looks for food among the algae on the sea floor. Wrasses often gather mouthfuls of sediment, which they then spit out, keeping only the edible organic parts.

C - Mullets intent on sifting the sediment with their barbels, in search of prey, can be seen in the patches of sand along the route.

D - The cardinal fish is quite common in poorly illuminated areas, and often forms large groups. This small fish is immediately recognizable by its colour and its large eyes, crossed by two narrow white bands.

E - The first part of the dive skirts a wall in which there are small caverns, and leads to masses of rocks.

F - Groupers of all sizes swim among the large rocks on the sea floor. Some of these fish are truly majestic.

G - Two scorpionfish have chosen the same place for their ambushes. Both have extremely mimetic colours, and only the light of the camera flash makes them easily recognizable.

H - The cuttlefish can change colour rapidly to match the colour of the sea floor. Here its dark colour means that it has perceived the presence of the photographer and considers him a potential danger.

A

B

C

D

LOCATION

These are the islands at the western entrance to St. Paul's Bay and this very popular dive site is located on the south-eastern corner of the outermost island. There is no access to the islands, so the only means of getting yourself and your diving equipment to this site is by boat.

THE DIVE

The dive boat will invariably anchor above a relatively shallow reef - an underwater ledge which is not far from the reef wall where the dive really

E

begins. The edge of the reef is clearly seen underwater and may be approached directly. From here the diver descends to the bottom of the wall, which is a fairly uniform depth of 34 metres. From here the divers turn left and follow the base of the wall where, once again, they will encounter some very large boulders which offer some very interesting formations in the way they appear to have been almost discarded by nature. Here, the goatfish and red mullets are found continually sifting for food amongst any small patch of sand they can find. Within the boulders

themselves are groupers of almost every size. There is also every chance of finding both cuttlefish and octopus. After something like 80 metres the divers are able to turn left and enter a massive large, and almost square, valley. The floor of this valley is covered with sandy ridges which are much favoured by large stingrays. The stingray hunts by digging itself into the sand until just its eyes protrude above the surface. Like this it will wait, absolutely motionless, until a suitable prey approaches to within a short distance of just in front of its eye. Quick as lightning the stingray then strikes the hapless fish with its tail before coming out of the sand to devour it. Unfortunately, stingrays are very wary of divers and often swim away long before they have even been seen.
As you get deeper into the valley, it begins to get slightly shallower and at some point the dive leader will ascend to the top of the wall and head back, above the reef, to the boat's anchor. Many divers spend a considerable time at the end of the dive enjoying the vast profusion of fishes found in 8-10 metres here.

PHOTOGRAPHY

Being at the entrance to St. Paul's Bay, there is a fair degree of medium-sized maritime traffic continually passing this point. Underwater visibility is not, therefore, always as good as one has come to expect. Fish life, however, is particularly prolific making this site absolutely ideal for close-up and macro photography. Scorpionfish, painted combers, rainbow wrasses and saddled seabreams are seen on almost every dive here but the real prize is to find either a seahorse or a nudibranch hidden amongst the seaweed.

F

G

H

HMS MAORI

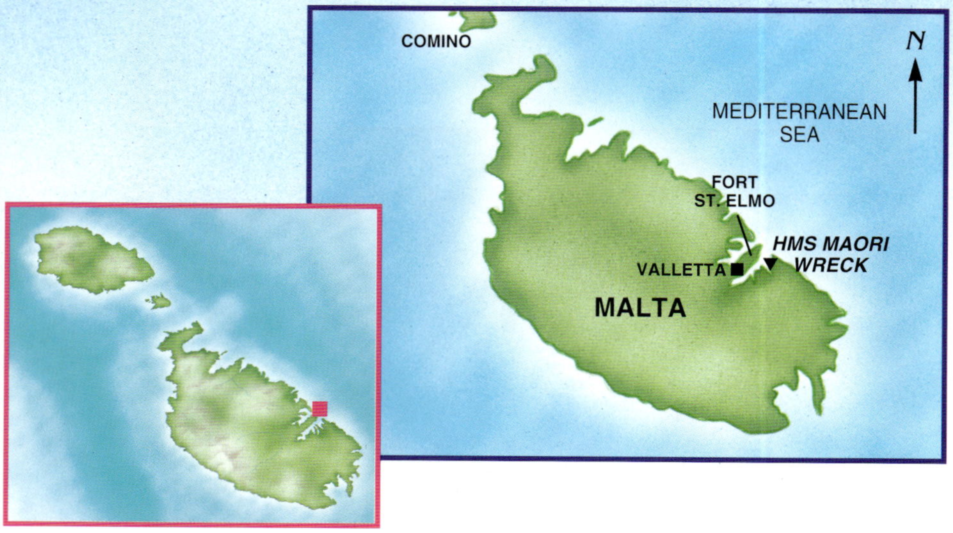
COMINO
N
MEDITERRANEAN
SEA
FORT
ST. ELMO
HMS MAORI
WRECK
VALLETTA
MALTA

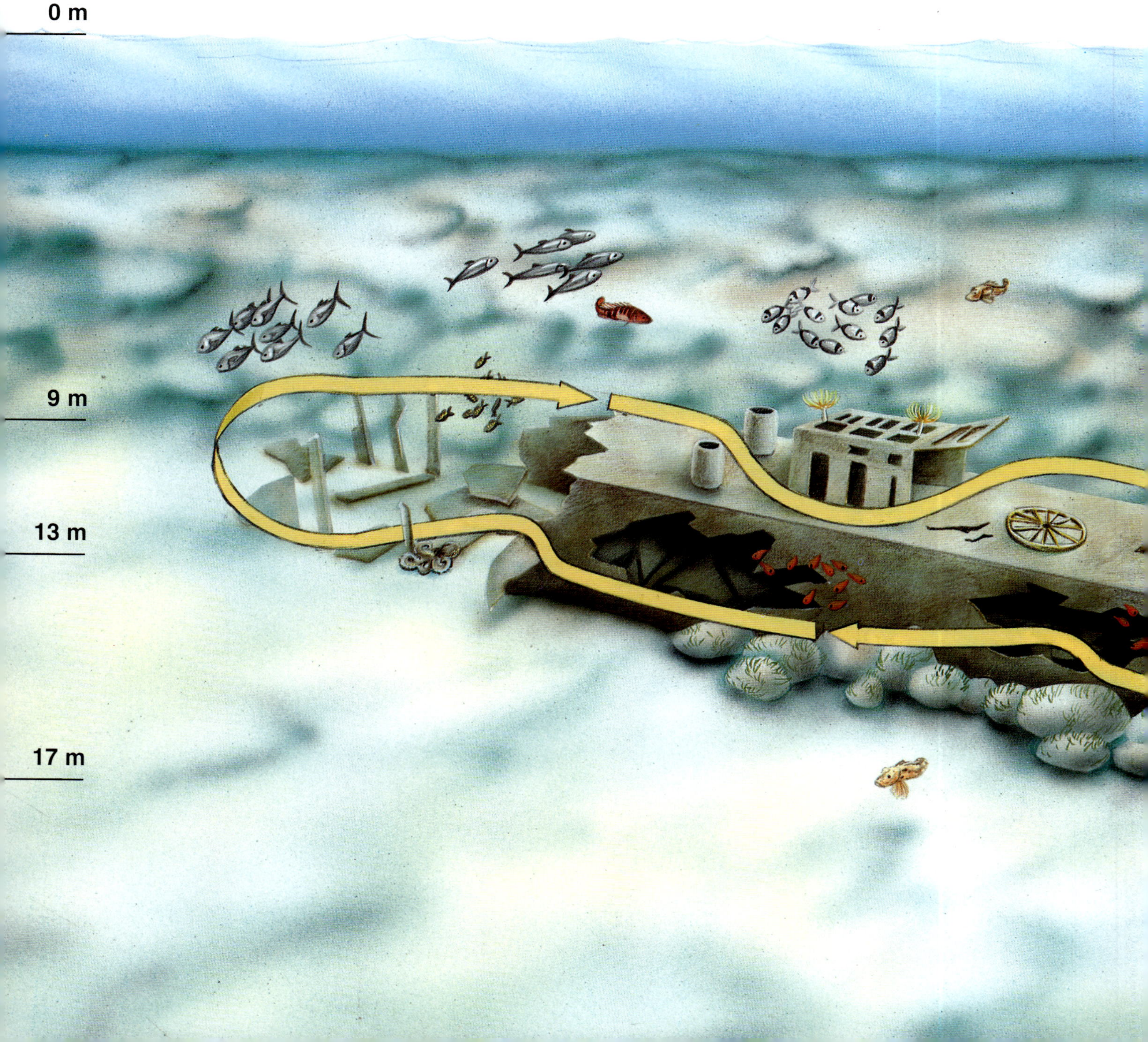
0 m
9 m
13 m
17 m

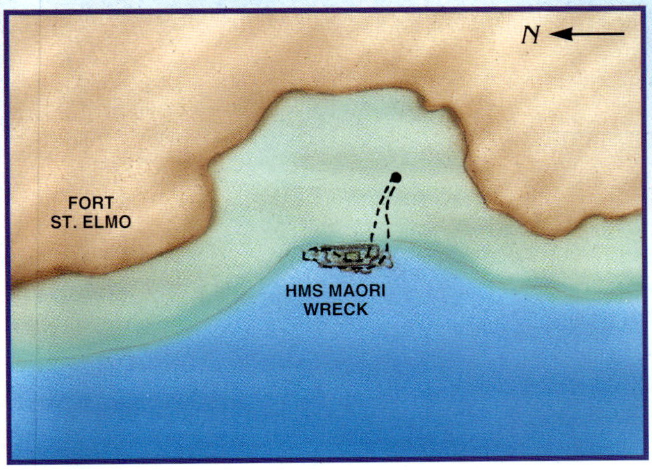
N
FORT
ST. ELMO
HMS MAORI
WRECK

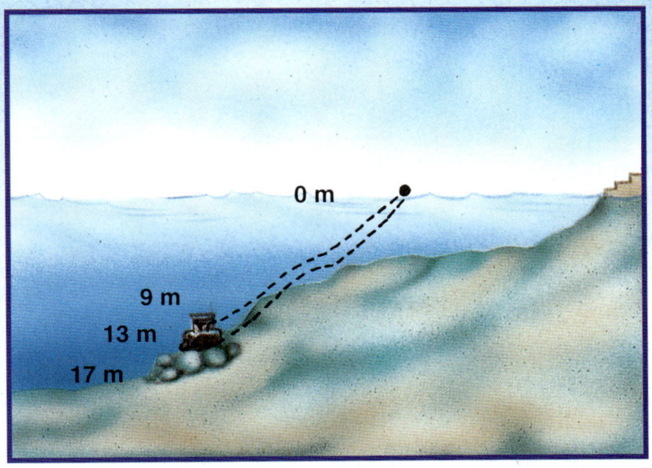
0 m
9 m
13 m
17 m

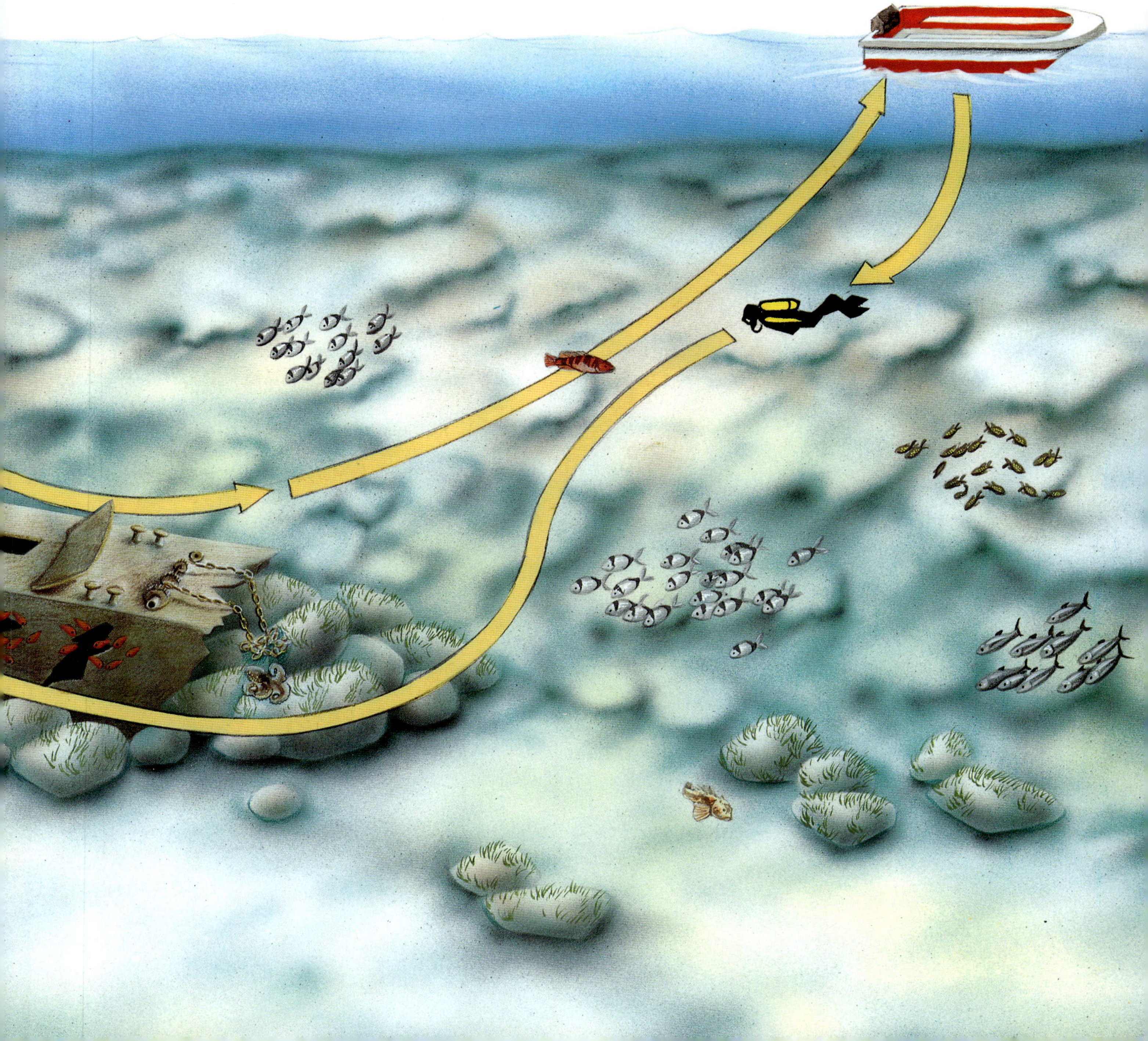

LOCATION

At the southern end of the small Bay below Fort St. Elmo, there is a cafe and on the outside walls of this building are painted a number of Destroyers - HMS *Kelly* (flagship of the group and former command of the late Admiral of the Fleet, Lord Mountbatten), HMS *Jersey* (blown up by a mine as she entered Grand Harbour on 2 May 1941) and HMS *Maori*. As you cross the narrow road right in front of this cafe, you will discover some steps leading down to the waters edge. HMS *Maori* lies approximately 120 metres north of those steps. The wreck is also clearly marked on Chart 974.

HISTORY

HMS *Maori* is probably Malta's most famous wreck and, although she is far from the best dive in Malta, a visit to this ship is a significant brush with the country's history. Launched in 1937, HMS *Maori* saw considerable action throughout her short life - the Mediterranean, the Norwegian campaign, Atlantic convoys and North Sea duties prior to returning to the Mediterranean in order to attack Rommel's supply lines and assist with the defence of Malta - to name but a few. In fact it was HMS *Maori* that re-established radar contact with the *Bismarck* and brought about the ultimate destruction of that ship in early 1941 - she even remained on hand to pick up survivors.
In late 1941, however, she was one of four destroyers, under command of Commander Stokes, ordered to reinforce *14 DF Squadron* in the eastern Mediterranean and thus, in the company of HMS *Sikh*, Legion and Isaac Sweers, came to be steaming in an easterly direction past Gibraltar in mid-December of that year. Coincidentally, at this time the two 5,200-ton Italian Cruisers *Alberico Da*

B

C

D

A - This old photo shows the torpedo-boat destroyer Maori *entering the bay of Malta. In 1941, in the middle of the Second World War, Malta was subjected to a massive invasion by the German air force.*

B - The Maori, *moored at Dockyard Creek, was hit by a bomb that struck its aft section, and it began to sink on February 2, 1942. All efforts to plug the leaks failed, and by the end of the day the ship had disappeared into the water.*

C - The wreck was moved from its original site because it interfered with navigation. Today it lies on a sandy seabed in the bay of St. Elmo, 13-17 metres from the surface.

Barbiano and *Alberto Di Giussano*, accompanied by a 789-ton torpedo boat, were known to have loaded cased petrol at Palermo before sailing at dusk for Tripoli. British torpedo bombers and *Force K* (the Malta based striking force of cruisers and destroyers) sailed to intercept this enemy force with Commander Stokes being ordered to position his destroyers between the enemy and Palermo - in case they turned back. Although the allied aircraft did attack, they did not damage the cruisers and the strike by *Force K* was cancelled. Realising that they could not get to Tripoli unmolested, however, the Italian cruisers did turn back. By now, it was dark and Stokes suddenly found himself facing the prospect of taking on a much larger fire-power than that possessed by his four ships. Stokes, therefore, carefully led his ships inshore and positioned himself between the land and the enemy craft so that he became well camouflaged against the shore. At 0225 hrs, on 14 December 1941, Commander Stokes ordered the attack.
Three torpedoes struck the *Alberico Da Barbiano* which sank immediately. Only one torpedo struck the *Alberto Di Giussano,* but this burst open many cans of fuel and burning petrol spread across the decks and flooded into the lower compartments. Within a few minutes the four destroyers had scored a spectacular victory and they received a heroes welcome when they steamed into Grand Harbour later that day.
By February 1942, however, Libyan airfields were once again in the hands of the Axis powers and the Germans opened a massive air offensive against Malta. The air raids were almost continuous with the harbours always their centre of attention. For this reason very few people remained on board those vessels

D - The upper portions of the Maori *are resting on the sand next to the hull. Sediment has partially covered the structures.*

E - The wreck offers many lovely views. Some parts of the ship are easily recognizable, while others remain a mystery. In order to get a full picture of the wreck, you'll need to make a number of dives.

F

G

E

F - Waters rich in suspensions reduce visibility considerably. Near the wreck it is therefore important to move cautiously.

G - You can enter the wreck from various openings and exit from others. If you are very careful, you can visit many parts of the hull.

A - Perfectly camouflaged scorpionfish can be seen on and around the wreck.

B - A squat lobster (Galathea strigosa) *has left its shelter among the wreckage. These little crustaceans live only in dark areas and move in rapid backward jumps.*

C - This group of giant sea lemons (Hypselodoris valenciennesi) *was probably photographed during the reproductive season. Although they are hermaphrodites, these molluscs always practice crossed mating.*

D - Violet gastropod molluscs, Flabellina affinis, *can be seen on the hydrozoans growing on the wreckage, as it feeds on the polyps of its host.*

which were necessarily in the harbour, and even the submarines spent much of their time submerged.
That is why only one man was killed at 0200 hrs on the morning of February 12th 1942, when HMS *Maori* - moored at the entrance to Dockyard Creek - received a direct hit as a bomb exploded in her engine room. Some of her own ammunition detonated and she quickly began to settle by the stern which was severely damaged. For many hours, as she stubbornly refused to sink, a skeleton crew worked furiously to seal all the water-tight bulkheads. They almost succeeded as the gallant ship endured the incoming water for as long as it was possible before finally slipping below the surface later that day.
Unfortunately, she then became a serious hindrance to shipping as she blocked almost the entire entrance to a number of Dockyards. She was, therefore

C

D

A

B

raised and salvaged before being set down in the quiet back-water of St. Elmo's Bay where she is now found on the sand at the foot of a sandy slope at a depth of between 13-17 metres.
The guns were removed and much of the superstructure is now found beside the vessel on the seabed. The stern is a mass of damaged and twisted steel but her bows remain proud and defiant to the last - just as they did when she lay half submerged with her guns still pointing at the enemy above. Parts of the hull can still be entered, although she is well silted up inside.

THE DIVE

On leaving the shore, the diver heads almost due north for approximately 120 metres across a rock strewn seabed at an almost uniform depth of 9 metres. Suddenly, this becomes a rocky slope down to a sandy seabed at 16 metres at which

E - A white gastropod mollusc (Flabellina babai) *moves sinuously along a carpet of algae and hydrozoans. Like all species of its genus, it feeds on the polyps of cnidarians.*

F - A cardinal fish (Apogon imberbis) *peers out from a dark crevice. These little fish have a strange reproductive behaviour: the eggs released by the female are hatched in the male's mouth.*

point the diver should turn right (east) and follow the slope for a short distance before finding the bows of HMS *Maori*.
At this point, the entire port side has been engulfed by a sandy slope and is, therefore, lost to view. What remains of the bows and part of the starboard side are, however, available for close inspection. Almost immediately the diver will discover what is left of the windlass and a certain amount of anchor chain. Astern of this, at deck level, are twin bollards - on both sides of the vessel - and then some form of splash guard stretches right across the deck. This was probably for the benefit of the forward gun crews - allowing them to continue their work in adverse conditions. Close behind this is a hatch and the framework on which the forward gun was mounted. Continuing towards the stern, the diver will now discover a structure often mistaken as the bridge. This, however, was sited at a level well below the actual bridge - which no longer exists - and was probably used for gunnery control. The sides of this structure are well rusted through enabling the diver to easily swim in and out, although the presence of so much silt often makes it difficult for a second diver to enjoy the same experience.
Immediately aft of this, are two round almost funnel like structures - the purpose of which I was unable to determine. These quickly give way to damaged decking which disappears altogether in a frantic array of twisted metal. Here, the diver can turn back and enter the wreck, which is also easily entered from various holes in the starboard side. With extreme care it is quite easy to enter any one of these access points and leave by another. Even further to the stern, the diver will find that the wreckage becomes more and more sparse until, eventually, just a few metal spars are found sticking upright from the seabed. Wrecks act as instant additions to any underwater reef formation and this one is no different. There are plenty of different species of fish and other, often more interesting, creatures in amongst the wreckage. There is also, surprisingly still a lot of wreckage to inspect and enjoy. This is covered with green weed and hundreds of tube worms. In amongst the weed are also a number of nudibranchs.
For me, however, the greatest delight is a close inspection of over 40 metres of the main wreckage, where I find it easy to pause and pay a silent, personal tribute to this small ship and her various crew members for all they saw and endured in the name of freedom.
Although silt is always a considerable problem, this only serves to spoil the dive. There is little or no chance of a diver becoming lost or trapped within this wreck. That said, one should always bear in mind that the older the vessel gets, the more unstable it might become.

PHOTOGRAPHY

Being at the entrance to Marsamxett Harbour (second only in size to the adjacent Grand Harbour), the *Maori* suffers from a reduced visibility which is only marginally better than the *Carolita*. As a wreck, the photographer will, presumably, wish to include certain identifiable features of this once magnificent vessel with and without the presence of divers. A wide-angle lens is, therefore, essential.
The diver will also be impressed by the marine life to be found within the wreck and nearby. A small number of octopus have taken up permanent residence and I could spend all day on this relatively shallow site with a Macro lens capturing these and other splendid creatures.

E

F

G

H

G - A white tip sea urchin (Sphaerechinus granularis) *grazes on algae on the seabed. The colour of these echinoderms can vary greatly, and some individuals have completely white spines.*

H - Saddled seabreams gather in large schools. Their name comes from the saddle-shaped black spot edged with white on the caudal peduncle.

CAROLITA BARGE

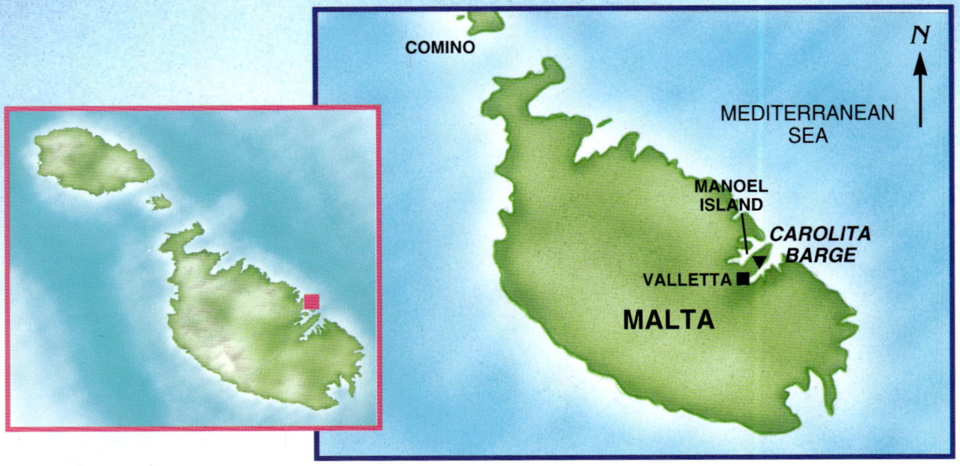

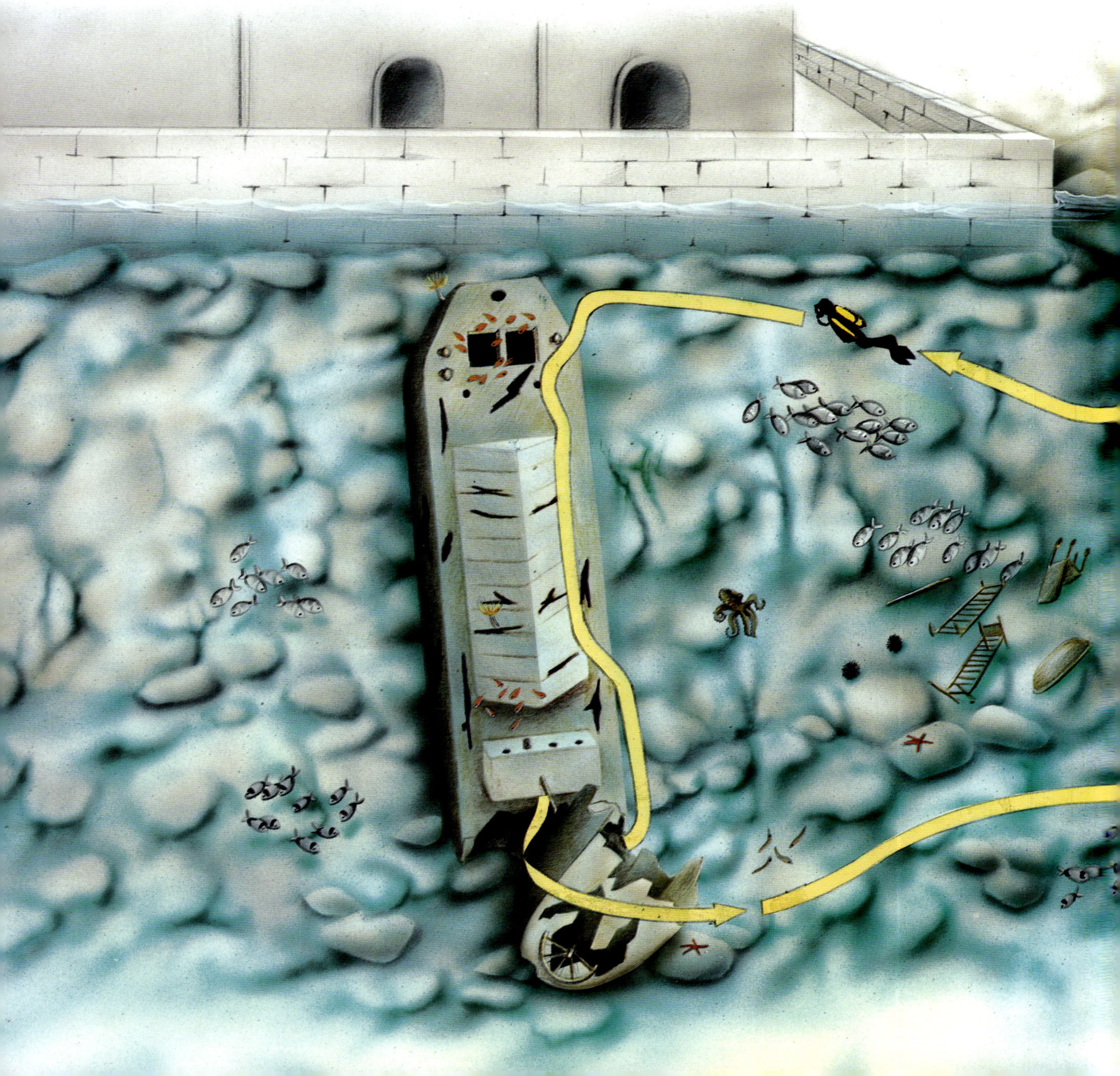

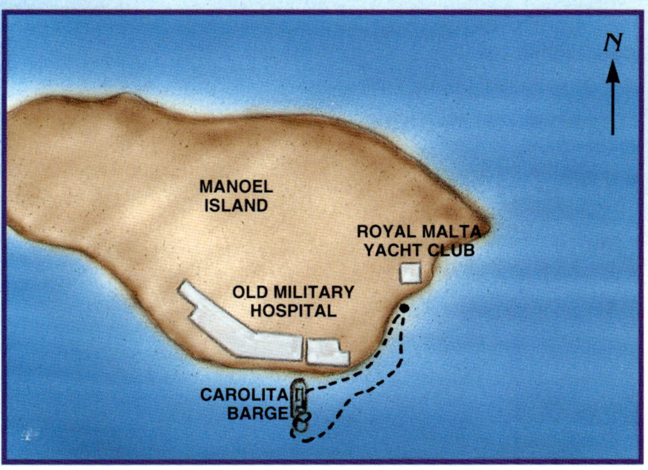
N
MANOEL
ISLAND
ROYAL MALTA
YACHT CLUB
OLD MILITARY
HOSPITAL
CAROLITA
BARGE

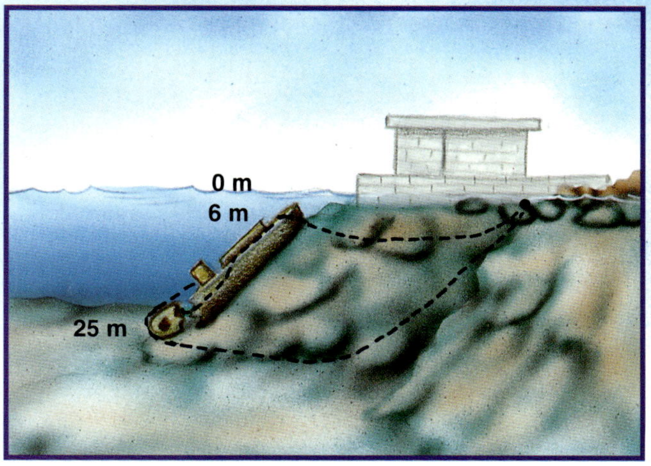
0 m
6 m
25 m

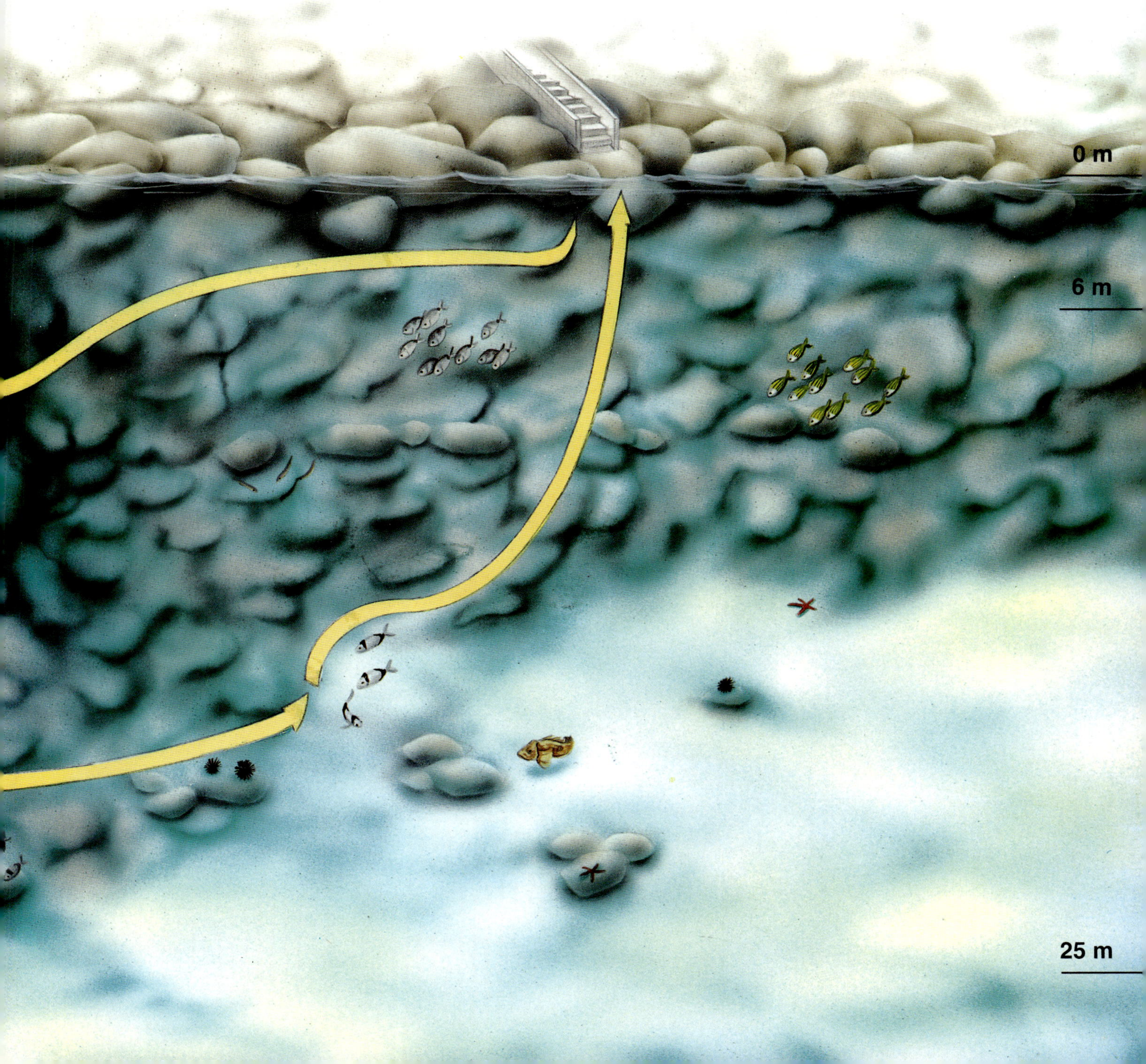
0 m
6 m
25 m

LOCATION

On the eastern side of Marsamxett Harbour - the opposite side from HMS *Maori*, is Manoel Island. An island in name only because it has, for many years, been connected to the mainland by a road which leads directly to the Royal Malta Yacht Club. Just before it reaches the club, there is sufficient space to park and prepare your diving equipment above steps which lead right down to the waters edge. Here the diver will find plenty of places for an easy entry and exit to and from the water.

Most divers walk as far as they can (in a south-westerly direction) towards the very prominent old Military Hospital building before a large wall prevents further progress at this point. In this way the underwater swim to the wreck is shortened. The vessel faces directly up a sloping seabed with the bows at a depth of 6 metres and the stern at 25 metres and is located right below one of the first windows of the now disused hospital. The wreck is clearly marked on Chart 974.

A

B

C

D

HISTORY

This vessel is sometimes mistakenly called *The Carolina* or *The Coral* and has even been referred to with an "HMS" prefix against any of its three names. All Royal Navy ships bearing the HMS prefix are well recorded and there are none bearing any of these names. Furthermore, although she was quite likely Royal Navy property, the HMS prefix was never bestowed on the many barges used to supply the various naval craft of her day. What is certain is that - on 21 April 1942, the vessel was moored at the submarine depot on Manoel Island. She was possibly mistaken for a submarine in the dark when a torpedo struck her in the stern and she sank immediately.

A - An old photo shows the submarine docking area at Manoel Island, where the Carolita *was sunk on April 21, 1942. Probably mistaken for a submarine, it was hit by a torpedo.*

B - The diving area at Manoel Island is near the old Military Hospital, which has remained practically unchanged since the war.

C - Several areas within the wreck can be visited, in particular the engine room and the steering compartment. Other passageways inside the wreck are too narrow and dangerous to explore.

D - A diver examines the interior of the hull from a gash in the wreckage, probably caused by the torpedo that sank the boat.

THE DIVE

To reach the wreck, divers should swim in a south-westerly direction at any depth between 10-15 metres. In this way, they will definitely find the wreck.
En route, the divers will encounter a variety of interesting artefacts such as bath tubs, hospital beds, wheel chairs, typewriters, various interesting bottles and other paraphernalia all thrown into the sea at some time during or after the war.
Throughout this dive, visibility can be poor - sometimes as little as 5-10 metres, but the effort is well worth the experience - especially when you arrive upon the wreck before anybody has had chance to reduce the visibility even further by stirring up the silt.
Although it is always best diving practice to start at the deeper part of any dive and proceed towards shallower water, it is always much easier to describe any vessel - beginning at the bows and working towards the stern. Despite being another casualty of WW2 and therefore, underwater for fifty years, *The Carolita* is in remarkable condition.
The bows are long and straight with double bollards on each side. As remarkable as it may seem the heavy mooring lines are still intact and in place leading from these bollards to some unseen secure point on the shore. The deck is flat with a small hole right at the front containing a resident octopus. Immediately behind this is a small double access hatch with a ladder leading downwards to the vessel's interior. This is such a tight squeeze that entry is not recommended.
Further towards the stern, is the large covered hatchway that once gave access to the cargo hold.
I am informed that the cargo was sacks of cement at the time of sinking, so *The Carolita*'s relevance to the submarine depot at this time becomes somewhat obscure - but then who knows what duties might befall any vessel during this time of considerable hardship.
Right behind the hatch, is the small wheelhouse which sits immediately above the damaged stern. The floor to the wheelhouse is missing, revealing the engine room below. It is quite possible to swim into the engine room from the damaged section and exit via the wheelhouse - a short journey which most divers discover for themselves.
The torpedo damage at the stern is the only visible damage to the entire vessel - although it is quite extensive. The stern section is almost completely broken away and leans over on its starboard side. The decking has also disappeared at this point revealing the steering mechanism.
Throughout this dive octopus, small groupers and thousands of damselfish are encountered although the diver can be forgiven for concentrating on the actual wreckage and, therefore, missing many of these and other creatures.

PHOTOGRAPHY

As with all wrecks, the main objective is to capture certain features of the vessel on film and, in this case I found it to be particularly difficult. Being located right inside part of the busiest harbour in the country, the wreck has become covered with a thick layer of silt which is easily disturbed whatever precautions are taken. After several attempts, I found the best method was to dive with a single partner on a day when the weather was such that other divers were likely to be visiting more popular sites elsewhere.
In this way, using the 20mm lens, I was able to photograph prominent features of the wreck without the silt being disturbed.
As for close-ups, a large octopus has taken up residence in the front of the wreck and appears to be quite happy to emerge to have its photograph taken, but this does take considerable patience.

E

F

E - The seabed around the wreck is muddy and scattered with objects of every type: hospital beds, chairs, typewriters, bottles and a large variety of objects thrown in during and after the war.

F - Many octopuses can be seen during the dive. One has chosen a small hole in the front part of the deck as its residence, while others hide among the wreckage scattered on the seabed.

BLENHEIM BOMBER

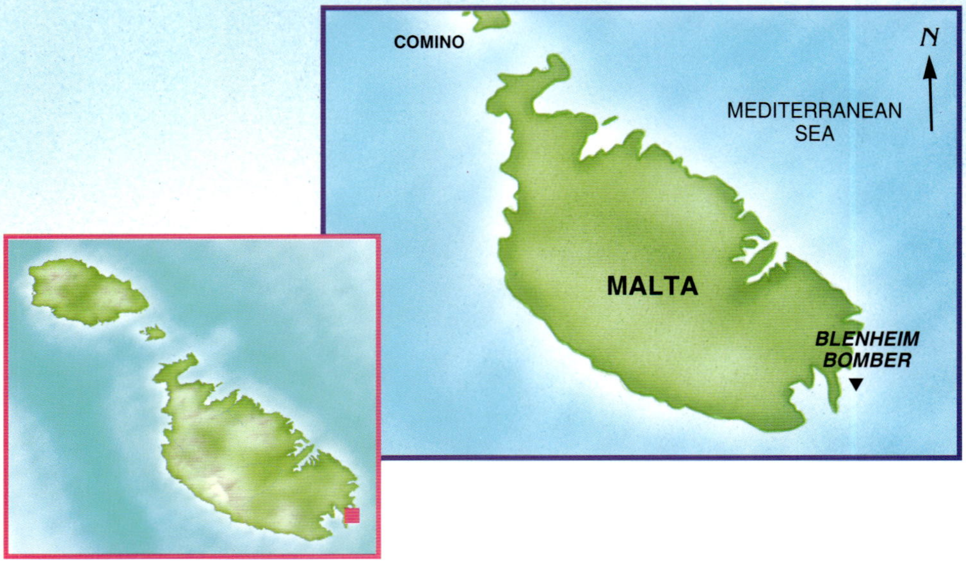

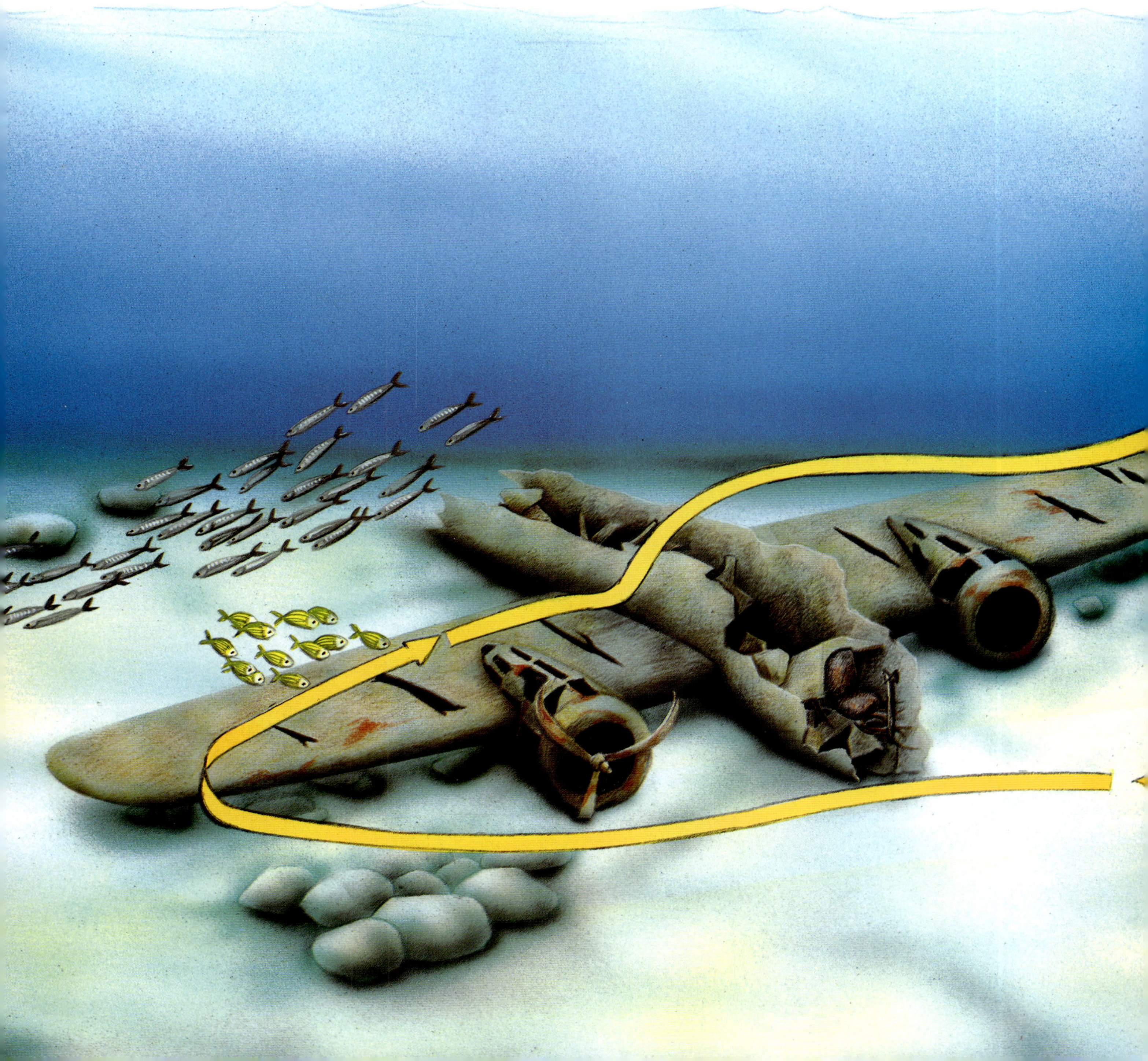

N
BLENHEIM
BOMBER

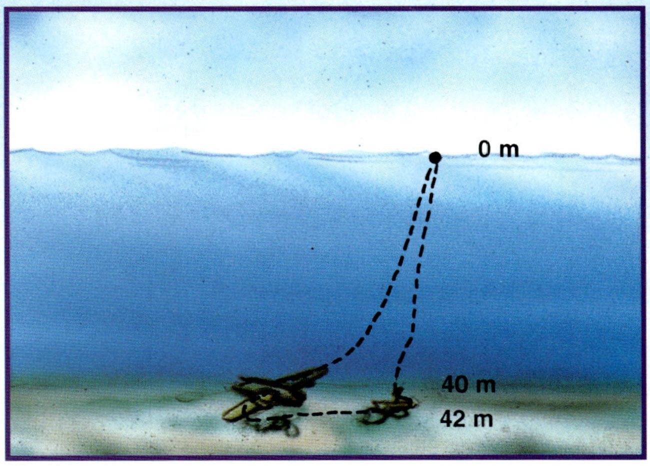
0 m
40 m
42 m

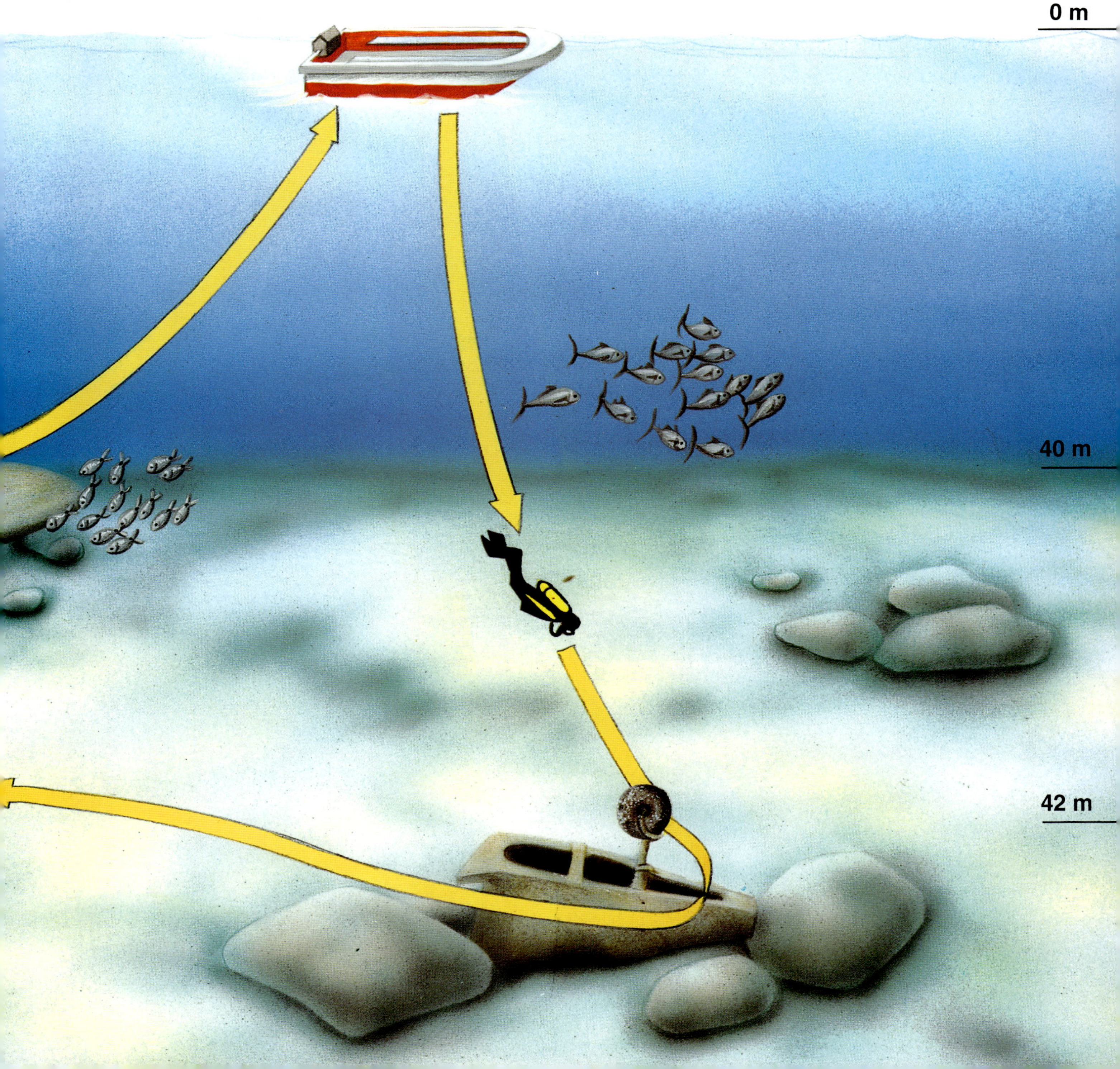
0 m
40 m
42 m

LOCATION

This aircraft is located approximately 800 metres due east of *Xorb Il-Ghagin* at a depth of 42 metres. The wreckage is not marked on the chart and - with its low underwater profile, will not be detected by position finding equipment. The precise location of the wreck is, therefore, known to very few people and you are advised to contact Ray Ciancio of Sport Diving Ltd in order to dive this wreck.
Ray has conducted considerable research into the aircraft and it was he who identified it as a *Blenheim* and not a *Beaufort*

B

A

C

A - This non-stop dive down to a depth of 42 metres requires careful organization. It is important to plan the length of the dive and consequent air consumption.

B - The Blenheim *was a light bomber in the English air force, equipped with two radial engines. It had a wingspan of 17 metres and carried a crew of 3 persons. It is not known when this plane, lying in the waters of Xorb il-Ghagin, was shot down.*

C - The great propeller of one of the engines, still in good condition, is covered with sponges and other benthic organisms. This wreck is of great historical interest.

D - The wreck lies 42 metres deep with its wings in flying position, while the fuselage is destroyed and partially covered by sand.

D

E

eventually replaced by the much smaller 3 man Mark IV Blenheim bombers. That said, although there is no doubt that the aircraft is indeed a Blenheim, the aircraft's specific identity and call sign has not yet been established. This will involve many hours of painstaking work in searching the wreckage for those important clues such as engine serial numbers. If the visiting diver should discover such information, it is vitally important, therefore, that they

G - One of the engines has lost the entire casing that covered it, revealing the complex structure of the Bristol Mercury, *a large, 920 horsepower radial engine.*

G

F

H

E, H - The control sticks are still in front of the pilot's seat. Although it's almost instinctive, you should not sit on the seat, as it would disintegrate rapidly

F - On good days visibility can exceed 30 metres, and you can get an overall view of the wreck, with its wings extended in flight position.

bomber. There are also the remains of a *de Havilland Mosquito* nearby - but that is another story!

HISTORY

Throughout WW2, Allied resources and manpower were always at a premium. At one point a squadron of Wellington bomber aircraft were stationed in Malta but, possessing a much greater range, were much needed elsewhere and were be pointed out to the dive leader but left exactly where they were found.

THE DIVE

This is a fabulous and very exciting dive and now rates as one of my own private Top Ten Dives - ever! The aircraft quickly begins to take shape as you descend. The wings and engines are virtually intact although the port side propellers are missing. The cockpit cover has also disappeared and this might suggest the crew safely ejected prior to ditching.
The pilot's seat and control column are quite intact and altogether these aspects form the main section.
The fuselage is detached and lies upside down a few metres to the front - mostly buried. In fact, it might not be recognised at all were it not for the single, non-retractable stern wheel which now sits upright and proud of the seabed - still occupying the extreme rear end of the aircraft. Altogether this allows divers to independently explore and inspect the entire area of wreckage without getting out of site of their buddies. The main wheels - retracted during flight, are still to be found on the underside of both wings still in that retracted position.
The engine covers have long gone thus enabling the diver to inspect the many parts that made up this type of 920 hp Bristol Mercury engine.
The control lever is directly in front of the pilot's seat and there is always a temptation for the diver to sit in the seat for a brief moment of fantasy. In this case, however, the seat is very small and any such temptation should be avoided at all costs because all the diver will achieve is to break the seat from its rather delicate mounting.
Irrespective of the depths involved, most of the dives in Malta allow the diver to follow the natural contours back towards shallow water for the

A

B

C

D

D - Careful and patient observation enables us to discover the extraordinary animal world that colonizes the structure of the wreck. This image shows a red crab that flaunts its long claws menacingly.

E, F and G - Perhaps attracted by the safe refuge offered by the most remote recesses of the Blenheim *bomber, some animals watch the approaching photographer curiously. In particular, we can observe below us a shy blenny, a courageous hermit crab and a red scorpionfish.*

E

F

G

A - The two engines of the Bristol Mercury *allowed the plane to reach 400 km per hour.*

B - A careful inspection of the wreck also enables us to admire the airplane's main landing gear.

C - The dive on the Blenheim *bomber is a fascinating experience: after some metres of descent we are able to make out the outline of the plane, and the light of our torch reveals complete metal parts that are still in good state of conservation.*

resultant decompression. Not so with this aircraft which is several hundred metres offshore. The only danger is therefore a badly planned dive where there is insufficient air for the necessary decompression.

PHOTOGRAPHY

This is one of those rare opportunities to photograph aircraft wreckage underwater - with and without the presence of fellow divers. When planning your photography you should remember that this is a deep, offshore dive and time on the wreck is, therefore, very limited before the commencement of the ascent and relevant decompression. A wide angle lens (20mm) will allow the diver to capture large sections of the aircraft in addition to filling the frame with those easily identifiable parts such as the port and starboard engines, cockpit and the upturned rear wheel.

DELIMARA POINT

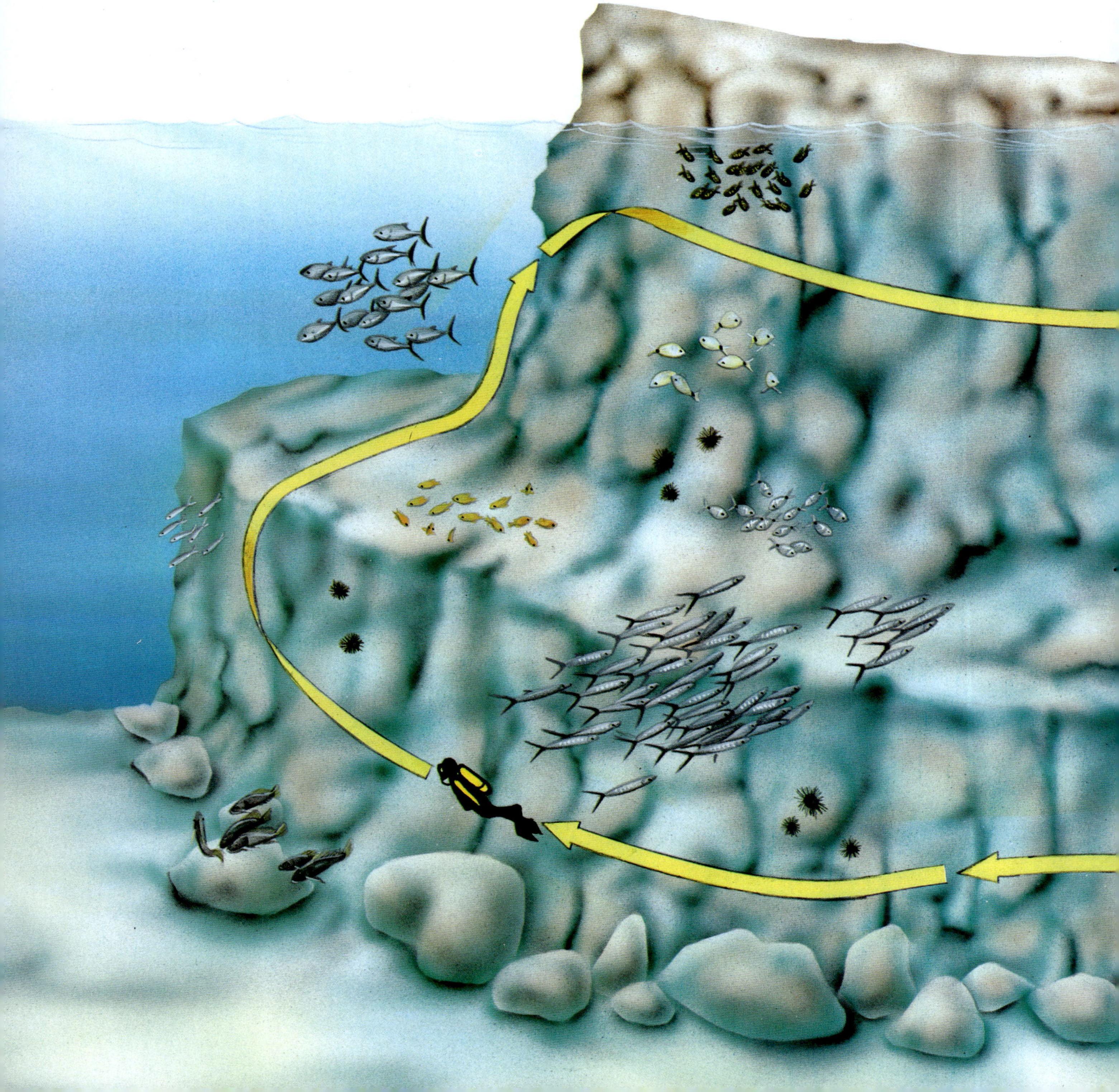

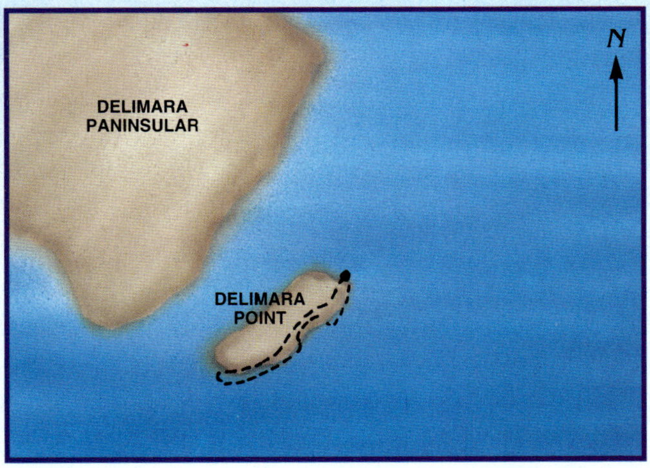
N
DELIMARA
PANINSULAR
DELIMARA
POINT
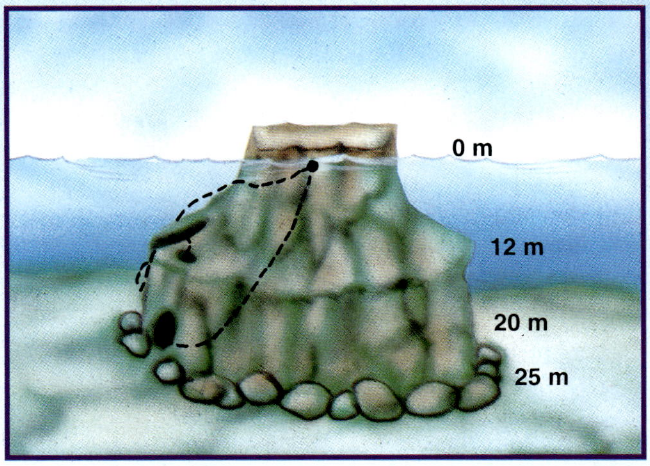
0 m
12 m
20 m
25 m
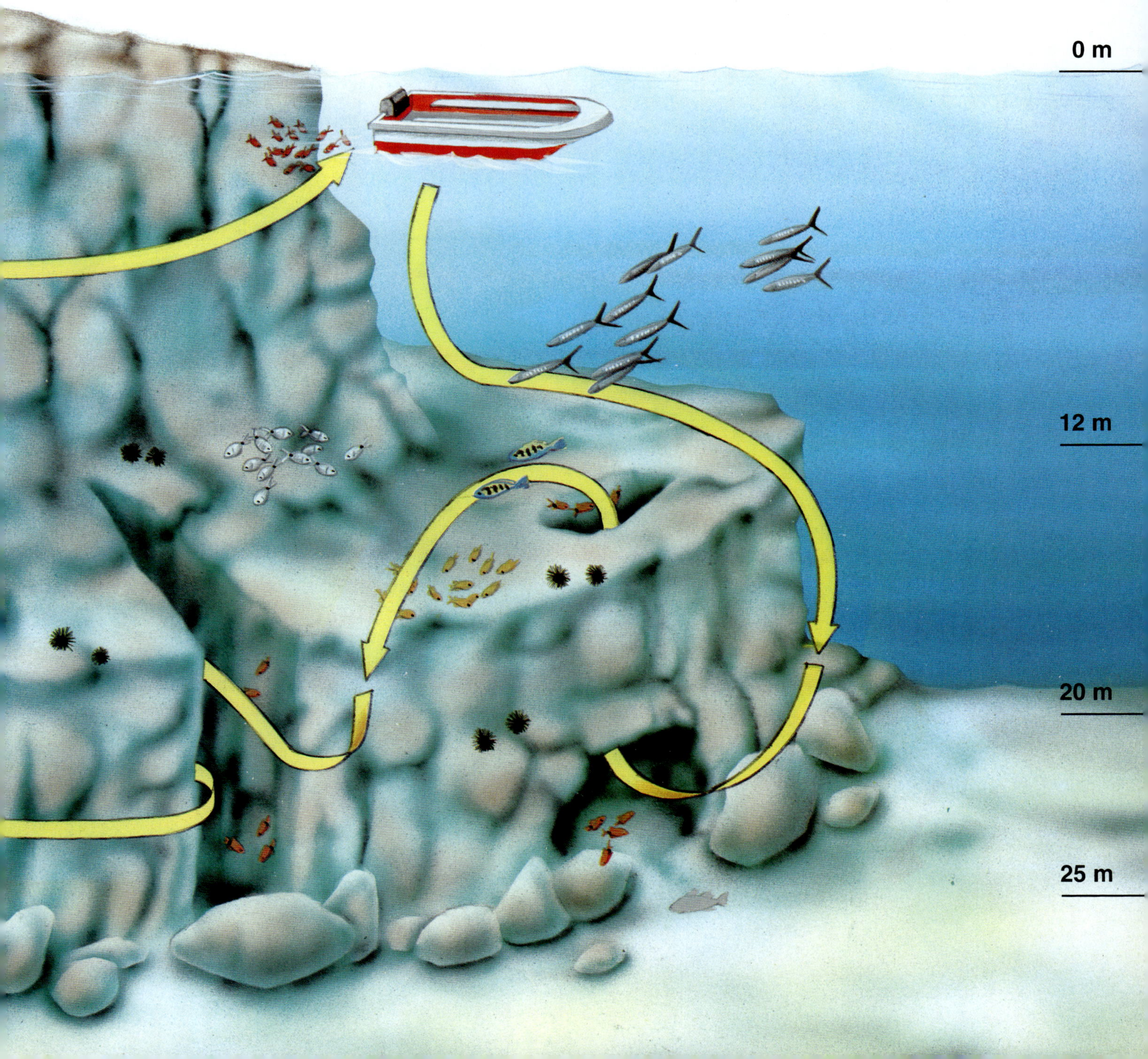
0 m
12 m
20 m
25 m

A - At the tip of the Delimara Peninsula, a small square rock indicates the diving area. The route winds through the open sea. You must absolutely avoid crossing the channel towards the mainland, which is continuously crossed by ships and boats.

B - On the walls near the surface, good illumination and strong hydrodynamics favour the presence of algae, which is well adapted to this environment.

C - Skirting the wall, you will come to a flat sandy area where rays are common, while elusive groupers can be seen in the distance.

D - A vertical tunnel leads from the deepest base of the wall to a depth of 12 metres, where the seabed slopes down. The walls of the cavity are covered with calcareous red algae, typical of poorly illuminated zones.

LOCATION

Right at the end of the Delimara Peninsular a small square-shaped rock barely breaks the surface. This rock provides the very best diving off Delimara Point. This is a boat dive and should not be attempted by swimming across from the shore - see notes on safety.

THE DIVE

The dive boat will anchor on an underwater reef which extends eastwards from the rock over a large area. This commences at a depth of about 9 metres and drops gradually down to 12 metres where the diver will discover a vertical cliff down to 25 metres. At the bottom of the north-east corner of this underwater plateau is a curious cave which rises up from the seabed to a ceiling at 20 metres. Here the diver will further discover a vertical tunnel right back to the top of the reef.
For those who know where to find the upper entrance to this tunnel, their dive often commences with a dive right through to the lower exit at the base of the cliff - an exciting start to any dive!
The cliff base is a fairly uniform 25 metres and is littered with some very large boulders close in. In amongst these, the diver will often see the elusive grouper disappearing into the distance. Beyond these the seabed is open sand on which the common stingrays are often seen. As the divers approach the south-east corner of the rock it is time to start the ascent back to the plateau. Here there are several parrotfish, scorpionfish and black sea urchins. Back at 12 metres the divers will encounter large concentrations of damselfish as they follow the edge of the cliff wall back towards the boat. About halfway there is a very interesting fissure in the rock and on the shaded side there are numerous cardinalfish, sea squirts, red sponges and those beautiful yellow soft corals in

A

B

C

D

E -
The Mediterranean parrotfish (Sparisoma cretense) *has gaudy colours like its tropical cousins. The individual in the photo is a female; males are less vivid.*

F - The groupers of Delimara are quite elusive and will rapidly seek shelter in crevices. The dorsal fin of the individual in the photo is extended in a typical sign of alarm, in this case due to the presence of the photographer.

G - A close-up of a scorpionfish shows its complex colours, which are perfectly adapted to the colour of the seabed. Scorpionfish use mimicry to surprise and capture their prey.

H - A large red star (Ophidiaster ophidianus) *crawls along the sea floor, with its long, purplish red, velvety arms. This is a temperate waters species which is easier to spot in the southern part of the Mediterranean.*

I - The branches of bryozoans (Porella cerviconis) *stand out among the sponges in a poorly illuminated area. Bryozoans are colonial animals which live within a communal hard skeleton.*

E

F

G

H

addition to the occasional moray eel and octopus. Elsewhere on the plateau, the diver will find many examples of those fishes common to these waters.

SAFETY

Fast boats continually speed between this rock and the shore creating considerable danger for any diver caught between the two. Divers must ensure, therefore, that they remain on the seaward side of the rock at all times - where it is absolutely safe. Divers are also advised not to attempt to swim across to this rock.

I

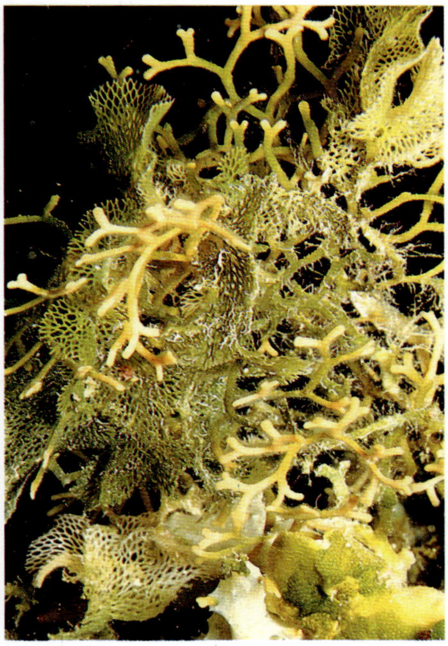

PHOTOGRAPHY

This site is at the extreme south-east of the country and is, therefore, able to command some of the best underwater visibility to be found anywhere. When the conditions are right, underwater visibility of 50 metres is not uncommon. The site is excellent for wide angle photographs of divers with a backdrop of dramatic scenery provided by steep cliffs and the tunnel.
At the top of the reef wall there is much to occupy the photographer seeking macro photographs of a wide variety of marine life. In short, there is something here for everyone.

WIED IZ-ZURRIEQ

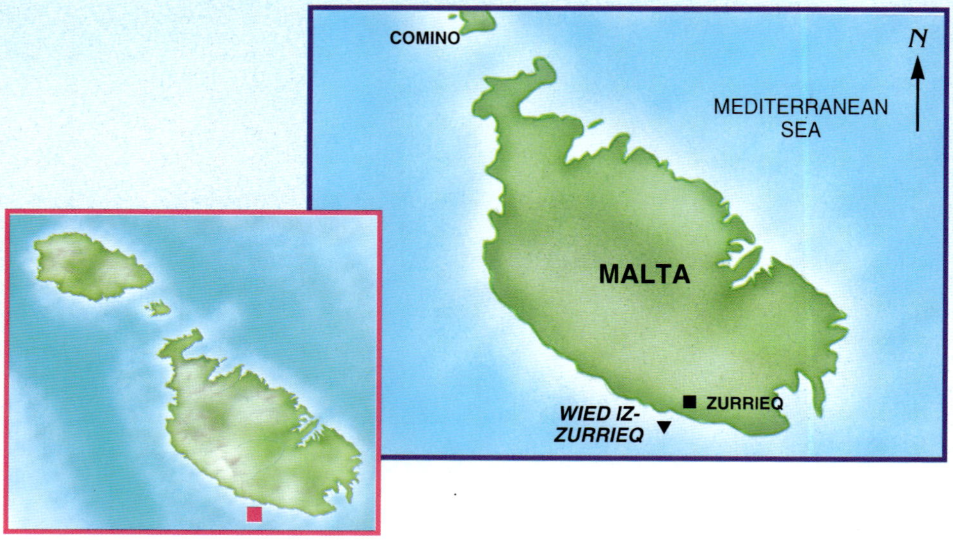

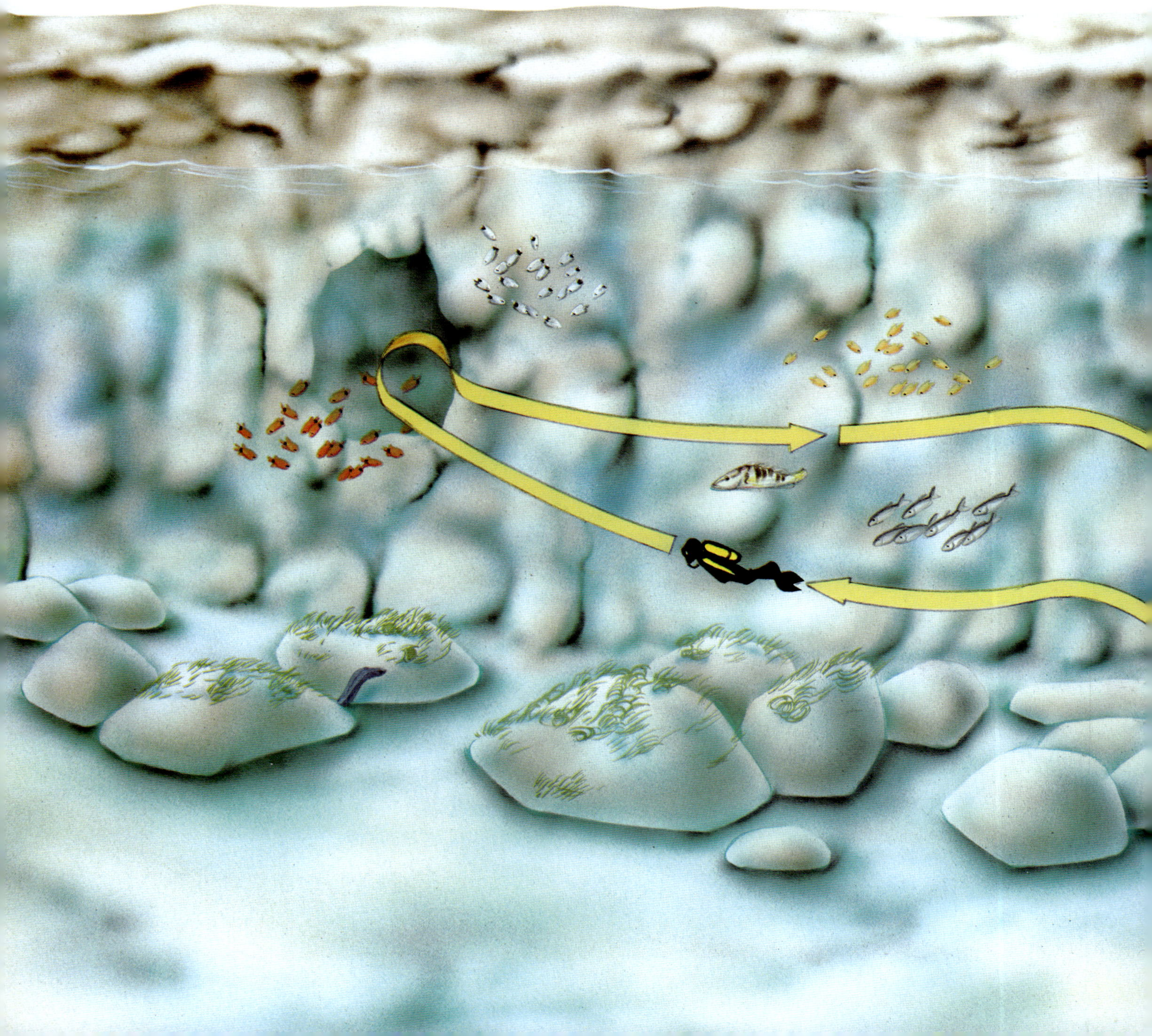

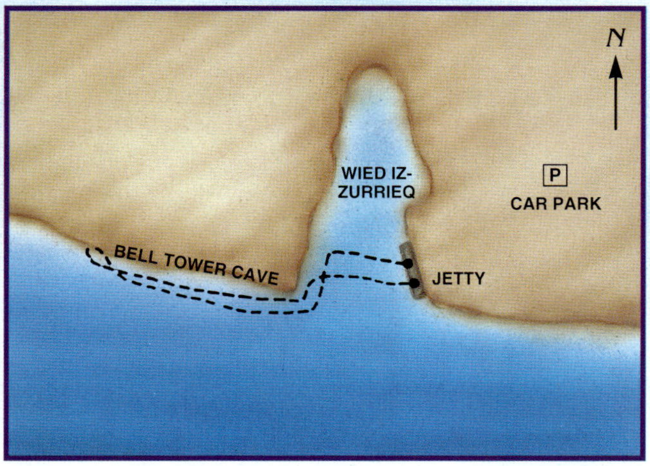
N
WIED IZ-
ZURRIEQ
P
CAR PARK
BELL TOWER CAVE
JETTY

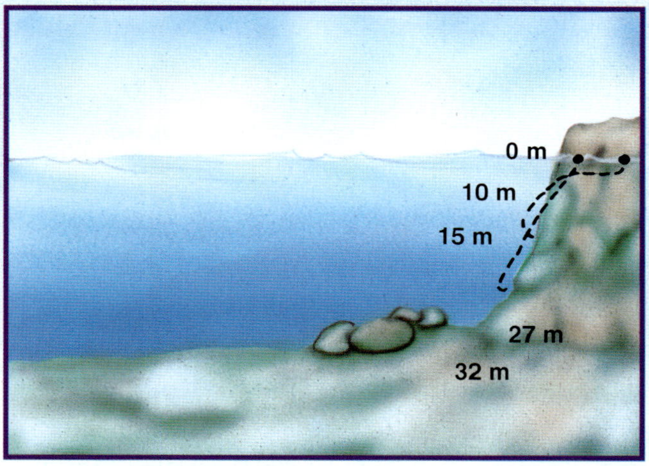
0 m
10 m
15 m
27 m
32 m

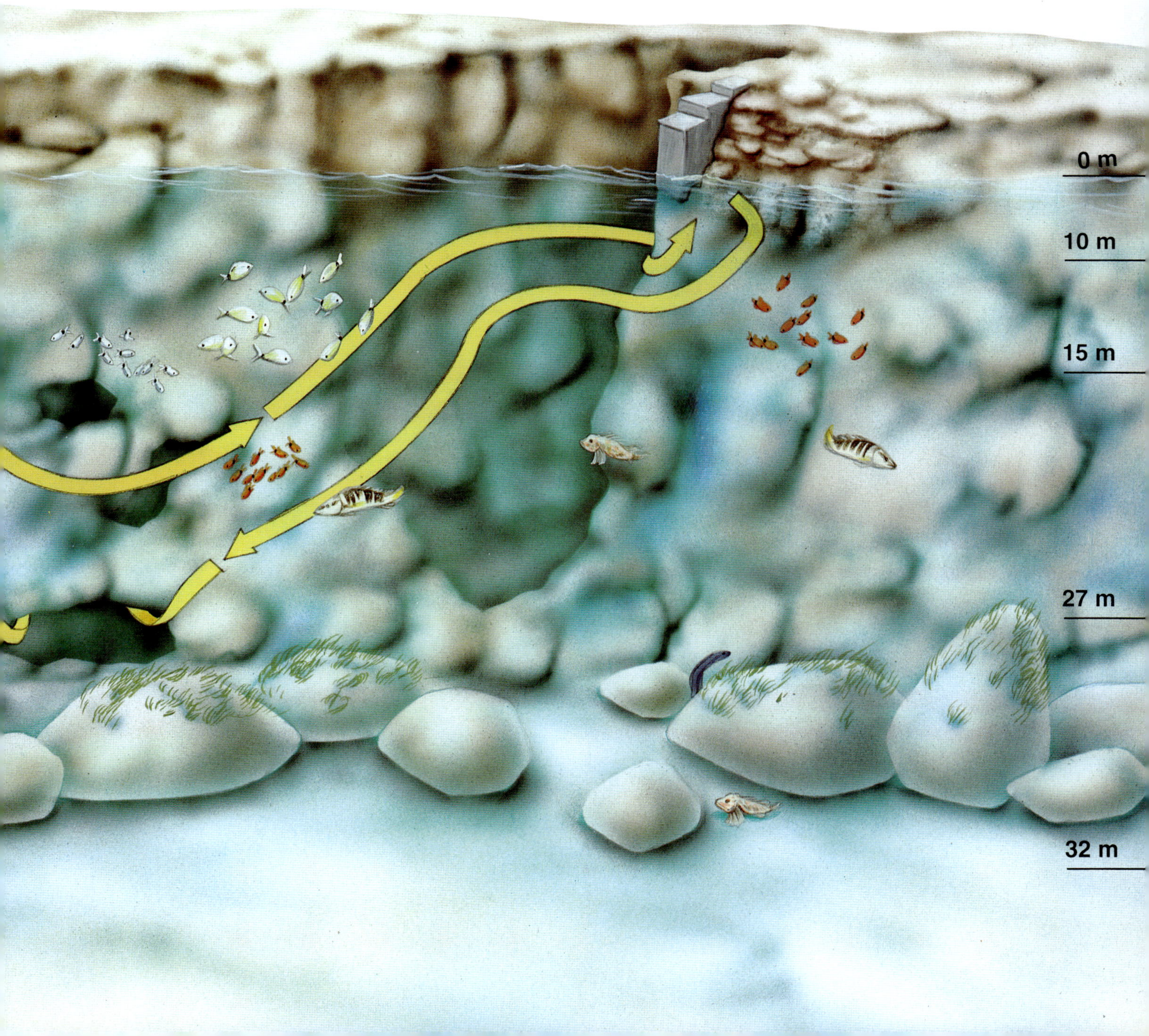
0 m
10 m
15 m
27 m
32 m

A - On the southern coast of Malta, a road ends right at the inlet of Wied iz-Zurrieq. This is a convenient place to prepare for the dive and enter the water, heading west.

B - At a depth of 27 metres is Bell Tower Cave with its three entrances. The cave owes its name to its almost perfect bell tower shape. The entrances are relatively narrow, and inside is a cloud of cardinal fish.

LOCATION

All the tourist maps clearly show the small inlet at Wied iz-Zurrieq on the south coast of Malta. Here the road comes to an abrupt end on the eastern side of this inlet and the diver will find plenty of space for parking, kitting-up and getting into the water. The dive commences by swimming across the inlet and out towards the open sea before turning and following the coast in a westerly direction.

THE DIVE

This is a very popular dive which commences with an entry into the water from a small, narrow quay very popular with anglers. On one dive we noticed one of these gentlemen getting a little upset with so many divers so we made a conscious effort to take a slightly longer route in order to lessen the disruption to his day. Throughout the dive we then just happened to find several lost fishing weights which we were able to give him at the end of the dive and suddenly all divers were his very best friends!
Having entered the water, you will reach a depth of 10 metres within the inlet as you cross over to the far side before turning left and heading out towards the sea. Keeping the rocky shoreline to you right on the outwards leg, you will exit from the inlet at a depth of about 27 metres and follow the natural contours around to the right. This is the base of another vertical cliff face - the top of which is well above the surface of the sea. A short distance along the diver will discover the incredible "Bell Tower Cave." Not a perfect "Bell" shape but it is very nearly so and has three very narrow entrances. The largest of these is right at the base of the cliff at a depth of 27 metres. It is a tight squeeze but the other entrances are even tighter. Inside, the cave has sufficient room for 2 or 3 divers at any time and is full of

C

D

A

B

C - Just below the surface, a compact school of salemas grazes on the rock, heedless of the presence of divers. Salemas are gregarious fish, and often several of them will remain at the edge of the group to act as sentinels and warn of any possible danger.

D - A moray peeping out of a crevice is being cleaned by a red shrimp. In exchange, the shrimp receives food and protection, as the moray will not in fact eat it.

cardinalfish. Leaving that cave behind, you progress further along the wall. This area is occupied by so many fish - painted combers, damselfish, rainbow and turkish wrasse, saupe, goatfish, scorpionfish and many, many that it is often referred to as "The Aquarium." All of which makes this one of the best sites for night-diving in the country.
Continuing further along in the same direction, the diver eventually finds another cave at 25 metres. This has a much larger entrance and thus is always thoroughly investigated by all the divers in the party. This point in the dive also marks the turning point for commencing the return journey.
Further inside the inlet is a slipway for small fishing craft that are often coming and going. Whilst the fishermen are aware of divers and take every care, the diver must also exercise extreme caution throughout the dive - but especially when in the inlet.

PHOTOGRAPHY

Like so many of the other diving locations, a number of different dives will be required to cover every aspect of photography available at this site. The area can also command excellent underwater - an added bonus for those engaged in wide-angle photography. With very little room inside the Bell Tower, the best photographs tend to be taken from the inside with your fellow divers on the outside. Elsewhere, this site is excellent for close-up and macro photography with all the common varieties of the smaller species found throughout the dive - and in good numbers. With the dive beginning and ending inside the harbour, there are many more species, including the occasional cuttlefish found amongst the detritus that is found in every similar inlet.

E

F

G

H

E - A cuttlefish extends its tentacles upward. This is a typical position used to camouflage itself as it prepares to attack.

F - The middle portion of the dive is in an area known as The Aquarium, *due to the great diversity of fish which can be seen here, especially at night. The photo shows a small scorpionfish among the algae.*

G - A solitary cardinal fish swims in the cavern, among sponges and false coral.

H - A tompot blenny resting among the rocks has a more faded colour than normal. This is one of the many examples of how fish can change their colours to match their surroundings.

GHAR LAPSI

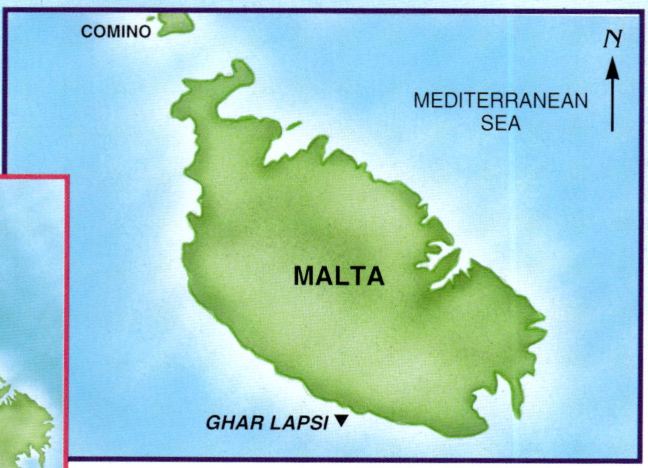

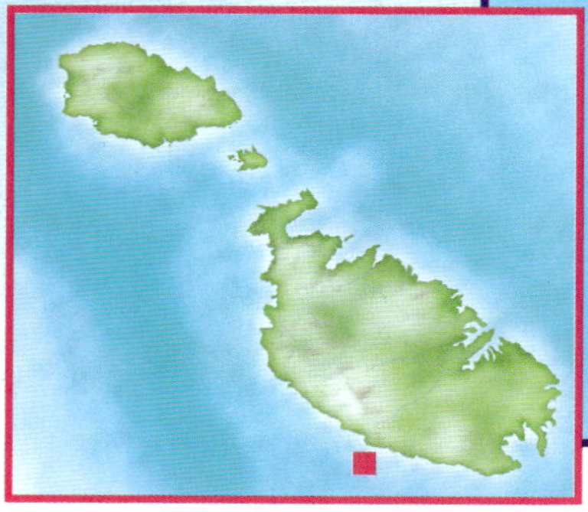

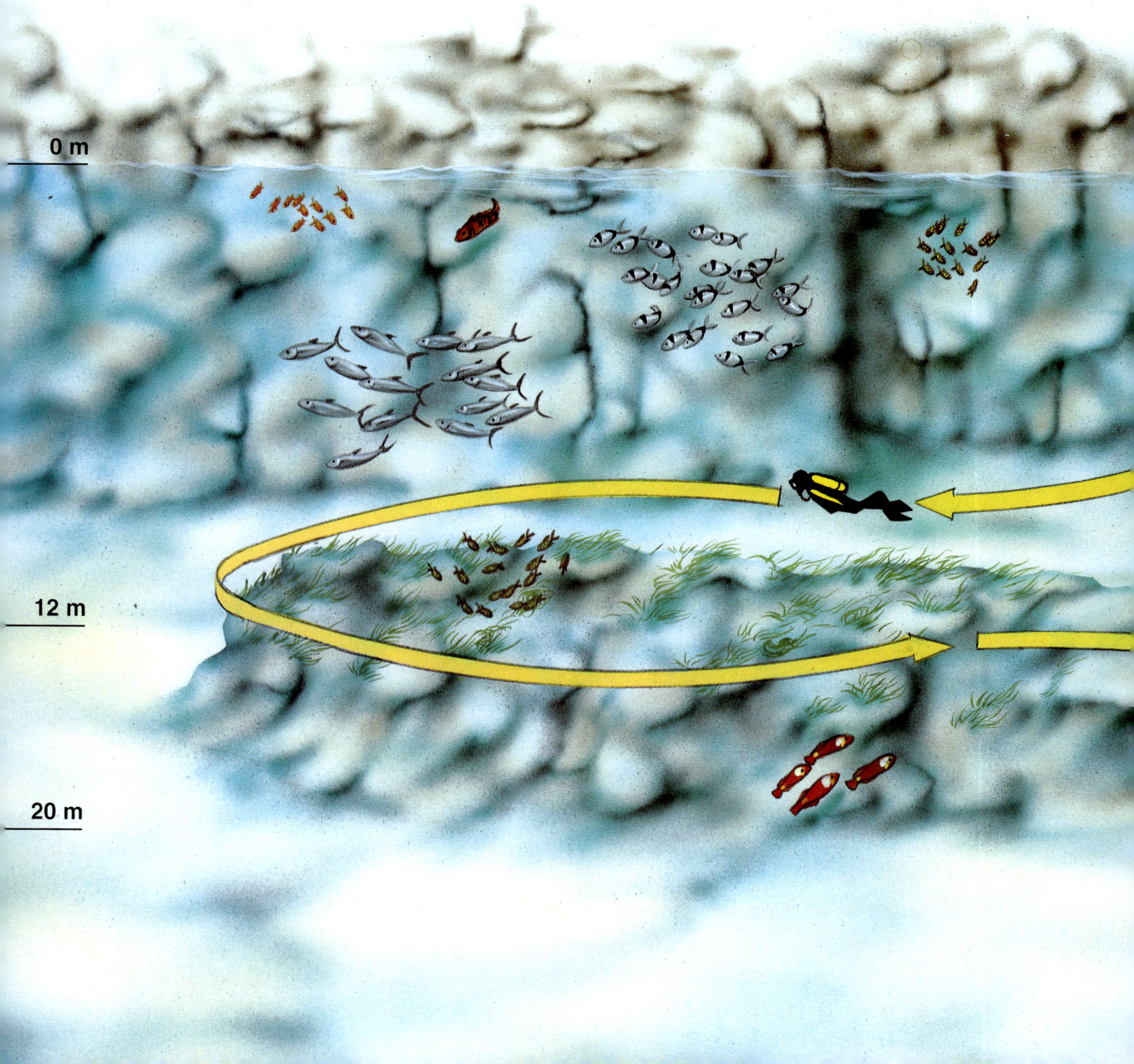

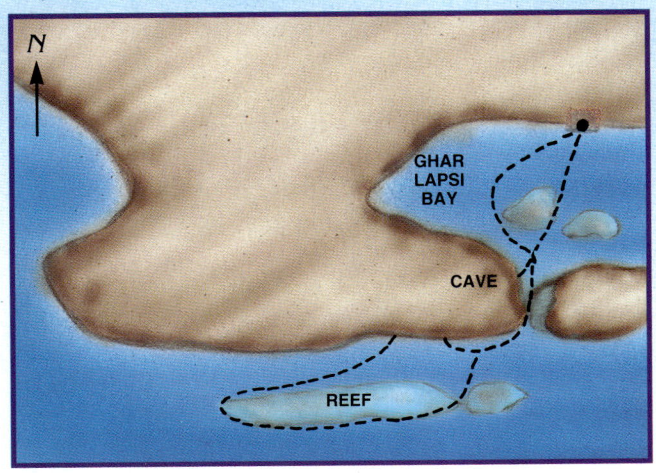
N
GHAR
LAPSI
BAY
CAVE
REEF

0 m
12 m
20 m

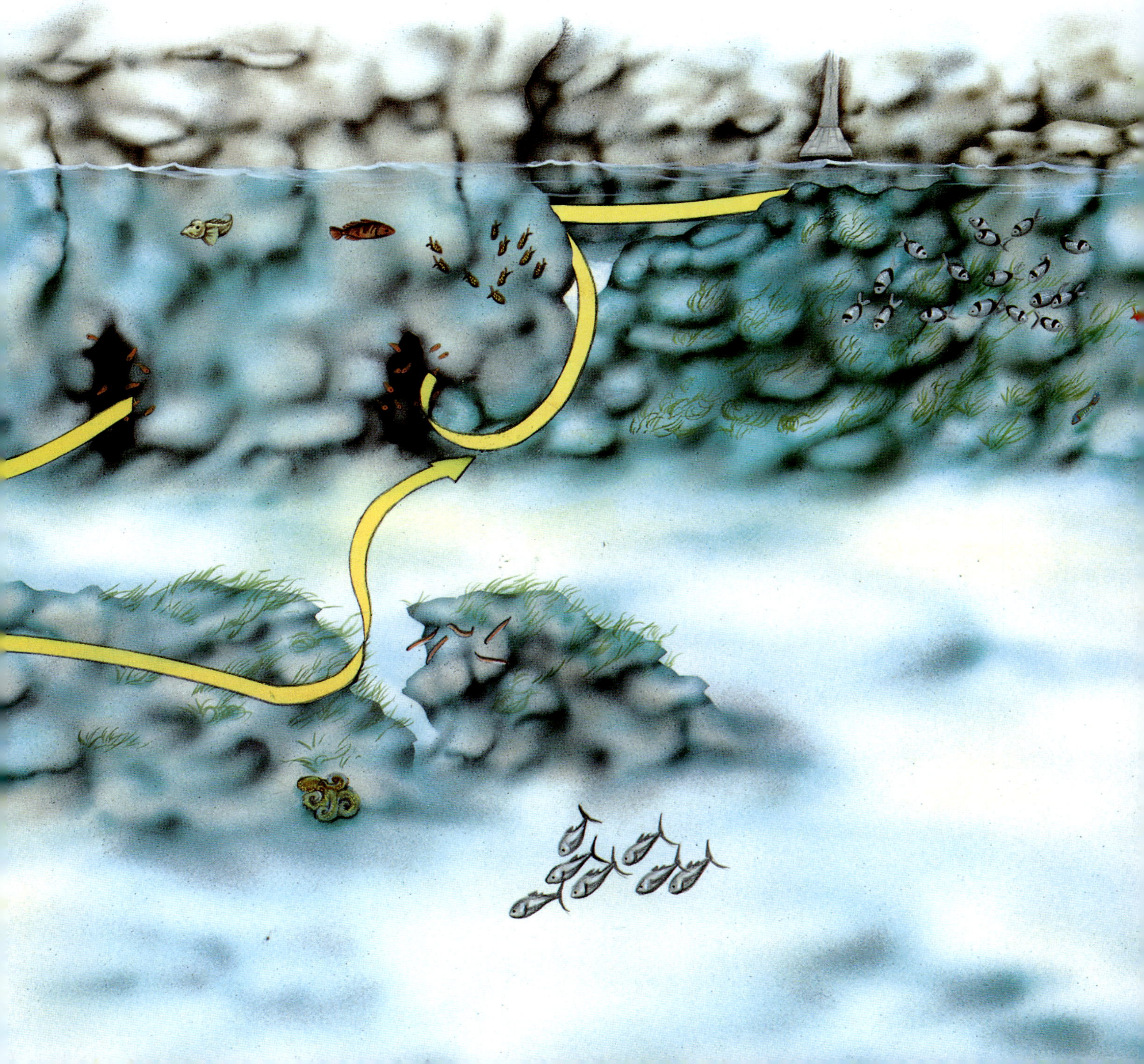

A

B

C

D

LOCATION

Ghar Lapsi is also well marked on the tourist maps and there is a good road leading right to an open carpark immediately above the access point. Here, the diver will find a wide slipway leading down to the water edge where a short swim across the bay brings the diver to a ladder right at the end of a concrete path. Although this was provided for swimmers, the ladder marks the entrance to a large, shallow cave system which is the beginning of this dive.

THE DIVE

The cave entrance is narrow and slightly complicated to find with the diver having to swim over one rock almost at the surface and then beneath another until all is revealed. The cave itself is rather wide and flat and there are a number of different entrances and exits - through which the sun reflects creating marvellous underwater images. On leaving the cave you exit from a steep, vertical cliff face at a depth of 9 metres and, swimming in south-westerly direction, you cross over to a large oblong reef a short distance away.
Between the cliff and the reef, large boulders litter a seabed which is 20 metres at its deepest. Occasionally some very rare fish

E

A - The entry point at Ghar Lapsi is indicated by steps which lead to a system of caves.

B - A long rocky ridge that rises to 12 metres from the surface is covered with algae. Here seahorses and nudibranchs, as well as a great variety of fish can be seen.

C - The dive winds through a varied, entertaining route, at a depth that never exceeds 20 metres.

D - A group of rainbow wrasses crowds on the rock in search of food. Sexual dimorphism is evident; in the centre the more colourful individual is a male, while the one below is a female.

E - The cave through which the dive begins has various entrances. The sunlight filters in through it to create beautiful underwater scenes.

F - A tangle of algae and hydrozoans seems to demonstrate how it is sometimes difficult to distinguish plants from animals underwater.

G - The delicate orange tentacles of the Astroides *turn some stretches of seabed into true flower meadows.*

H - A front view of a tompot blenny shows its protruding, independent eyes and its large mouth.

I - A Tylodina perversa *sponge feeding gastropod crawls along the seabed in search of its favorite sponge.*

have been sighted here so stay alert. The reef has a long shape rising up from the seabed to within 12 metres of the surface and stretches for over 100 metres before coming to an end. Large areas are covered in seagrass where there is every chance of the diver discovering some of those rather special smaller creatures such as seahorse, nudibranch and even sea hare. All the usual common fishes are found throughout the entire length and breadth of this reef. Circumnavigating the reef eventually brings the diver to a position opposite the cave entrances in the cliff wall and at this point he should cross back

H

F

I

G

in order to complete the journey, thus creating another opportunity to enjoy the cave system - by the same or another route to the bay or, if preferred, the diver can continue in a westerly direction and enter the bay by avoiding the cave altogether.
Not generally known for its currents, this dive has been known to produce fairly strong easterly currents of 1-1,5 knots which can make the return journey very hard work indeed.

PHOTOGRAPHY

The most outstanding feature of this dive is undoubtedly the cave - through which most dives start and end. As with all caves, however, silt is a serious problem so, once again, the photographer should enter the cave first and position himself in readiness for his fellow divers as they proceed through the cave. For this a 20mm lens is essential as is adequate lighting in a very dark environment.
Remaining with wide-angle photography, the best shots are, however, taken at the end of the dive. Once again you should position yourself inside what was the cave exit (and is now the entrance as you proceed through in the opposite direction) and capture each diver as they approach.

ANCHOR BAY

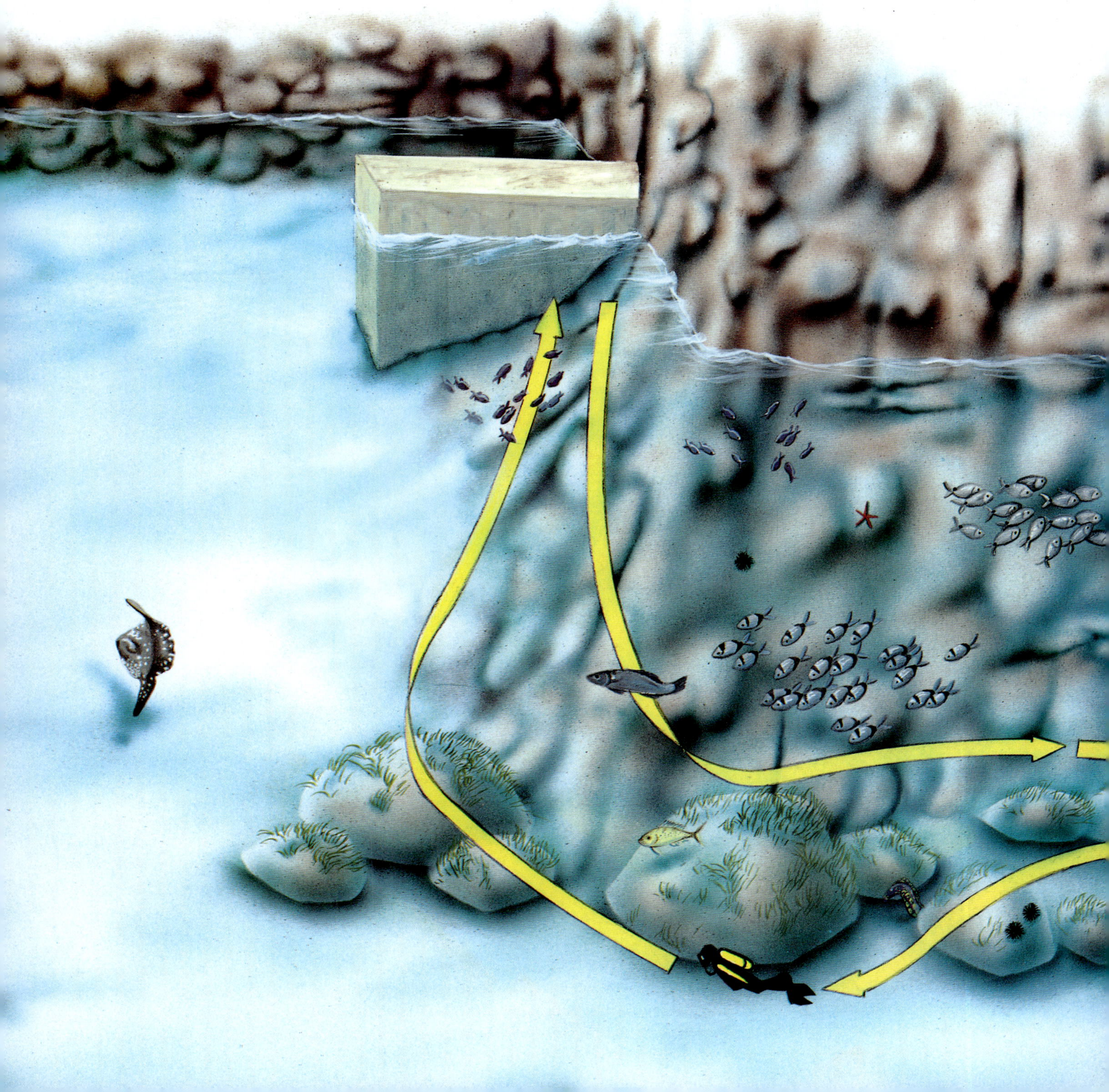

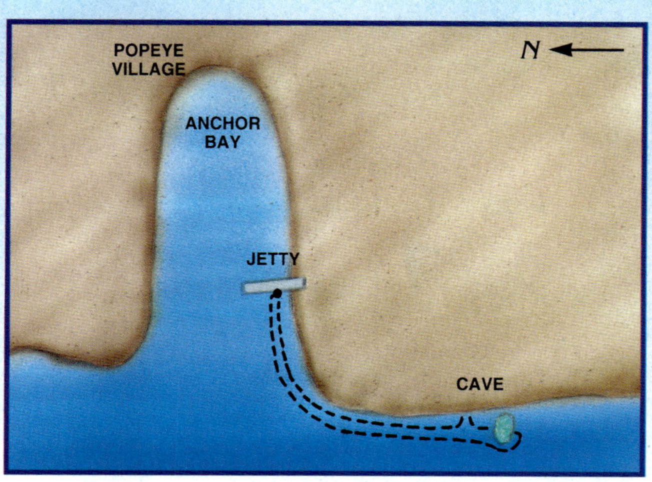
POPEYE VILLAGE
N
ANCHOR BAY
JETTY
CAVE

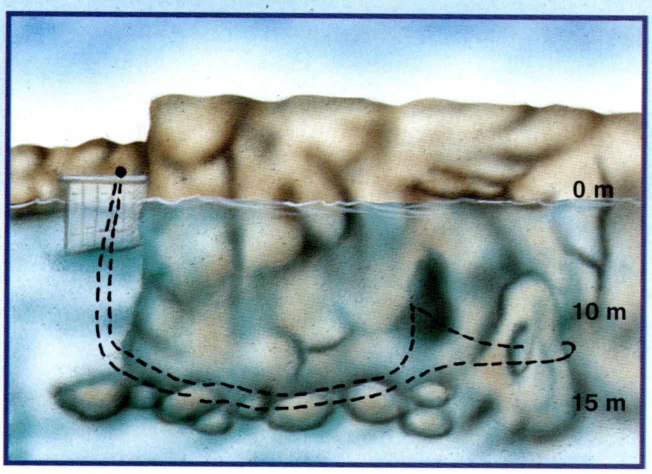
0 m
10 m
15 m

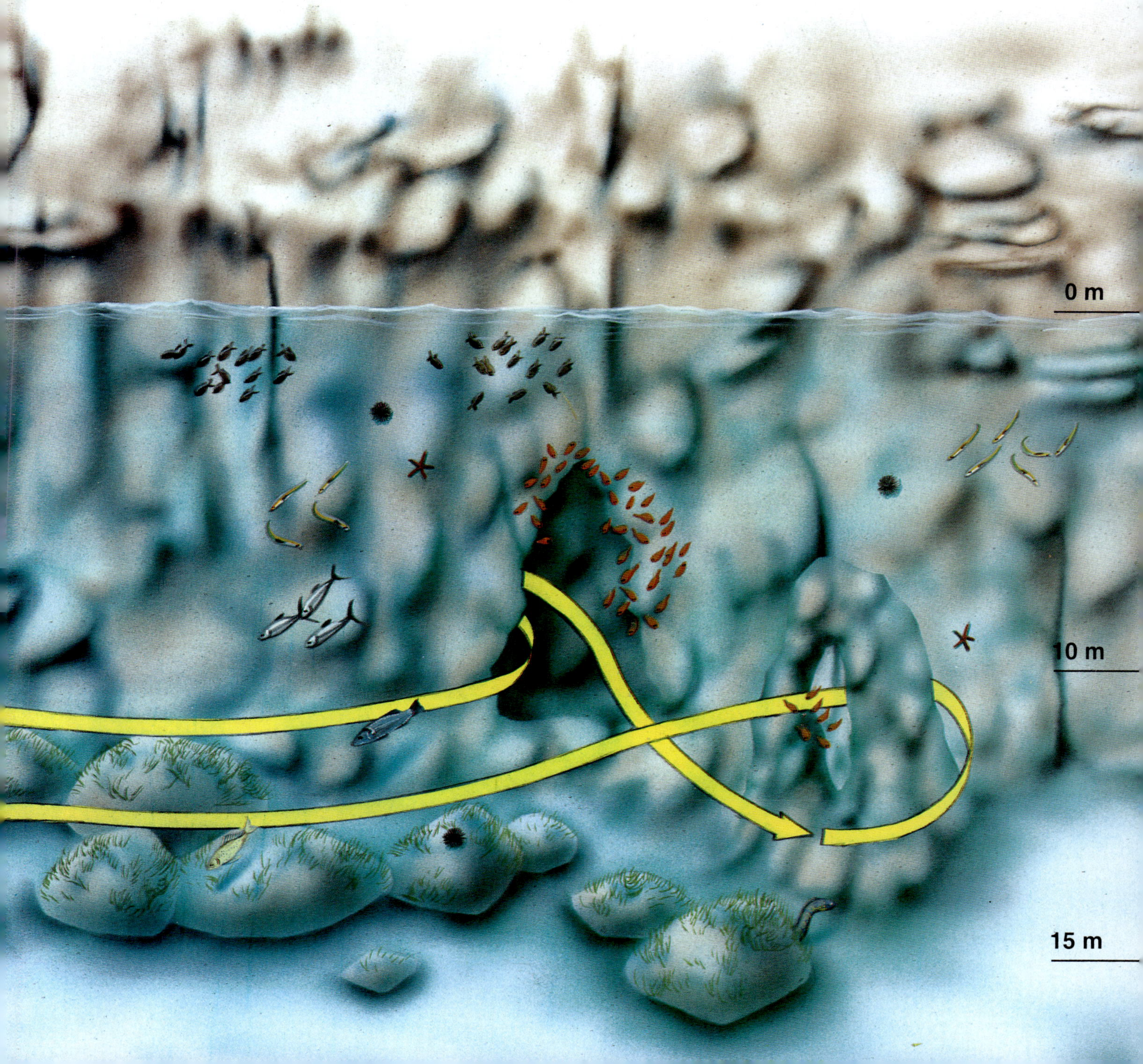
0 m
10 m
15 m

A - The coast of Anchor Bay changed its name after the set for the film "Popeye", with Robin Williams, was built here, and now maps show it as Popeye Village. The bay takes its name from a great anchor abandoned on the sea floor.

B - The dive begins at a place called Jetty, following the south side of the bay and then turning left.

C - Visibility within the bay is generally poor, but increases noticeably as soon as you head out to the open sea.

D - After about 150 metres along the wall, you will see a cave with a floor 10 metres deep. You can surface in the cave and observe the stupendous vault of the emerging cavity. Farther on, you'll see other beautiful passageways.

LOCATION

Almost as soon as the set for the Robin Williams film *Popeye* was built right on the shores of Anchor Bay all the local road signs were changed to read "Popeye Village". Follow these signs but carry on right past the tourist entrance to the village, at which point the road begins to wind down to a very substantial concrete jetty reaching out from the southern shores of the bay. Incidentally, this jetty provides one of the very best views of Popeye Village - across the bay - and is rarely enjoyed by anyone other than divers and fishermen! Anchor Bay gets its name from the actions of a captain in command of a warship. Apparently the anchor was dropped to assist in slowing the vessel down on entering such a shallow anchorage. The vessel was safe but the anchor was lost and can still be seen on the seabed - at the end of a very thick chain. Further anchors are found on the shore.

THE DIVE

Entrance into the water is from the jetty from where the diver follows the southern cliff face out of the bay and round to the left (south). Within the bay itself visibility is generally reduced by wave action on the sandy seabed but quickly improves as soon as the open sea is reached and the divers leave the bay behind.
Here the seabed is covered with some extremely large boulders. Many of these are found to be sitting one on top of another - providing some very interesting swim-throughs and curious formations. This is ideal country for octopus and groupers as well as other reasonably large fish that prefer to have a dark hole in which to escape should the need arise. It was here that I saw the largest scorpionfish I have ever seen and it was the less common red scorpionfish.
A large cave is located

A

B

C

D

E - A good close-up of a moray shows its eye and the characteristic protuberance of the nostrils on the front part of the snout.

F - A small lobster seems to show off all its complicated apparatuses: its long antennae, its claws and the extended telson.

approximately 150 metres from the bay - although it is almost hidden away in a corner of the cliff face and is, therefore, quite easily missed. The floor of the cave is at 10 metres and the divers are quite easily able to surface inside, where they will marvel at the magnificent dome shaped ceiling. A little beyond the cave is a large window right through the top of a prominent rock and most divers seem unable to resist the temptation of swimming through it.
The window generally marks the turn around point for this dive although there is no reason why other divers should not investigate even further.
Octopus and parrotfish are very common throughout the dive as are some medium sized groupers - the dive being too shallow for the really big ones. Moray eels are also occasionally seen and, although not encountered by myself, the area is renowned for stone fish - so beware.

E

F

G

H

PHOTOGRAPHY

Before commencing the dive, the photographer should bear in mind that the jetty provides one of the best views of "Popeye Village" seen across the Bay. The village is a very popular tourist destination but few visitors take the trouble to get away from the actual buildings to enjoy such a good view. Surface Camera, Natural Light, 55m lens for panoramic view - longer lenses for close-ups of individual buildings as required. Once the diver has left the bay and is following the cliffs around to the left (south), the visibility improves and the large rock formations, cave and window provide excellent situations for wide-angle photography involving your fellow divers. Throughout the entire dive there is also sufficient marine life to satisfy the close-up and macro lenses with the most outstanding creature being the splendid red scorpionfish.

G - A small brown scorpionfish among the vegetation on the sea floor extends its dorsal fin. This is a sign of alarm, perhaps because the photographer has come too close.

H - This close-up of a grouper shows its large lips, nostrils and big eye. Medium-sized groupers can be seen during the dive.

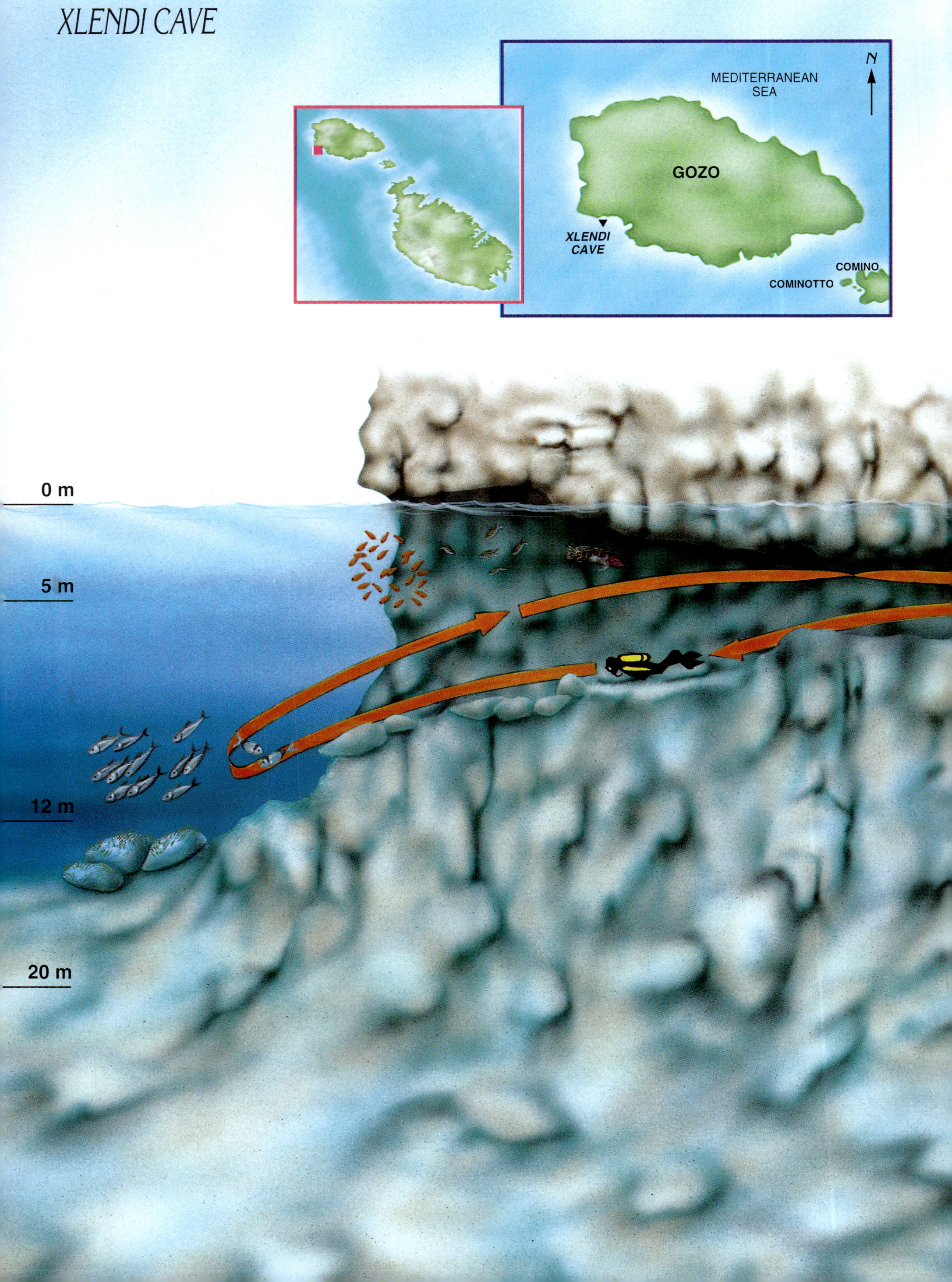
XLENDI CAVE
MEDITERRANEAN SEA
N
GOZO
XLENDI CAVE
COMINO
COMINOTTO
0 m
5 m
12 m
20 m

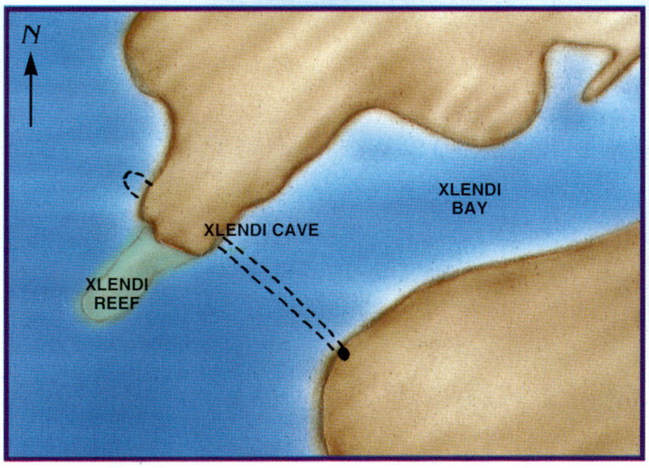
N
XLENDI BAY
XLENDI CAVE
XLENDI REEF

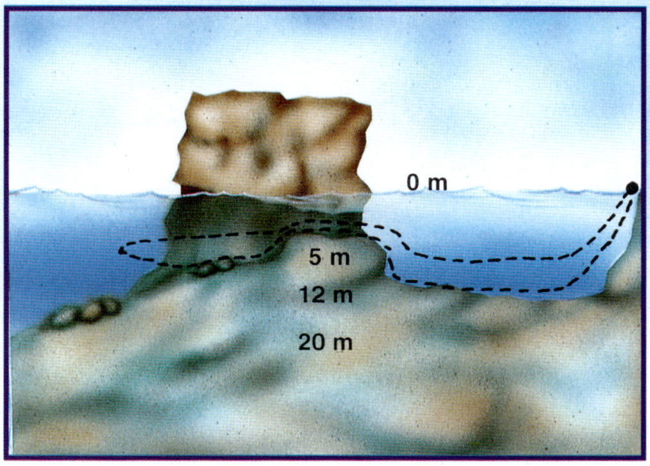
0 m
5 m
12 m
20 m

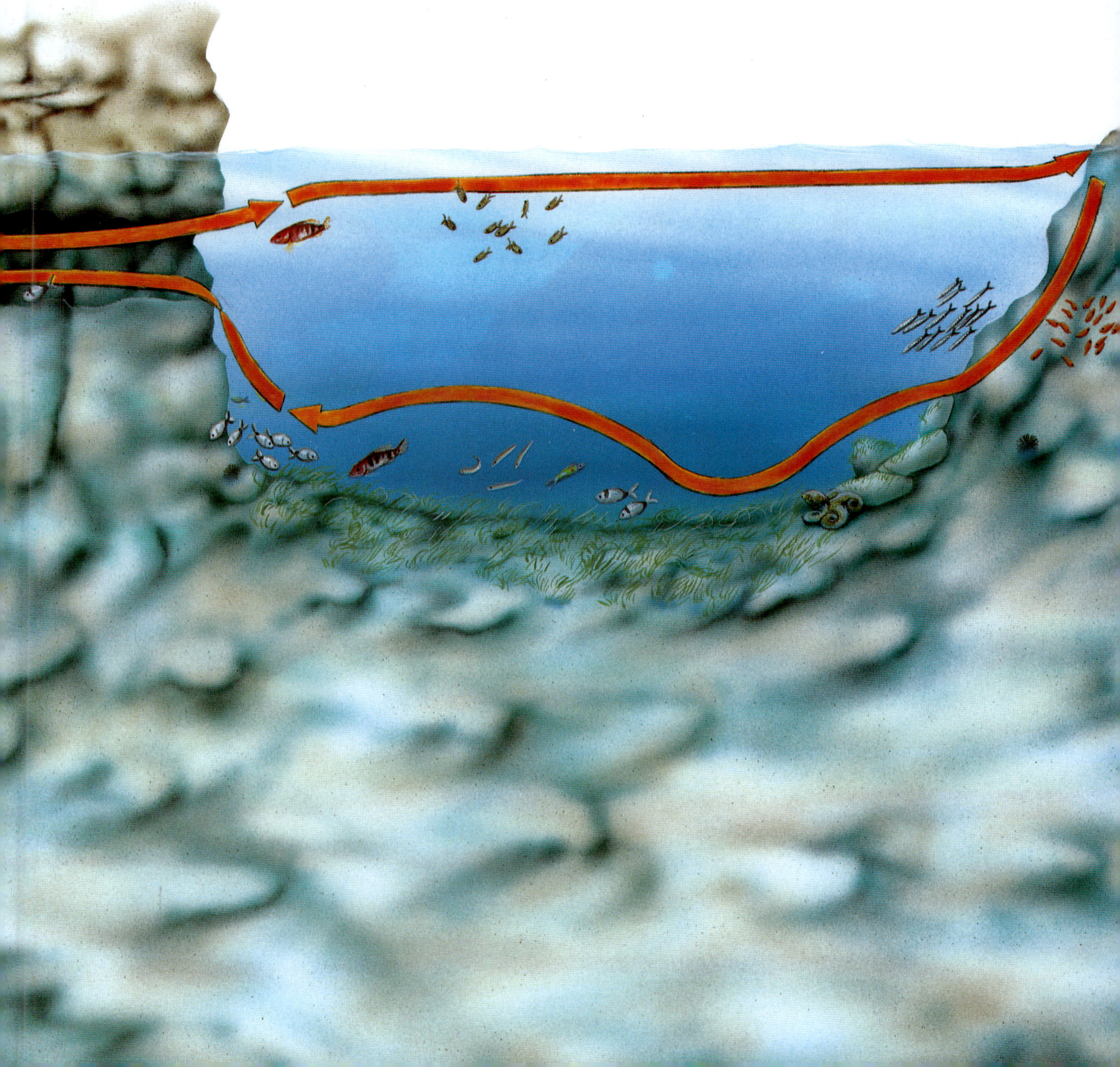

A

B

C

D

A - Xlendi Bay is long and narrow: the cave where the dive takes place is on the north side, where a rock wall descends vertically into the water.

B - The dive is not very deep, and given its simplicity, it is recommended for anyone who wants to try a cave dive for the first time.

C - Formations of beautifully coloured red calcareous algae are surmounted by concretions of coral in the outside area of the cave.

D - A group of bearded fire worms crowds on the rock, probably contending for food. Bearded fire worms feed mostly on dead animals.

LOCATION

Xlendi Bay is long and narrow and faces south-west. The northern shores comprise of fairly steep rocks which drop vertically at the waters edge. The southern shores are, however, quite different with buildings and, of course, the main road. Below these, a wide pathway runs right along the shore. Because Xlendi Cave is just below the surface on the northern shore, it is quite inaccessible from that side so the diver is required to follow the pathway to any point roughly level with the cave and swim across the bay - either on the surface or underwater.

THE DIVE

This is a shallow dive with much to recommend to those who are relatively new to cave diving.
In fact the deepest part of the dive is on either side of the cave with a maximum depth of 12 metres found at the bottom of the bay during the crossing. This contains large areas of seagrass on a soft, sandy bottom where the diver will find many different species of fish - especially juveniles. Small barracudas at only 5-6 centimetres in length are very common at certain times of the year.
Xlendi Cave has a really splendid entrance where the diver will find goatfish and painted combers actively feeding on the cave floor with numerous damselfish and cardinalfish above these. Apart from the cardinalfish, very few fish are found beyond this sunlit entrance in the darker confines of the cave itself.
Xlendi Cave is in fact a large bent tunnel which joins both sides of the rocky promontory which forms the northern extremity of Xlendi Bay itself. As the divers proceed through the tunnel, they begin to rise above large boulders and get progressively shallower. In fact, there are many places throughout this journey where the diver can surface before continuing with the dive. About halfway through, the diver will encounter three distinct features. To begin with, the tunnel bends to the left. As it does so, it suddenly

E

F

E - A small blenny (Blennius zvonimiri) *peeps out of its shelter. The smaller species of this group often use holes or dead shells for their dens.*

F - A porter crab rests on a carpet of yellow corals (Leptosammia pruvoti) *on the vault of the cave. Porter crabs take their name from the habit of younger individuals of covering themselves with a piece of sponge.*

drops three metres over a large rocky ledge. The cave floor at this point is covered with smooth, sea-washed rocks and shingle. It is at this point that the large exit comes into view and altogether, these features give the divers a feeling of adventure and of having entered something very large and very spectacular - which they have.

Although the far side of the cave marks the turn around point for this dive, it is also the start of another adventure which is covered in the next dive. Far from being the end of dive even, the return journey through the cave is very different from the outward leg as the diver encounters the steep rock wall and then swims around and over the large boulders which make this return trip different.

The most serious danger facing any diver undertaking this dive is from surface traffic. Do not surface in the middle of the bay unless it is vitally important and only then with extreme caution.

PHOTOGRAPHY

A photograph of a diver inside a cave could be a photograph of that diver inside almost any cave. This is not so with a cave entrance. Photographed from within, with natural sunlight in the distance beyond, each cave entrance reveals its own distinctive shape and pattern. Xlendi Cave has two such entrances. The inclusion of a diver in the foreground - and throughout their journey to the other side, adds dimension and scale to the photograph for which the wide angle lens is essential. Macro photography is, however, quite possible within the daylight zones of each of the two entrances. Red sponges, soft corals, goatfish, cardinalfish and other species are found here including some that are not normally known as "cave dwellers".

G - A large spiny starfish slides among the orange coral cushions. This starfish can become quite large, and its body is covered with spines and tubercles.

H - In the cave, among yellow corals and net sponges, the antennae of two small lobsters peer out. The antennae have a tactile function.

G

H

XLENDI REEF

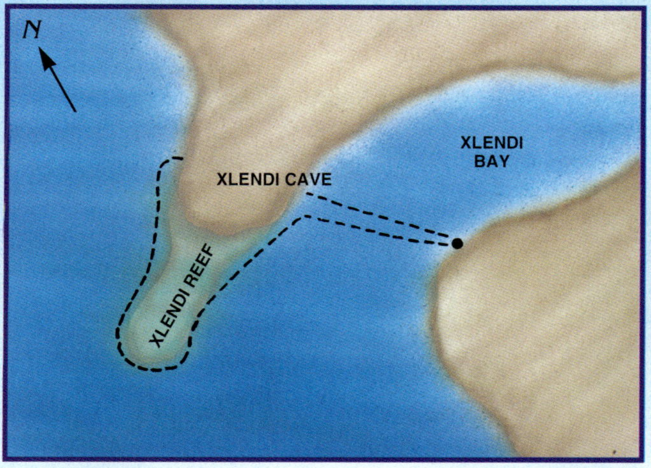
N
XLENDI CAVE
XLENDI BAY
XLENDI REEF

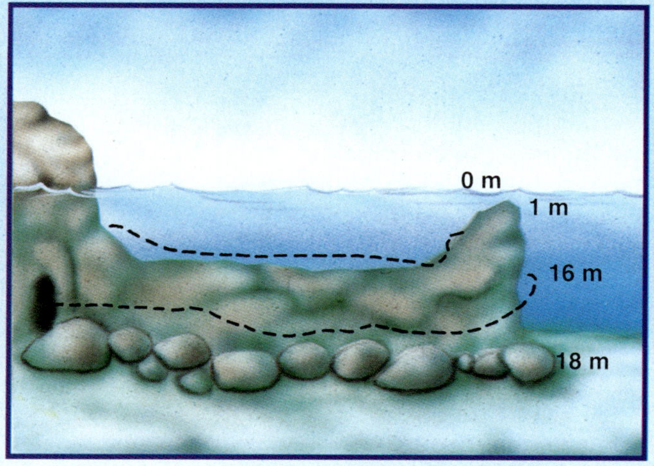
0 m
1 m
16 m
18 m

0 m
1 m
16 m
18 m

LOCATION

Xlendi Reef is located in the middle of the final approaches to Xlendi Bay. Of interest to divers is the fact that boat users deliberately avoid the reef because part of it reaches up to within a very short distance of the surface. Finding the reef is easiest from the far side of Xlendi Cave (see previous dive site). On leaving the cave, follow the rocky cliffs round to the left and it will lead you right to the reef. Keep the reef to your left throughout the dive and you will circumnavigate the entire structure and be well placed for a return direct into Xlendi Bay.

C

A

D

B

THE DIVE

After enjoying the exciting confines of Xlendi Cave, the diver emerges into an area rich in marine life. Beyond the cave, the seabed is immediately covered with extremely large boulders which provide refuge for groupers, octopus and scorpionfish. Just beyond these, the diver will also encounter several large amberjacks.
Above the surface, the rocky headland dips steeply down to the sea where it disappears. Underwater, however, this structure continues for quite some distance but in a different format altogether. The steep rocky reef is covered with light seaweed of green and gold with all manner of smaller fishes enjoying everything the area has to offer. There are large numbers of damselfish, small groups of grey mullets and many individual fishes such as painted combers, and various species of wrasses and seabreams.
The base of the reef continues to be littered with large boulders where many more interesting creatures are often observed. Soon, however, the diver will reach the end of the reef and this is marked by a large

A - During this dive you may encounter many species of fish: damselfish, groups of grey mullets, wrasses and seabreams.

B - A dive on Xlendi Reef begins just beyond the caves. By following the wall to the left you can circumnavigate the entire rock structure.

C - A good flashlight makes it possible to discover an endless variety of interesting organisms seeking refuge in the dark. All around, swarms of saddled seabreams swim frenetically in search of food.

D - Even the rocks near the surface are covered with sponges and orange corals. Swarms of damselfish can be seen in the blue depths.

E - Xlendi Reef is the entry to the bay of the same name. The longest portion almost reaches the surface, and is therefore avoided by passing ships.

F - A painted comber (Serranus scriba) *waits for prey on the sea floor. The scientific name for this fish comes from the complicated design on the upper part of its head.*

G - Octopuses can easily be spotted among the masses you'll pass at the beginning of the dive. Their mimetic abilities are not limited to just changes in colour, but in the form of their mantle by adding protuberances and furrows.

H - The red scorpionfish is easily distinguishable from other species by the protuberances under its jaw which do not exist in the brown scorpionfish and the small red scorpionfish.

pinnacle which reaches up to within a metre of the surface. On the extreme edge of this pinnacle the diver will enjoy several shoals of different species of fish.
As the divers swim around the end of the reef they are now facing into Xlendi Bay itself and automatically commence the return leg of the journey.
The species of fish found on both sides of the reef are fairly identical but garfish (always found at the surface) and very small barracudas (5-6 centimetres long) only appear to be found on this side.
Eventually, the reef comes to an end as the diver reaches a point directly below those steep cliffs seen above the surface.
To return via the cave at this point involves a very long swim indeed and is not recommended - it is also unnecessary because the entrance to the cave (on Xlendi Bay side) is now very close. As you continue to keep the vertical rock face to your left you are entering the bay along its northern shores and at any time you can surface and swim across the bay to one of the many exit points or continue underwater until you reach shallow water and leave from the beach.
The most serious danger facing any diver undertaking this dive is from surface traffic. Do not surface in the middle of the bay unless it is vitally important and only then with extreme caution.

PHOTOGRAPHY

In order to record the site on film a wide-angle lens is necessary. This will allow the photographer to capture the unique design of the reef - especially that part which almost breaks the surface.
The sheer variety of fish and other sea creatures in and around the reef have to be seen to be believed and the site is quite ideal for close-up and macro photography.

E

F

G

H

FUNGUS ROCK

MEDITERRANEAN SEA
N
DWEJRA BAY
GOZO
FUNGUS ROCK
COMINO
COMINOTTO

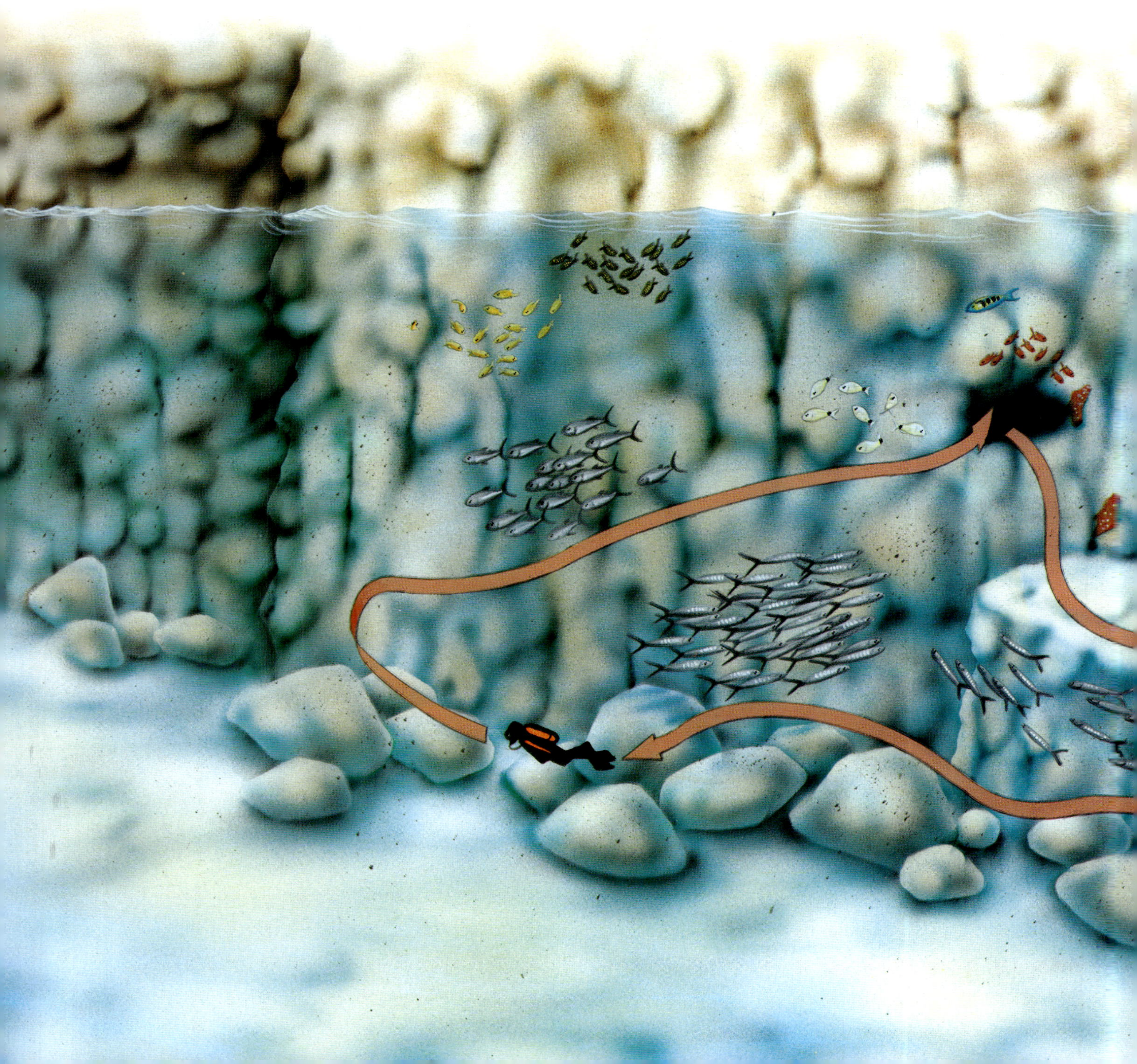

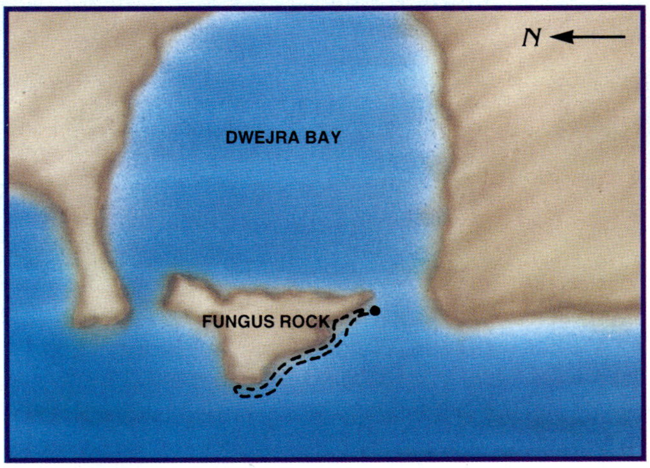
N
DWEJRA BAY
FUNGUS ROCK

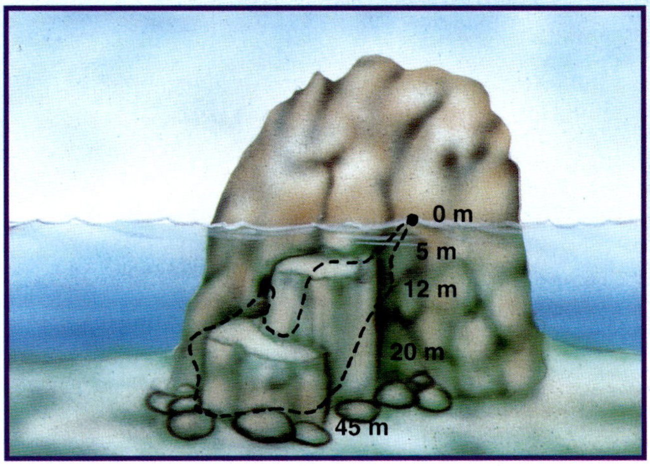
0 m
5 m
12 m
20 m
45 m

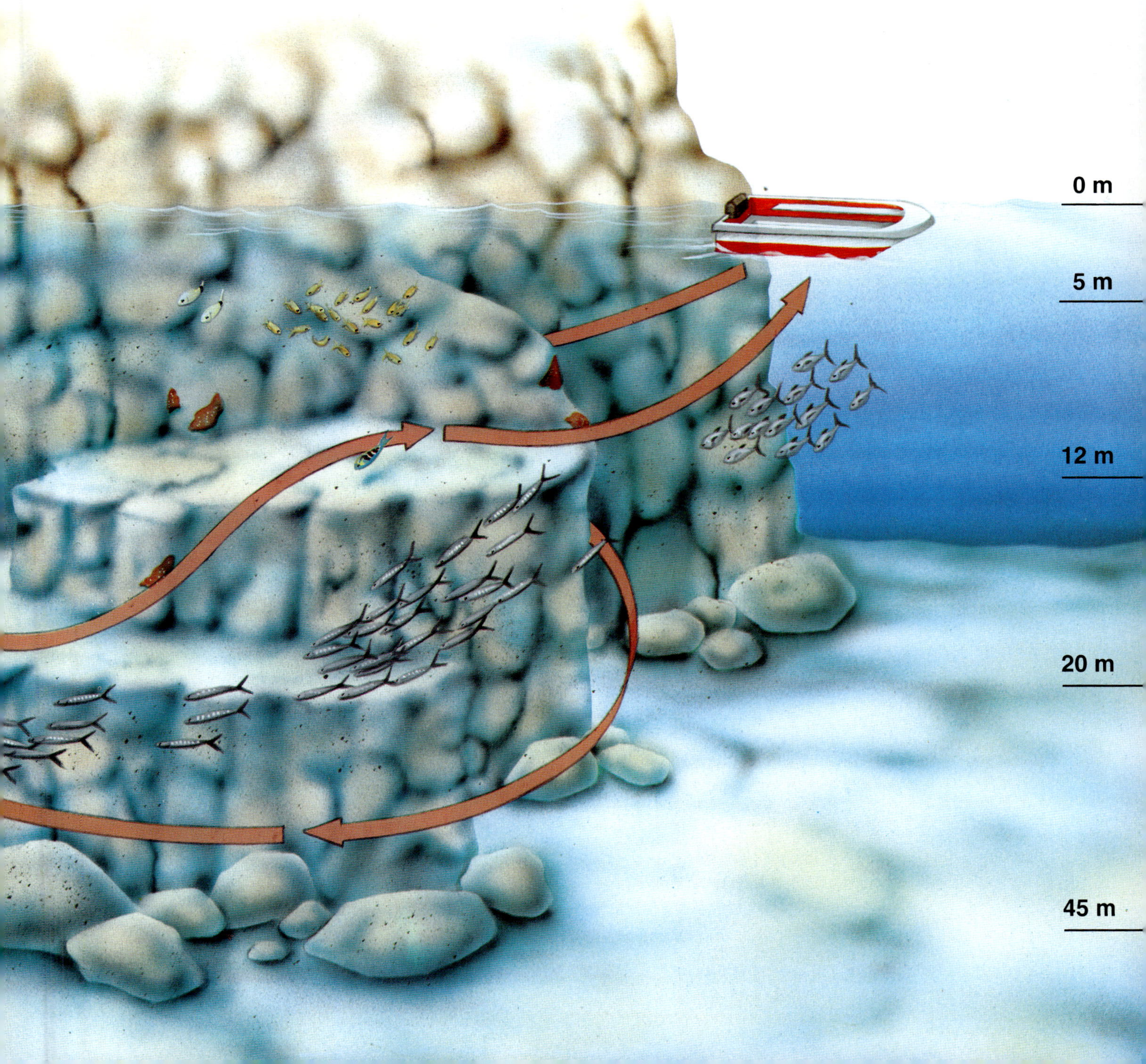
0 m
5 m
12 m
20 m
45 m

A - On the western coast of Gozo, across from the Bay of Dwejra, the vertical walls of Fungus Rock rise up vertically. The best point to drop anchor is at the southern tip of the rock.

B - A hole passing through the rock, illuminated against the light, creates lovely reflections on the water at the base of the reef.

C - The dive is quite popular and fascinating, especially for photography buffs. The most exciting encounters are those with large pelagic fish such as tunas, barracudas and amberjacks, which patrol the waters around the reef in groups or as solitary individuals.

D - The deepest part of the dive, at a depth of about 40 metres, is characterized by large masses which provide shelter for large groupers. Groupers are common along the west coast of Gozo.

LOCATION

Fungus Rock is an isolated and prominent feature in Dwejra Bay on the western coast of Gozo. It is clearly marked on chart 2537 and most tourist maps. The rock can only be reached by boat.
A suitable anchoring point is found close to the southern tip of the rock from where the dive commences and continues in a north-east and then northerly direction - remaining on the seaward side of the rock at all times.

THE DIVE

This is a fascinating dive to a maximum depth of 45 metres. Immediately below the anchorage point, there is a small cut in the rock - like a vertical gully. This enjoys the shade most of the time and it is quite possible to find small moray eels hunting here - although a closer inspection is best left to the end of the dive. The rock wall drops absolutely vertically to a depth of 45 metres where, once again we find the area covered in sizeable boulders - often sitting one on top of the other.
These, coupled with the depth involved, provide excellent habitat for the largest groupers - which are often a feature of the west coast of Gozo.
Looking upwards, the diver will almost always discover tuna, amberjacks and barracudas - usually as individual but occasionally in shoals.
On reaching the north-eastern corner of the rock, it is time to begin a slow ascent as you turn and commence the return journey. Here the underwater features become much more interesting as ledges and gullies present themselves for closer inspection. From 20 metres the diver will begin to encounter small shoals of saddled seabreams and two-banded seabreams before discovering the brilliantly coloured red sponges and equally bright yellow soft corals within the small cave at 15 metres.

A

B

C

D

E - In the small cave you'll find on the return trip, at a depth of 15 metres, you may encounter narval shrimp, elegant little creatures with a long rostrum.

F - A small scorpionfish seems to crown a projection, which is also adorned by Haliclona mediterranea *pink tubular sponges.*

The cave is set back in a large cut in the rock and is, therefore, almost hidden from view - it is, however, well worth finding. Immediately south of the cave the diver will discover two horizontal underwater plateaux carved into the vertical rock wall. These offer a further dimension to a truly interesting site and I never cease to be amazed at the sheer variety of marine life - from the very largest to the very smallest - always found here. The upper plateau points almost directly to the anchor and, being only 8-9 metres deep at its southern-most edge, provides an ideal location for decompression at the end of a very rewarding dive.

G

PHOTOGRAPHY

Fungus Rock is a popular site with all divers, especially with photographers. The sheer cliff walls, large boulders, craggy outcrops, small caves and two plateaux combine to provide excellent frames and back-drops for the wide-angle lens - with or without the addition of your fellow divers. In addition to those creatures already mentioned, there is every chance of encountering the larger pelagics - so always keep an eye to seaward.
A closer inspection of the underwater cliff will reveal plenty of material for the macro lens - cardinalfish, red sponge and cup corals are found on almost every one of those surfaces that rarely, if ever, sees direct daylight.

E

F

G - The contrast between the higher zone covered by Neptune grass and the dark part of the reef is evident in the flashlight beam, which also shows up the long red arms of the red star.

CROCODILE ROCK & CORAL CAVE

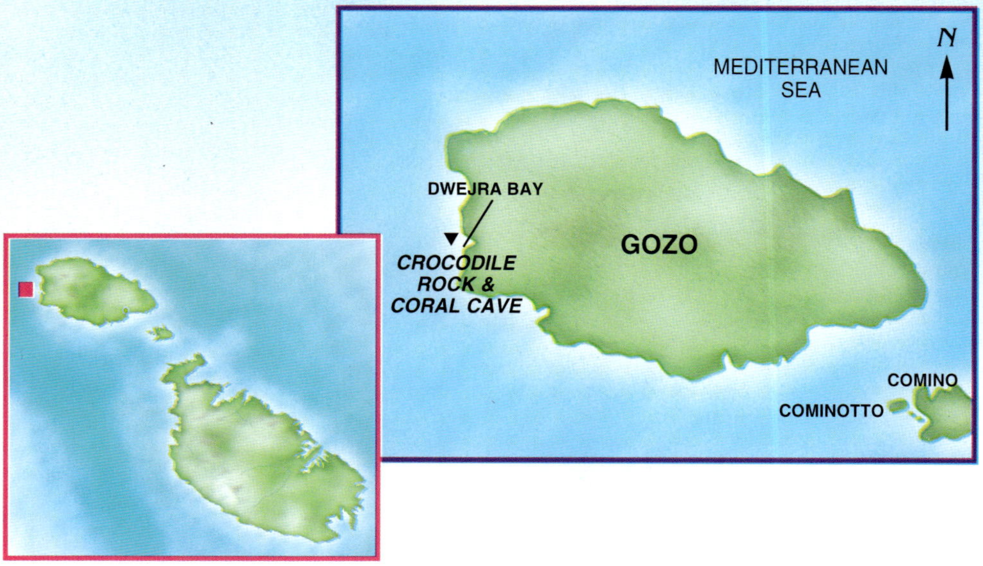

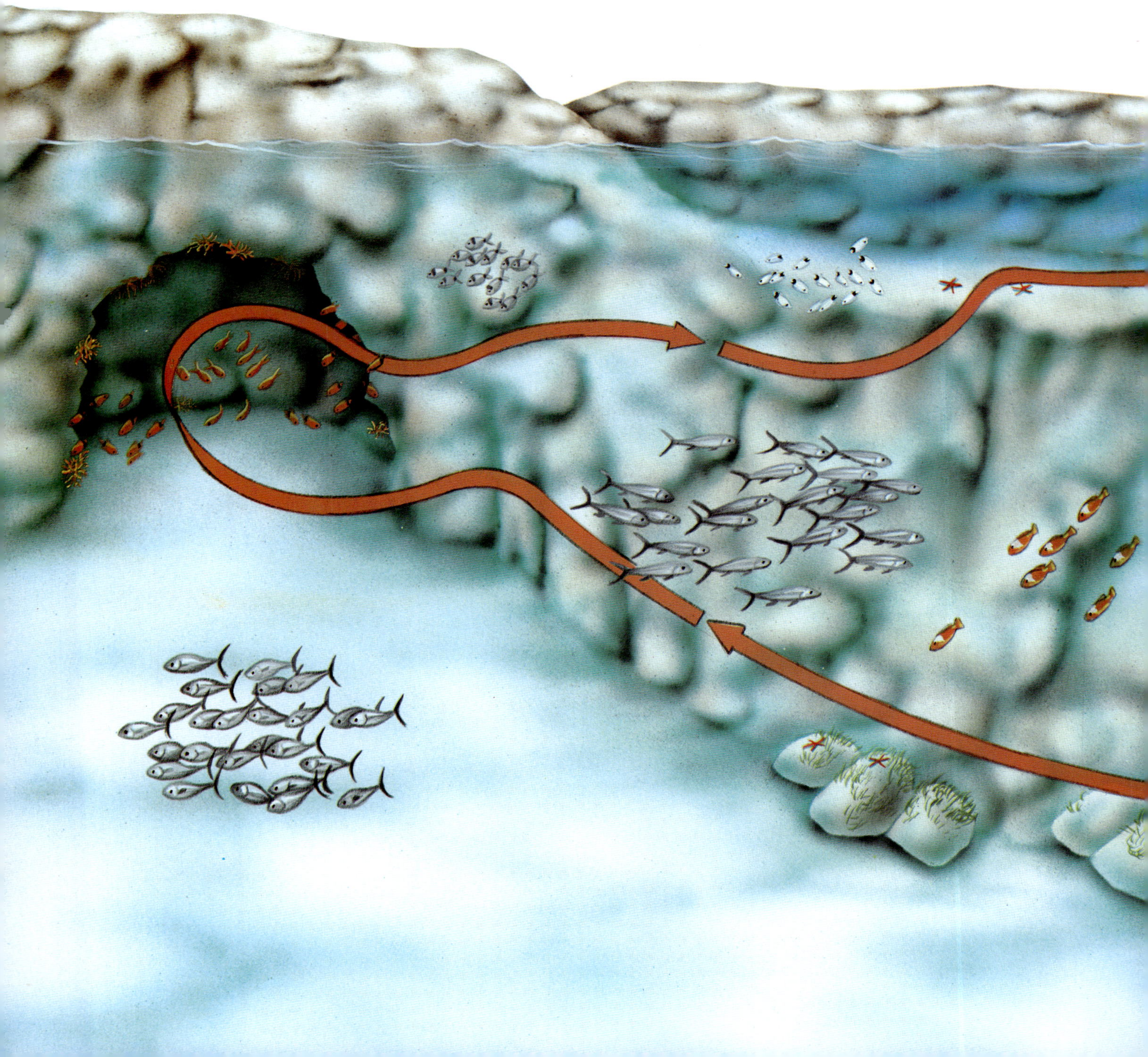

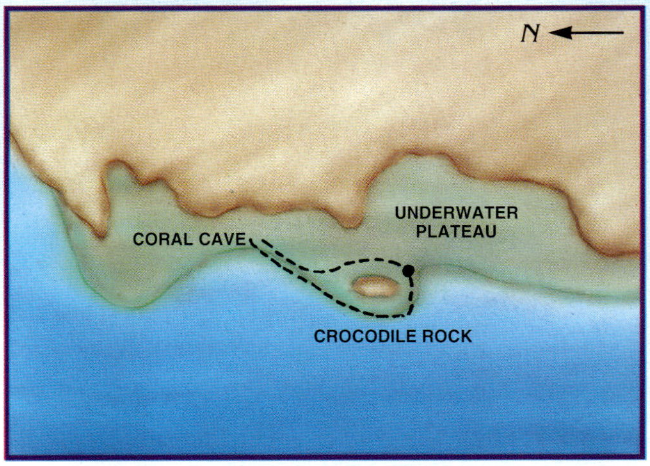
N
CORAL CAVE
UNDERWATER PLATEAU
CROCODILE ROCK

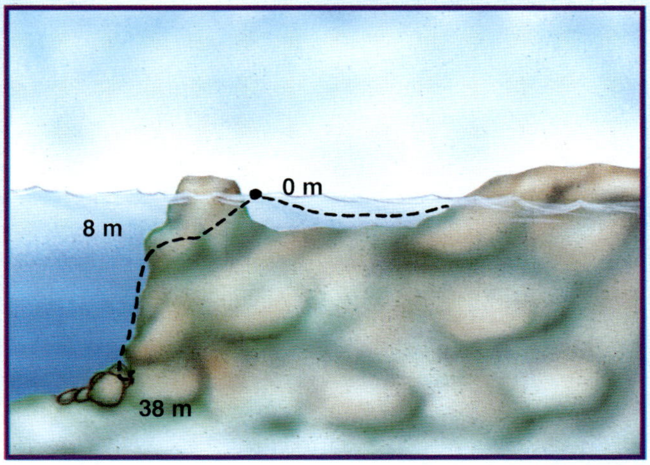
0 m
8 m
38 m

0 m
8 m
38 m

LOCATION

Viewed from a certain angle, Crocodile Rock takes on the distinctive appearance of something resembling a crocodile and is found a short distance north of Fungus Rock. The dive can be tackled from the shore but is usually a boat dive. Between the rock and the shore is a vast expanse of relatively shallow water ideally suitable for anchoring although the dive really starts on the seaward side of the rock.

THE DIVE

Commencing from the sheltered side of the rock, the diver heads in a westerly direction towards the left of the rock where a square shute points towards the deeper water and reveals a steep cliff directly below the seaward side of the rock. Here the cliff drops vertically down to 38 metres where a collection of boulders is found at the base. Beyond these boulders a seabed of sand gently slopes away into the distance.
At the bottom of the cliff the diver turns to the right and heads in a northerly direction. Here the occasional moray eel is found amongst some medium-sized groupers and a large number of green wrasses. Eventually the boulders almost disappear as the base of the cliff cuts back towards the land and gets slightly shallower. Here the diver will find some of those curious fish which prefer life on the sand such as lizard fish, flounders and once in a while a common stingray.
At this point the diver should also remember to look all around as there is every chance of seeing small shoals of grey mullet, amberjack and tuna.
Keeping the cliff-face to the right at all times, the diver will eventually reach the truly splendid Coral Cave. This has a very large round entrance which is a full 20 metres across at the bottom which is at a depth of approximately 22 metres. The top is only five metres from the surface and, inside - as the roof slopes gently down at the back, so the cave floor rises gently

A

B

C

D

A - The low profile of Crocodile Rock rises out of the water a little to the north of Fungus Rock. The diving site is along the north side of the rock, facing the open sea.

B - The rocky shallows around the emerging rock can be explored during your safety stop. You'll see small organisms which colonize the rocks and the sloping seascape.

C - The delicate forms of peacock's tails (Padina pavonica) *stand out on the carpet of algae that covers the rocks close to the surface. Peacock's tail is a brown alga that has a whitish colour due to the high content of calcium carbonate.*

D - A pair of red mullets (Mullus barbatus) *rests on the sea floor. They can be distinguished from striped red mullets by their variegated colour and spots.*

E - A large colony of false corals (Myriapora truncata) *grows on the walls of Coral Cave. False corals are bryozoans, colonial animals that live in a hard skeleton, and are quite different from true corals.*

F - A large red scorpionfish lies on the sea floor, with its large pectoral fins extended, almost as if trying to balance itself. Due to its stocky body's stocky structure, the scorpionfish is capable of attacking its prey in extremely rapid darts.

G - The white seabream (Diplodus sargus) *is a typical den fish, which nevertheless often frequents open areas in search of food among the vegetation which covers the rocks.*

upwards until they both meet. Within the cave the diver's torch brings to life the many different types of encrusting coral sponges, virgin lace and other corals all with masses of cardinalfish and even anthias seeking refuge amongst them. From amongst the little holes and gullies spider crabs and shrimps, with their eerie looking eyes, peer back at the diver.

Inside, the cave is a fairly uniform shape and for some divers is less interesting because there are no tunnels leading off and, once inside, you cannot surface. For me, however, this is a magnificent cave because of its fairly unique covering of corals and it remains the only site in Malta where I saw the beautiful anthia. Perhaps all divers should pause and reflect when they are inside these wonderful structures - carved by nature, and realise how privileged they really are.

On leaving the cave, the diver begins by heading back towards the start point but progresses up to the top of the cliff face and onto the fairly extensive plateau that extends towards Crocodile Rock - which is now far over to the right and the shore which is away to the left. Here the diver is in 8 metres of water - ideal for decompression amongst all the usual species of fish one expects to find.

PHOTOGRAPHY

Crocodile Rock and Coral Cave is a site that provides scope for many different photographic requirements. A wide angle lens is essential if the photographer wishes to capture on film the entrance to a truly magnificent cave, or the drop-off below Crocodile Rock itself.

On the other hand, there is such a wealth of material for macro photography throughout the entire dive - especially on the roof and sides of the cave which are literally covered with various small young corals. Unfortunately, these, especially the virgin lace coral, are so delicate that they are easily dislodged from the ceiling of the cave by divers' bubbles.

E

F

G

THE BLUE HOLE & THE CHIMNEY

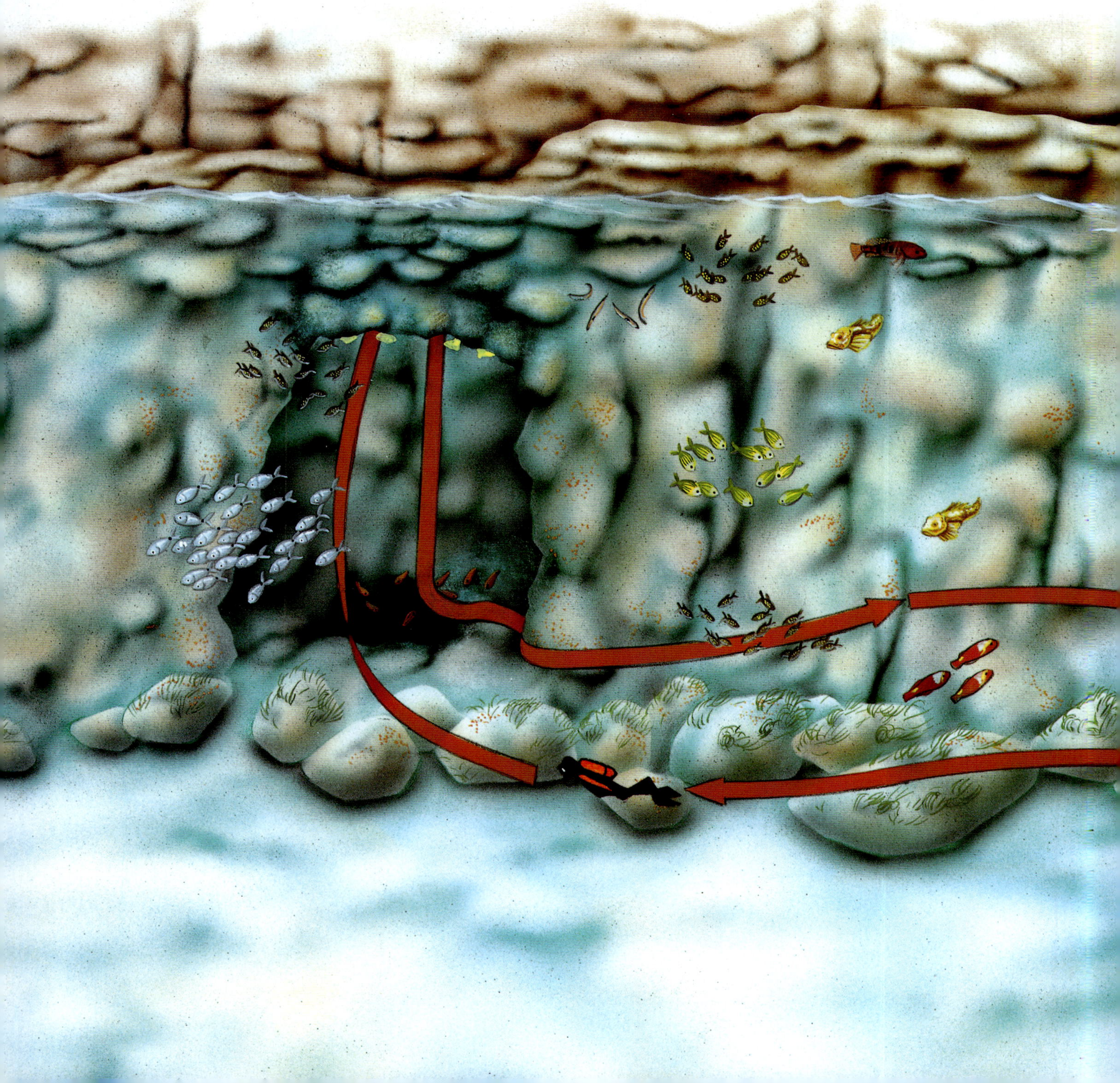

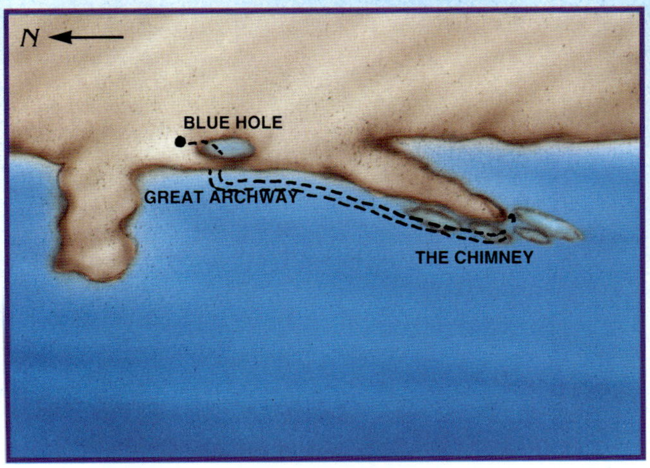
N
BLUE HOLE
GREAT ARCHWAY
THE CHIMNEY

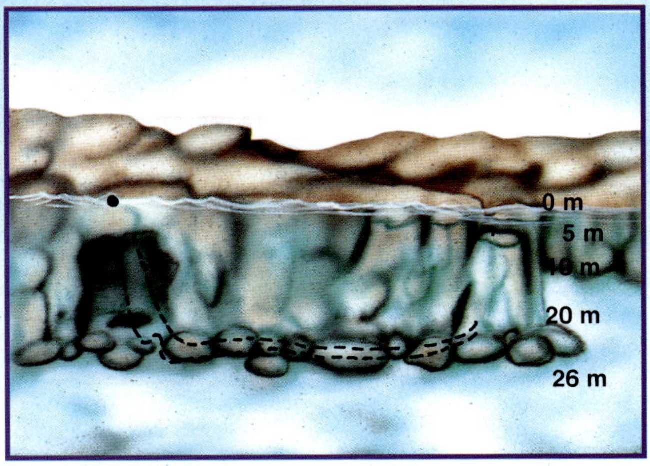
0 m
5 m
10 m
20 m
26 m

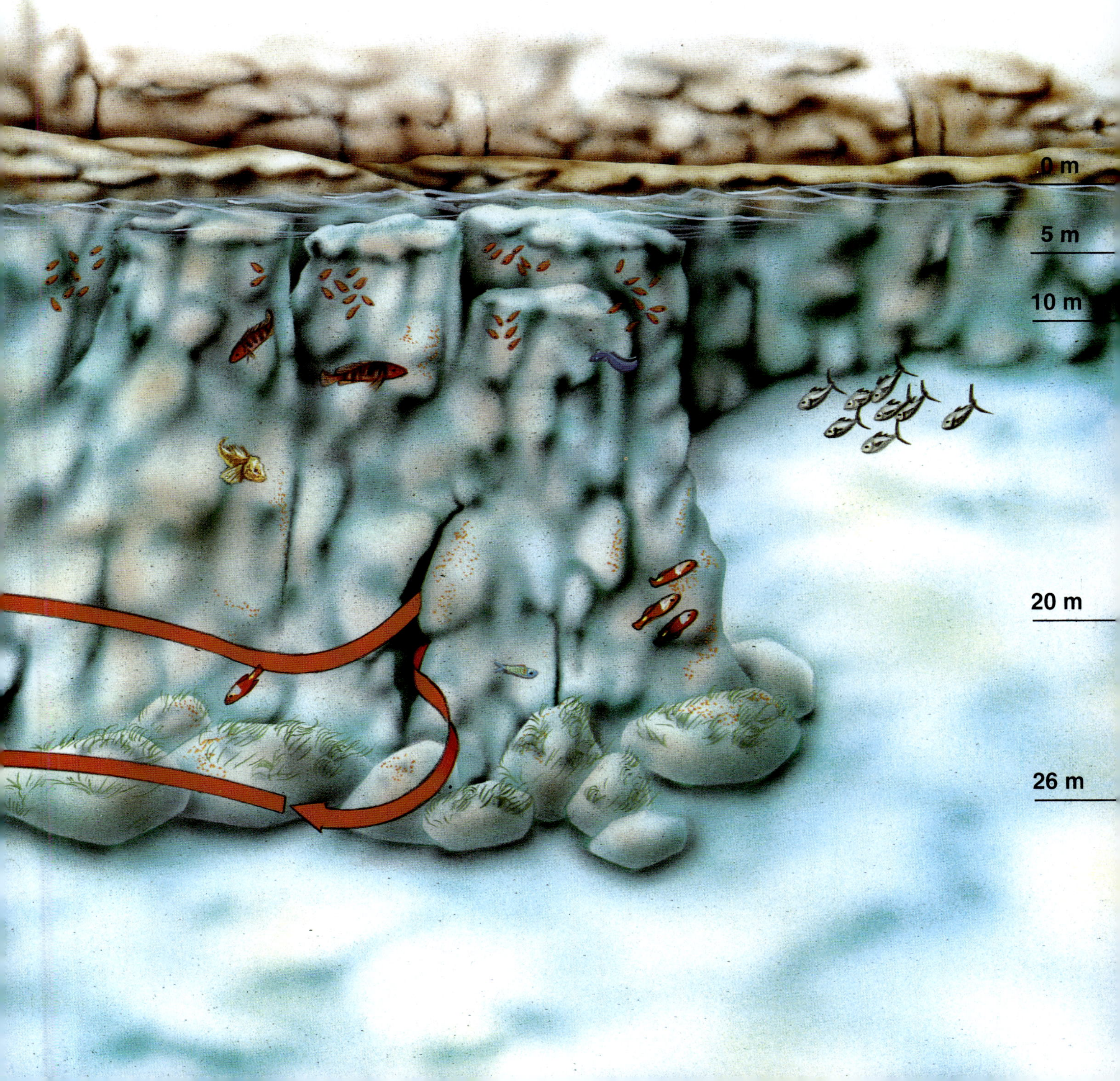
0 m
5 m
10 m
20 m
26 m

LOCATION

The Blue Hole is a shore dive easily reached by vehicle and then foot. The only road south from San Lawrenz ends at Dwejra Point where the diver will find a church, a cafe and ample parking. When ready, the diver has only a short walk along the rugged shoreline - where steps have been carved into the rocks to aid his journey, until he arrives at the Blue Hole. Please note that the rocks are sharp and a pair of hard-soled bootees or separate sandals are essential.
Geologically, this is not a true Blue Hole - which are submerged limestone caverns found in such countries as Belize and the Bahamas. This blue hole is simply a beautiful rock formation carved by nature. At the surface, it is a large circular hole in the rock about one metre above sea level. On entering this "hole" the diver has entered a formation resembling an upright tube that drops vertically to 26 metres.
A few metres down, however, and the seaward side of this tube of rock disappears to give unlimited access to the sea in the form of a great archway. At the bottom, cutting back into the rock, there is also a large cave. This may not be a true blue hole, but I can think of no better name - especially, when viewed from the surface where anyone can see that it has a blueness all of its own.

THE DIVE

The Blue Hole is a spectacular and memorable beginning to any one of a different number of adventures that all commence with a somewhat deceptive beginning as the diver enters what appears to be nothing more than a rock pool that is no more than 10 metres wide and 5 metres across. The first of these adventures involves turning south (i.e. left) after exiting through the Great Archway above some huge boulders where the occasional moray eel is found. As the diver continues further south, the vertical rock is kept to the

A

B

C

immediate left. This is home to various species of fish, octopus, starfish, and bristle worms.
At night-time their numbers are significantly increased and sleeping parrotfish are often encountered. In amongst the many little cavities and crevices the diver will find cardinalfish, sea urchins - even the long-spined sea urchin and colourful sponges and tunicates.
Further along, the diver is eventually confronted by a crevice which juts out almost

A - A single image sums up the outside and underwater surroundings at Azure Window. The diving area is characterized by arches and cavities.

B - Blue Hole is an almost round opening about one metre above the surface of the sea, and leads to a long vertical chimney that goes down to a depth of 26 metres.

C - The vaults of the arches and caverns are covered with sponges, corals and bryozoans. A flashlight is indispensable both to visit the cavities and to illuminate the depths.

D - The Chimney is a vertical crack in the rock that can fit one diver at a time. The views from the inside are quite lovely.

E - A large number of bright orange Astroides *completely cover this rocky wall.*

F - After descending a few metres, the outer part of the entry chimney leads out to the open sea in a great arch. This is a spectacular dive from start to finish.

G - A small blenny (probably Blennius zvonimiri*) peeps out of a cavity in the rock. Blennies rarely leave the sea floor.*

H - It is not uncommon to encounter quite sizeable octopuses, well hidden and camouflaged in rocky crevices.

at right angles to the wall. Here, there is a fissure in the rock which happens to be the entrance to "The Chimney". This entrance is rather deceptive - a few metres from the bottom it narrows to a point that divers cannot enter. The secret is to enter The Chimney immediately above this narrow point.
This is a perfectly safe dive but can only be undertaken in "single file". About halfway up this narrow tunnel there is a hole in the base of the rock large enough for a diver to stand in. This is ideal for the photographer who wants to capture his diving buddies who follow on behind. Once photographed, the photographer can stoop down and allow them to continue their journey by swimming over his head. Divers emerge from the chimney at a depth of 8-10 metres and this marks the turn around point of the dive.
Most divers prefer to swim back through the Chimney but another route around the rock is also available.
On returning to the Great Archway most divers pay a brief visit to the cave - almost secretly tucked away at the back. It is a circular structure about 20 metres across. It has a flatish ceiling and the floor is covered in soft silt. During the day it is quite easy to see the entrance from within because of the light outside - not so at night-time when a torch is essential. Most important of all, however, it is easy to disturb the soft silt and quickly obscure the entrance and spoil the dive for other divers.
The under side of the archway and the cave entrance are festooned with numerous bright yellow soft corals, tubeworms, red sponges and the ever-shy cardinalfish are always present.

SAFETY

Should the diver disturb the silt and found himself "lost" inside the cave at the bottom of the Blue Hole, it should be remembered that the cave is circular and not that large. Swim towards the side

D

E

of the cave, select a mid-range height between ceiling and floor and, keeping in contact with the wall, slowly work your way around the cave. It will not be long before the entrance is found.

PHOTOGRAPHY

Underwater, this is very dramatic scenery to which the presence of divers adds dimension and scale to the subject. The Great Archway and the Chimney are ideal for wide angle photography.
A 20mm lens with diver in the foreground and Archway in the background should prove an ideal combination. The same lens when situated within the Chimney could be put to equally good use with the divers returning down the Chimney and swimming towards the photographer who also manages to include the well-lit surface far above everyone.
It is always interesting to compare the marine life found during the day with that available at night-time on the same dive site. During the day, a Micro-105mm is ideal for capturing most, if not all the subjects available at this site. During a night-dive, however, I preferred the Micro-55mm lens but found that I ran out of film in a very short time due to the abundance of marine creatures.

F

G

H

SAN DIMITRI POINT

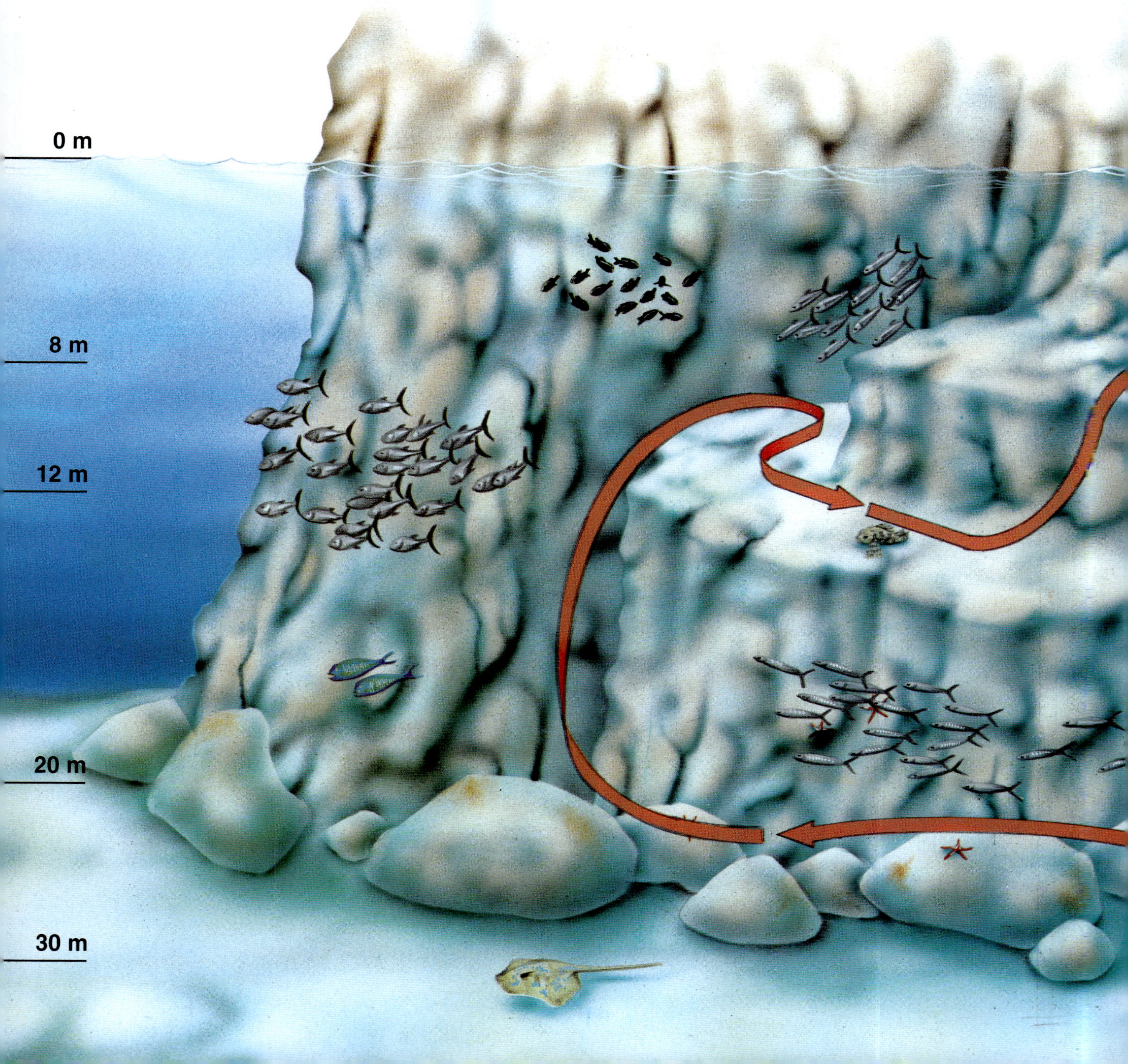

N
SAN DIMITRI POINT

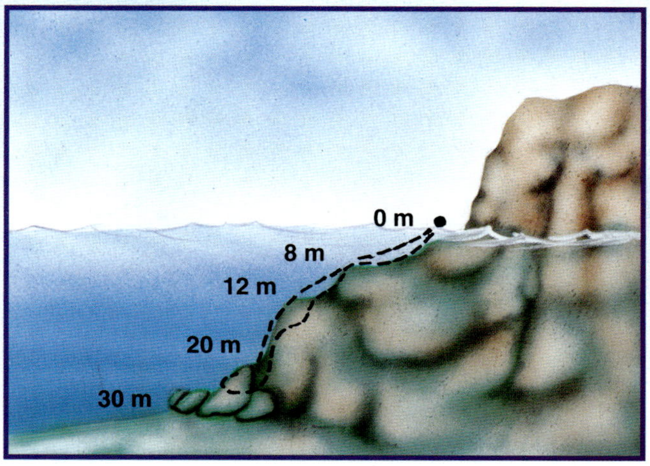
0 m
8 m
12 m
20 m
30 m

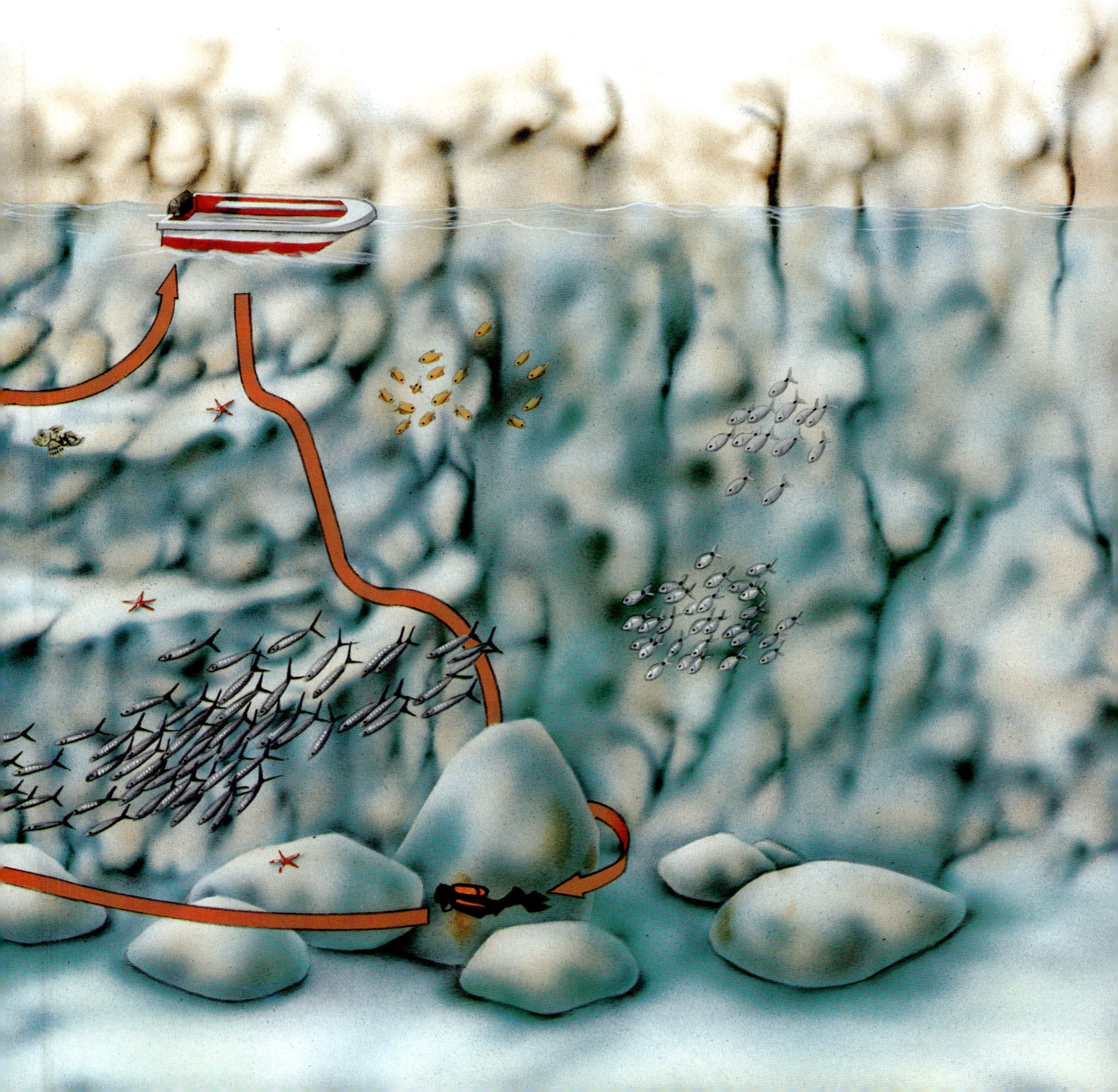

LOCATION

The coastline of the north-west corner of Gozo comprises vertical cliff faces with large, individual rocks jutting out from the shore. One of the most imposing of these is called San Dimitri Point and is only accessible by boat. The number of similar, prominent rocks nearby means that one is quite easily mistaken for another - local knowledge is, therefore, essential for finding the right rock - directly below which is a truly outstanding dive site. Very good anchorage is provided by relatively shallow boulders and other rock formations close inshore.
A very long time ago an old

A

hermit built a small chapel right at the edge of the rocks.
He dedicated the chapel to Saint Dimitri and here he lived - devoted to his faith and his meditations - until one day the rocks collapsed sending his chapel to the bottom of the sea. Fortunately, the Hermit lived to build another - this time 100 metres further inland where it is found today. In the meantime a popular legend has grown up - in that the original chapel can still be found underwater - directly below what is now called San Dimitri Point, and a light still burns in the window!
Looking upwards on a clear day

B

C

D

E

A - The elongated silhouettes of a school of barracudas stand out against the light. You may encounter tunas, schools of seabreams, and even swordfish during this dive.

B - San Dimitri Point offers exceptional visibility that sometimes exceeds 50 metres. Few areas in the world offer such clear waters.

C - A crescent-shaped rock surrounds the outside wall of the final portion of the route. With the excellent visibility, you'll be able to spot many species of fish here.

D - A dense group of salemas shimmers as it reflects the light of the camera flash. Salemas always move in large schools, searching for food on the rocks closest to the surface.

E - An amberjack swims in search of prey. This typical pelagic fish is easily recognizable by the dark band that runs diagonally across its eye, giving it a sinister appearance.

F - A small goby (Gobius geniporus) *resting on the seabed allows the photographer to approach. This close-up shows its emerald green eyes and the intricate tracery of small pores on its head.*

the sky appears to be blue - but there is nothing actually blue up there! The blueness is an effect of density - created by looking through many thousands of metres of air. Water, however, is a much denser medium and appears blue much sooner - instead of several thousand metres it takes just 50 metres. The human eye is quite incapable of seeing beyond this "Blue Barrier" no matter how clear the water or how excellent the conditions. I have never, therefore, claimed underwater visibility of more than 50 metres for any of the many dives in my log-book. It says much for this site, however, that I recorded "Depth - 50m plus." This is simply because it is here that I experienced quite the best underwater visibility I have ever known - anywhere in the world.

THE DIVE

The steep, vertical cliff face above the surface belies that which the diver experiences just as soon as the dive commences. At a depth of 4 metres a long finger of rock juts out from the cliff wall at an angle of something like 45 degrees. This reaches slowly down to 8 metres where it forms an underwater plateau on which the dive boat anchors. Dropping down onto this finger of rock, the divers proceed directly over its side where they will find another level underwater ledge between 12 and 14 metres. Beneath this is a very prominent large boulder which sits well above the others that litter the seabed at a fairly uniform depth of 30 metres - from where the diver turns right and heads in a northerly direction.
Throughout this dive there is every chance of seeing large shoals of truly spectacular fish such as barracudas, tuna and large seabreams in addition to a rare sighting of a pelagic. On one occasion I saw a rather large swordfish swimming past in the far distance. Amongst the rocks, however, the diver is continually confronted by octopus, moray eels and groupers but the most fascinating discovery has to be the presence of small nudibranchs at this depth. Nudibranchs are delightful and colourful sea slugs with exposed gills. Normally found in the shallows, they rarely exceed lengths of 2-3 centimetres.
The underwater terrain eventually curves round to the right and this generally marks the point for beginning the ascent. Here the diver will see some splendid examples of parrotfish - always busily feeding in small groups of up to six or so, as he ascends towards another underwater ledge.
This is shaped like a half-moon and surrounds the outer edge immediately below the plateau mentioned earlier. It is a fairly uniform depth of 12 metres and home to some of the smaller fishes one has come to expect in these waters. Above this the plateau provides an excellent opportunity for decompression with the added interest of being amongst a wide variety of marine creatures.

PHOTOGRAPHY

The underwater visibility is so good at this site - it has to be experienced to be believed.
It is not just a matter of picking a good days or even chance. Perhaps it is the location in relation to prevailing conditions - I really do not know. What I do know is that this site is outstanding for wide angle photography.
Divers pictured against a dramatic background or in amongst the rocks, windows and swim-throughs created by large fallen boulders are all part of the overall excitement in addition to the presence of large shoals of barracudas, tuna and seabreams. The diver must also remember to look out to sea periodically because there is every chance of seeing the occasional pelagic.

F

G

H

G - A red squat lobster (Galathea strigosa), *photographed at night, seeks food among the algae. During the day these small crustaceans are always sheltered among the dark crevices.*

H - An ornate wrasse in the intermediate sexual phase swims along the sea floor. Ornate wrasses are born female and become males as they mature. During the transition phase they have vertical green stripes.

GHASRI VALLEY

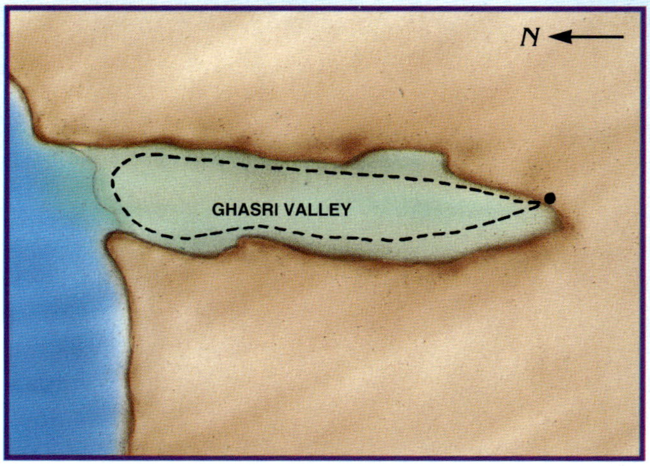
N
GHASRI VALLEY

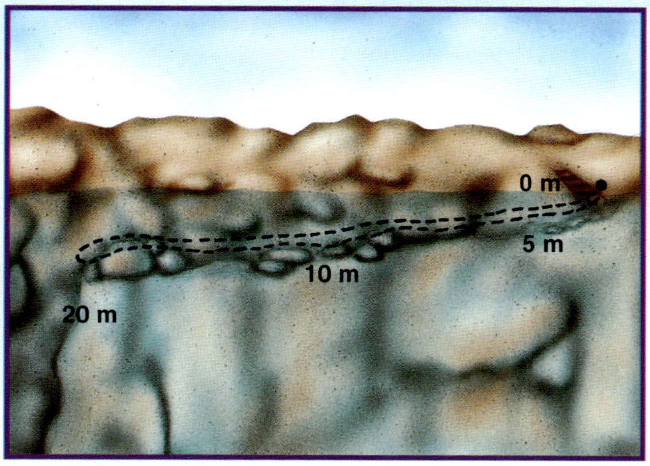
0 m
5 m
10 m
20 m

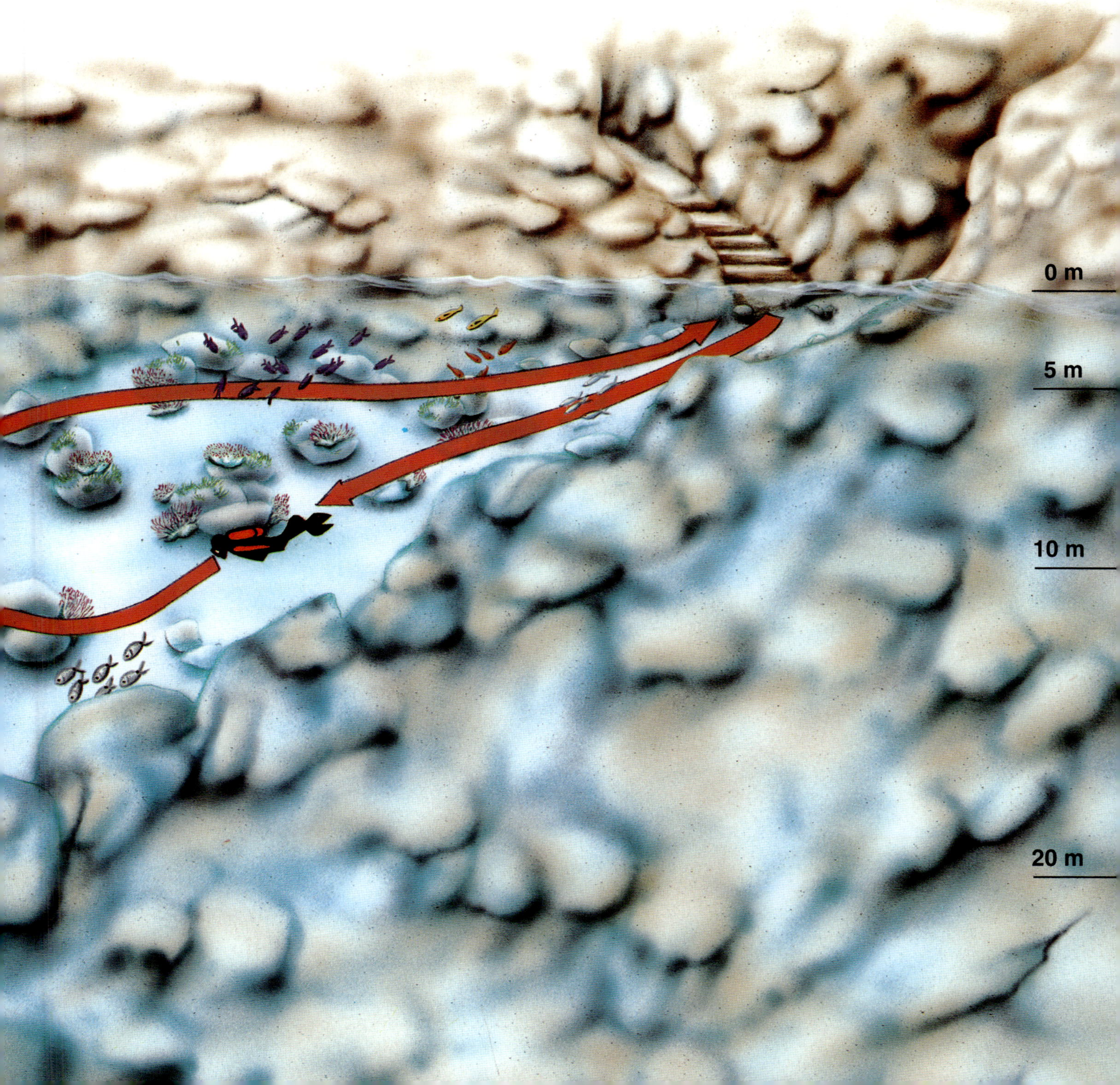
0 m
5 m
10 m
20 m

A - The reef on the northern coast of Gozo is divided by a narrow gorge that widens toward the open sea. This is Ghasri Valley, and the point of entry for the dive can be reached by following a path along the rock.

B - This close-up of a damselfish (Chromis chromis) *shows this fish's characteristic yellow spots and violet-edged fins. When seen from a distance, damselfish appear totally black.*

LOCATION

On the North coast of Gozo, west of Marsalforn between Forna Point and Reqqa Point, lies the beautiful Ghasri Valley - a spectacular narrow gorge which widens as it reaches the sea. Approximately 500 metres inland, a series a steps have been cut into the solid rock and stretch all the way down to the water edge. From here, there is only one direction the diver can take - almost due north, as he heads towards the sea.

C

D

THE DIVE

This is a long, gentle dive which commences on a shingle beach. At first the water is shallow but, over the entire length of the valley, becomes progressively deeper. One of the most outstanding features at the beginning of this journey is the profusion of anemones - quite frankly the seabed is literally covered with these to such an extent that I was expecting to see a clownfish appear at any time.

A

B

As global warming continues, I cannot help but wonder how long it will be before such fish are a feature of the Mediterranean in general and this site in particular. The shingle eventually gives way to small rocks and these in turn eventually give way to larger rocks and then the big boulders which are such a feature of Gozo waters. Each of these provides home and refuge to a variety of creatures such as wrasses, seabreams, scorpionfish, goatfish and many more besides. There is also every opportunity of finding seahorse, seahare and even nudibranch in any area which, for me at least, seems quite different from anything else found in Maltese Waters.
Towards the end of the valley the diver will find himself at a depth of approximately 20 metres and, as it gives way to the opens sea, so the type of fish encountered are clearly much larger. Here are the octopus and groupers that always seem to generate an excitement of their own. This is

C - The dark walls provide favorable conditions for orange corals (Astroides calycularis) *and carnation corals. A sea cucumber can be seen to the right.*

D - An anemone shrimp (Periclimenes sagittifer) *perches among the tentacles of a fat anemone* (Cribinopsis crassa)*: this is a classic case of symbiosis in the Mediterranean.*

E

F

G

H

the turn around point and a good chance to give the walls of the valley a closer inspection on the return trip.

All along the eastern wall are little cuts - too small to be called caves, into the rock where red sponges and yellow soft corals are brought to life by the divers torch. Suspended amongst these, almost like a study in still life, are the brilliantly coloured cardinalfish and closer inspection might even reveal the occasional shrimp. Damselfish are particularly prolific throughout the Maltese Islands and here the diver will find very small specimens in great quantities.

At this size 1-2 centimetres long) these fish have a neon-blue colouration - what a pity that this bright colour is lost as they grow bigger.

PHOTOGRAPHY

Ghasri Valley is one of those rare and beautiful places that is only appreciated by the privileged few. Underwater, those people are even fewer in number and, despite the hard work of getting to and from the site, I can fully recommend the effort. When there have been storms and gales from the north-west, I have watched large waves bouncing furiously from side to side - smashing their way down the entire length of the valley. Perhaps it is that destructive power which creates a seabed so popular with all the small varieties of fish. Whatever it is that makes Ghasri Valley what it is, it is quite magical.

This site is ideal for close-up and macro photography - and, with all the many different species of fish to occupy the camera, the anemones should not be overlooked. Though occasionally encountered elsewhere, they are not overly common - and certainly not in the vast numbers found here.

E - Portions of a wall of smooth rock are covered with orange encrusting sponges and sparse orange corals.

F - Two small hermit crabs seem to be doing acrobatics on the slender branches of a gorgonian (Eunicella singularis)

G - A beautiful white gastropod mollusc (Flabellina babai) *feeds on the polyps of a colony of hydrozoans. Common in the Mediterranean, it is one of the largest species of western nudibranchs, and can reach 5 cm in length.*

H - A saddled seabream swims in the open water. Saddled seabreams can be found in various areas of the marine environment, but they are nevertheless one of the members of the Sparidae family least dependent on the sea floor.

BILLINGSHURST CAVE

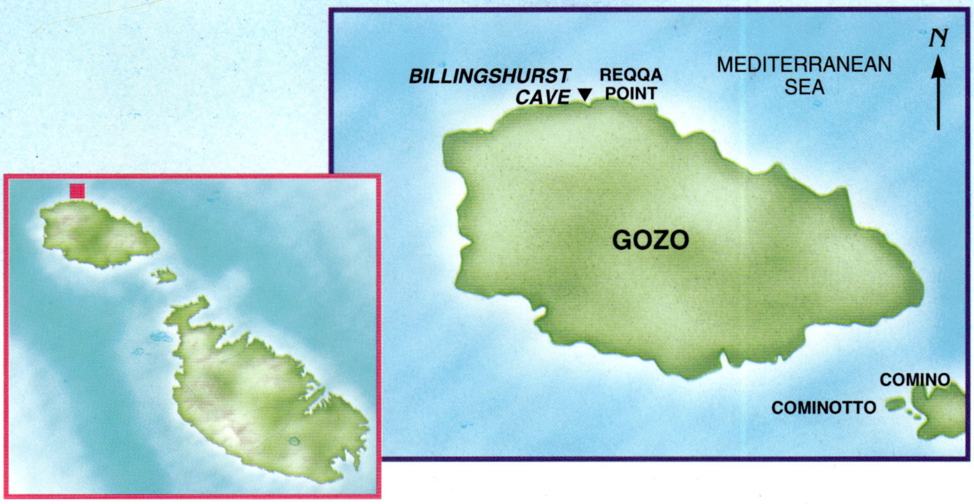

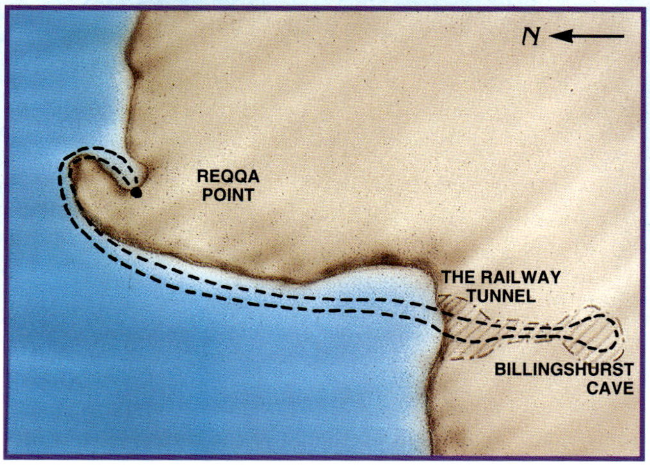
N
REQQA
POINT
THE RAILWAY
TUNNEL
BILLINGSHURST
CAVE

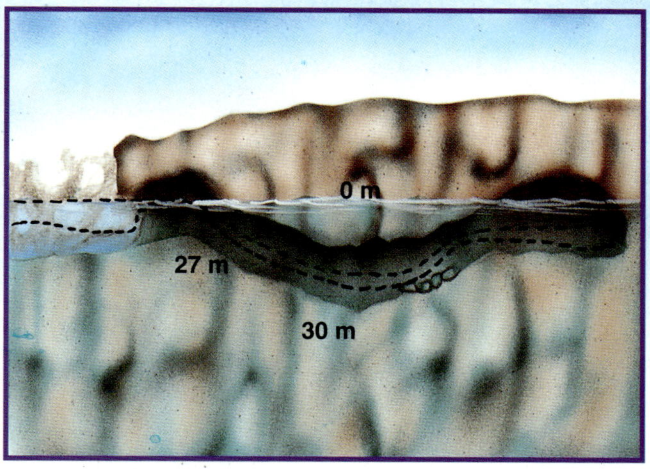
0 m
27 m
30 m

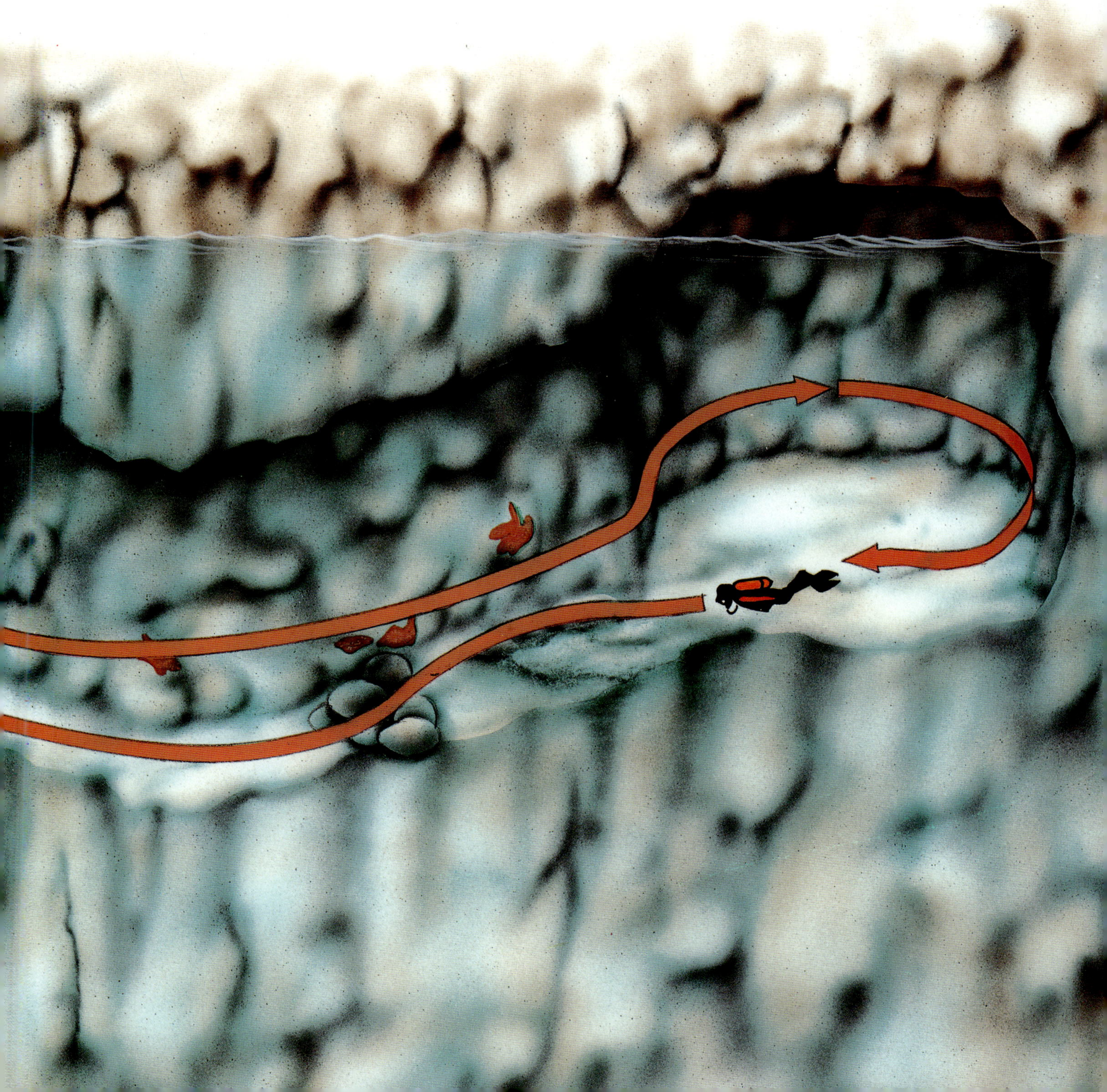

A

B

C

D

LOCATION

Billingshurst Cave is found to the west of Reqqa Point. The top of the cave entrance is just above the surface and the bottom is at 27 metres. A long tunnel - called "The Railway Tunnel" on account of its size - leads to a further cave deep inside the rock where the diver can surface. Entry is from Reqqa Point, although some divers prefer the long jump (3-4m or more!) into the sea from rocks immediately above the cave. Whatever entry method is preferred - Reqqa Point remains the nearest exit point. Large sea swells create a booming sound as they crash into the outer cave giving that part of the cave the appropriate nickname "Booming Cave." From here, the story goes that in 1984 a team of divers decided to explore this Tunnel and, after a distance of some 50 metres, found they were able to surface where they found a message wrapped in a plastic bag. The message said that the cave had already been "discovered" and explored by "Billingshurst Sub Aqua Club" and invited divers to add their names before re-sealing the plastic bag. Thus Billingshurst Cave came into being.

THE DIVE

Today, the entire structure is called Billingshurst Cave and, with an entrance that is easily the largest of all the caves in the country, it is easy to understand why this cave is the most exciting. Immediately inside the entrance to the cave there are plenty of red sponges, soft corals, cardinalfish and other delightful creatures for those interested in marine life - but divers come here for one purpose only and that is to explore the entire length of this amazing creation of nature.

To begin with the cave is located in a tight corner of a rocky coastline. Facing due north, it sees little or no direct sunlight and there is, therefore, very little natural light penetration - even within the immediate entrance. Furthermore, this is deep and the seabed here comprises soft sand and fine shingle which is easily stirred up - facts that remain vitally important throughout the dive.

After only a very short distance, the large cavern shape of the entrance quickly sweeps down to meet the

A - The entrance to the cave is on the north side of Gozo, and can easily be seen outside the water due to the long, crescent-shaped vault just above the surface.

B - The widest part of the cave is known as Railway Tunnel. It leads to another cavern in which divers can surface.

C - The cave gets its name from the diving club that first explored it thoroughly, but it is also known as Booming Cave, due to the noise of the waves entering the cavern.

D - A horizontal crack opens into a shadowy wall. In it swims a forkbeard, a fish in the cod family common in dark areas.

E - Two small scorpionfish seem to face off within a niche; note the different colouration.

F - Inside the cave are numerous zebra seabreams (Diplodus cervinus). *This is the most common species in the southern Mediterranean and is easily distinguishable by the large dark bands on the sides of its body.*

G - A tiny red fish swims under the lee of a rocky wall.

rising cave floor at the back. Already it is very dark and torches are essential. Here the contours of the entire cave become somewhat funnel-like as they draw the diver towards the "Railway Tunnel" which is very easily found. As soon as the tunnel is entered, the seabed slopes gently downwards and, at the start of the journey, gives the impression of an ever downward journey. For this reason, many divers decide to return to the entrance before they find themselves deeper than planned. In fact, there is only a further 3m drop to a maximum depth of 30m over a distance of something like 25m before the tunnel commences its upwards journey towards the final cave. On this upwards slope there are several loose boulders just after which the diver enters the final cave and is able to surface in the large air pocket. This is a massive cave totally enclosed in rock. The ceiling is five metres above surface and the furthest walls are well beyond range of torchlight! Occasionally the diver will encounter a hot and heavy mist above the surface of the water. Remarkable as it may seem, divers are continually entering and swimming the length of this cave without the aid of a line fixed from the entrance to the furthest point - a small aid that I would regard as an essential item for this dive. We may all think we know what we are doing but this site is so very popular that it may well be divers from another group who destroy the underwater visibility. That said, I am aware of no recorded accidents or incidents involving this particular dive site.

PHOTOGRAPHY

This is an ideal subject for wide-angle photography providing the photographer with group shots of the divers as they approach, enter and leave the cave. Inside the cave, however, it is a most difficult subject. On the one hand, it is a most exciting location but poor light penetration makes focusing extremely difficult. This is further exacerbated by those divers who always seem intent on reducing the visibility even further by disturbing the silt in great quantities. The photographer must, therefore, have a very powerful modelling light - either as an integral part of the strobe or attached to that strobe - so that he can clearly see in order to focus.

E

F

G

REQQA POINT

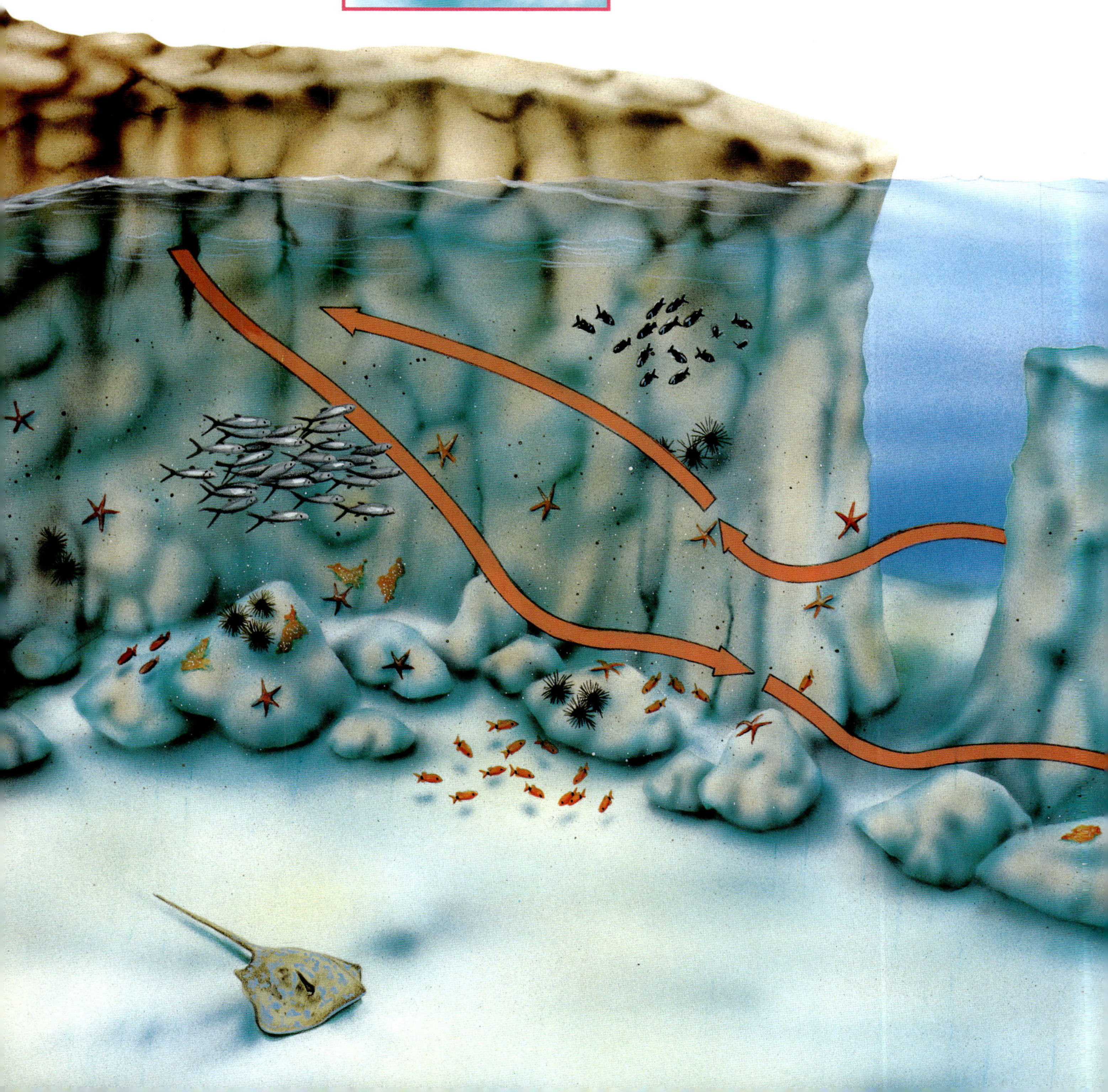

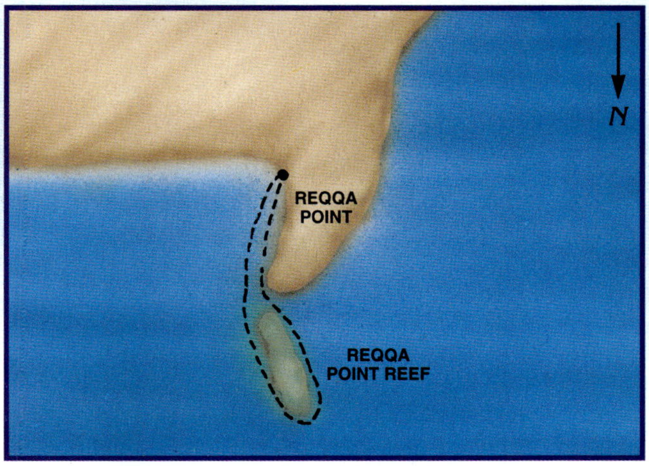
N
REQQA
POINT
REQQA
POINT REEF

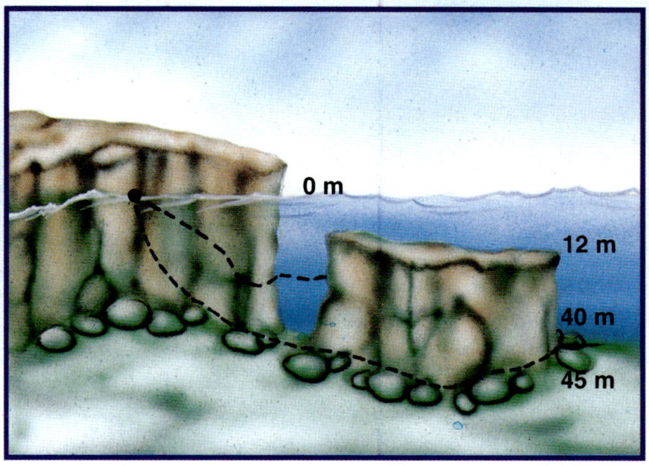
0 m
12 m
40 m
45 m

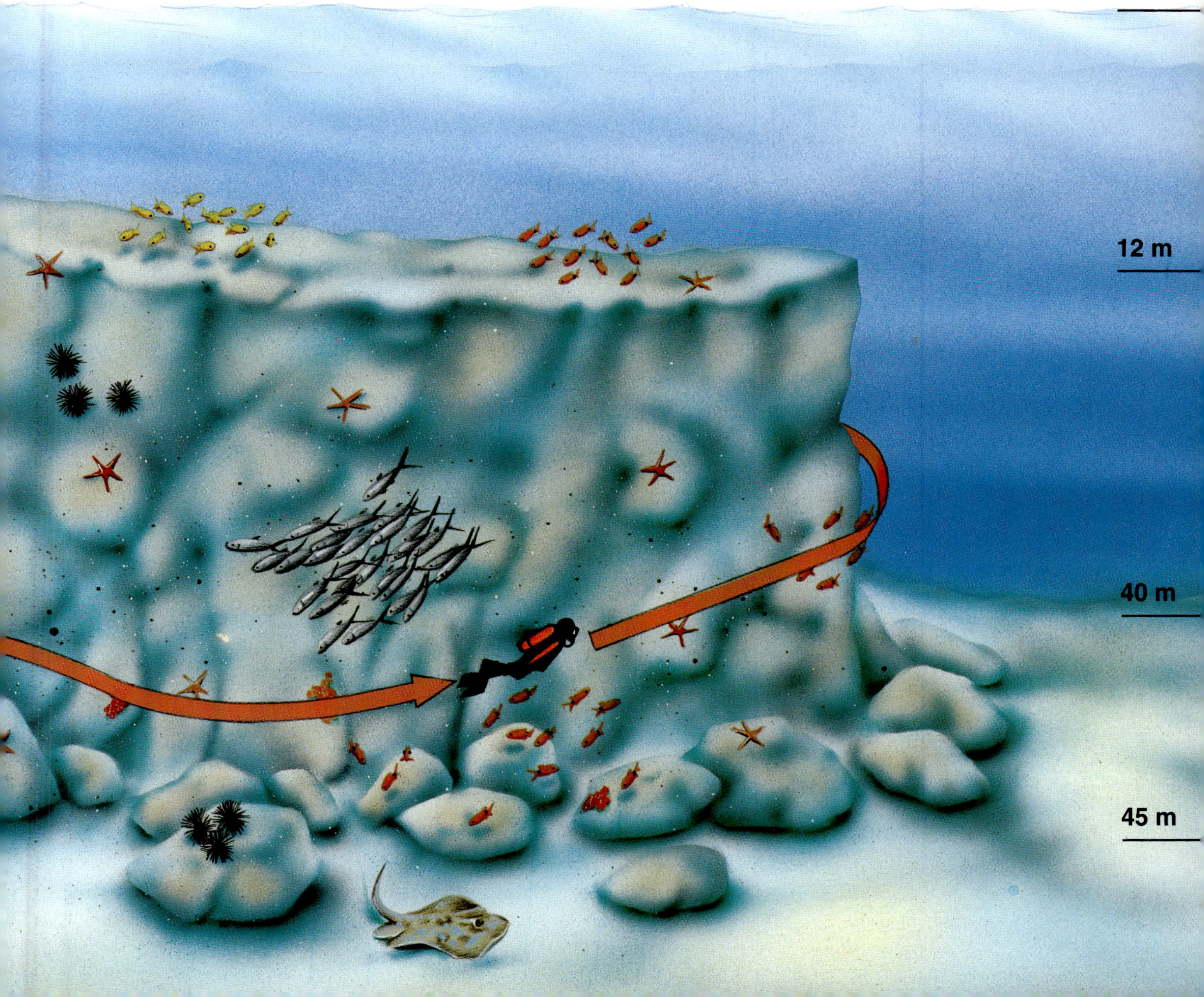
0 m
12 m
40 m
45 m

A - The walls descends vertically to the sea floor, at a depth of over 40 metres. The rays of the sun filter through the limpid water and create an enchanting atmosphere.

B - The long promontory that juts out from the northern coast of Gozo continues underwater in a rocky formation, where the dive takes place to the north.

C - The end of the rocky spur where the dive takes place is an imposing vertical rock. You should stop to watch the seascape.

LOCATION

A rocky promontory on the north coast of Gozo - clearly marked on all maps. The rocks are very sharp so care must be taken not to slip and fall when approaching the entry/exit point. The water is very deep all around the point and the diver will set off in an almost northerly direction with the cliff face to the left. This eventually stretches down underwater and leads to a long, steep underwater column of rock. This is Reqqa Point Reef and is actually an underwater extension of those rocks seen above the surface.

THE DIVE

This dive commences on the right hand (eastern) side of the Reqqa Point. This is generally regarded as the sheltered side of this outcrop of curved rock which is perched directly above depths of over 40 metres. The diver sets off in a northerly direction gently dropping down to 40-45 metres by the time the gap between Reqqa point and Reqqa Point Reef is reached. Here the large boulders appear as though they have been deliberately propped against the vertical underwater cliffs and are an excellent refuge for groupers, octopus and large scorpionfish. Beyond the boulders a sandy seabed provides an ideal hunting ground for the "not so" common stingray and the even rarer anglerfish.
As the divers progress round the reef, they are continually shadowed by large numbers

B

C

A

D

D - If you swim along the wall, you'll find numerous groups of amberjacks, who will approach divers curiously and fearlessly.

of greater amberjacks. These fish are very curious and often approach the diver as though looking for food. The cliff wall itself, however, is festooned with very large bright red and bright orange starfish in addition to many different varieties of sea urchin.
The far end of the reef is a very imposing and vertical rock which is actually admired by many of those divers who take the time to pause and look at it. The base of this rock is at 45 metres and represents the deepest part of the dive. From here the divers continue in their circumnavigation but commence an upward journey at the same time.

E

F

G

H

E - A close-up of the bearded fire worm shows its parapodia with their slender white bristles, which can cause painful stings if you accidentally touch one.

F - A spotted nudibranch (Marionia blainvillea), *with ragged appendages on its back, crawls along the sea floor. This is a common species in the Mediterranean; it feeds on cnidarians.*

G - The vertical wall of Reqqa is covered with large red stars, with their characteristic purple red colour and velvety appearance.

H - An octopus tries to make itself less visible by changing the colour of its mantle. Groups of orange corals grow on the rock.

Eventually the divers will reach the gap once again and here they must cross back to the sheltered side of Reqqa Point in order to complete the journey. There is usually, however, time for an inspection of the top of the reef. This is 10-12 metres deep and hosts many different species of wrasses in addition to scorpionfish that are smaller than those found earlier. There are also many, many thousands of damselfish throughout the entire dive.
As the diver completes the journey back to the start point, Reqqa Point reveals yet another side to its rich and diverse character. The shallow waters right along this part of the rock are often overlooked and conceal a profusion of bright colours - red sponges, yellow soft coral, orange corals, some virgin lace coral and all of these richly decorated with numerous cardinalfish.

PHOTOGRAPHY

The eastern side of Reqqa Point is sheltered from the sunlight in the mornings as is the western side in the evenings. This light differential - even on the sunniest of days - can make a big difference to photography - especially wide-angle shots of divers. Away from the shore, however, the problem is much lessened.
A wide-angle lens is essential for including the often dramatic natural underwater features - with and without the inclusion of divers. In addition, there is also much scope for close-up and macro photography - especially in the shallower reaches towards the end of the dive.

DOUBLE ARCH REEF

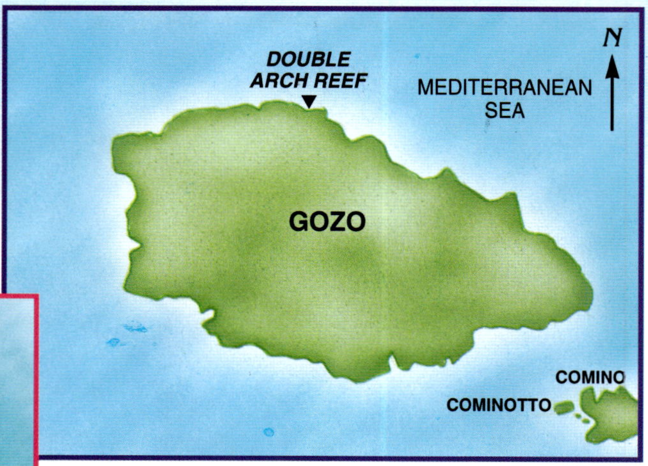

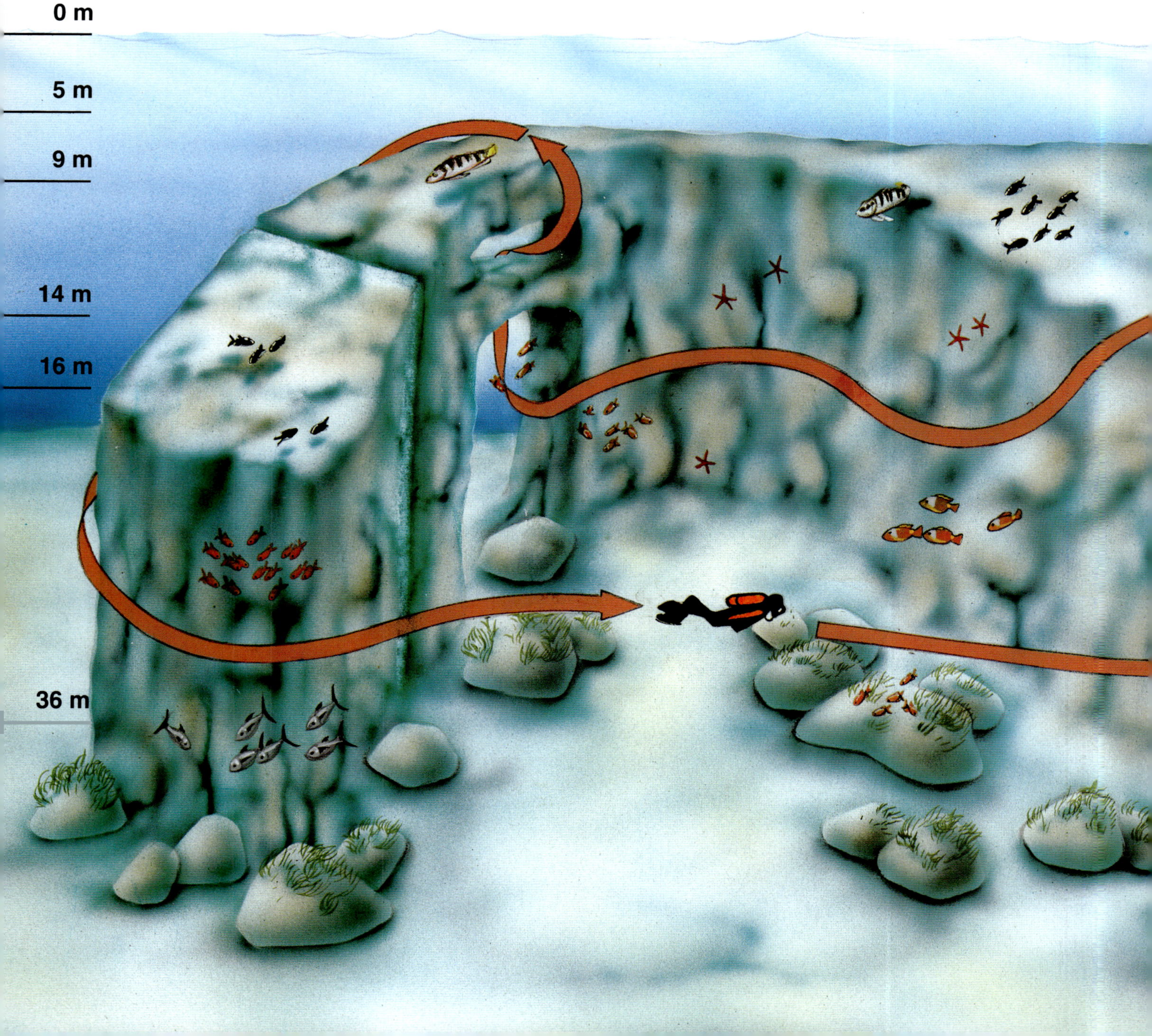

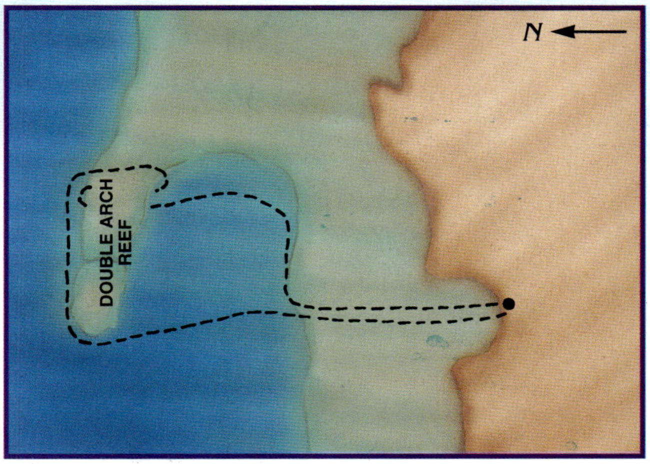
N
DOUBLE ARCH REEF

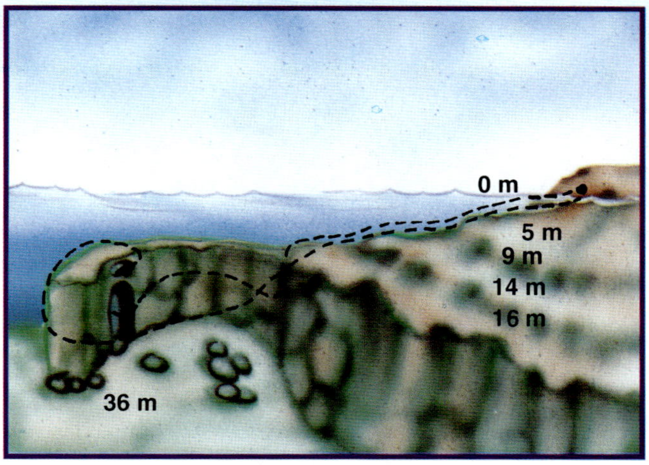
0 m
5 m
9 m
14 m
16 m
36 m

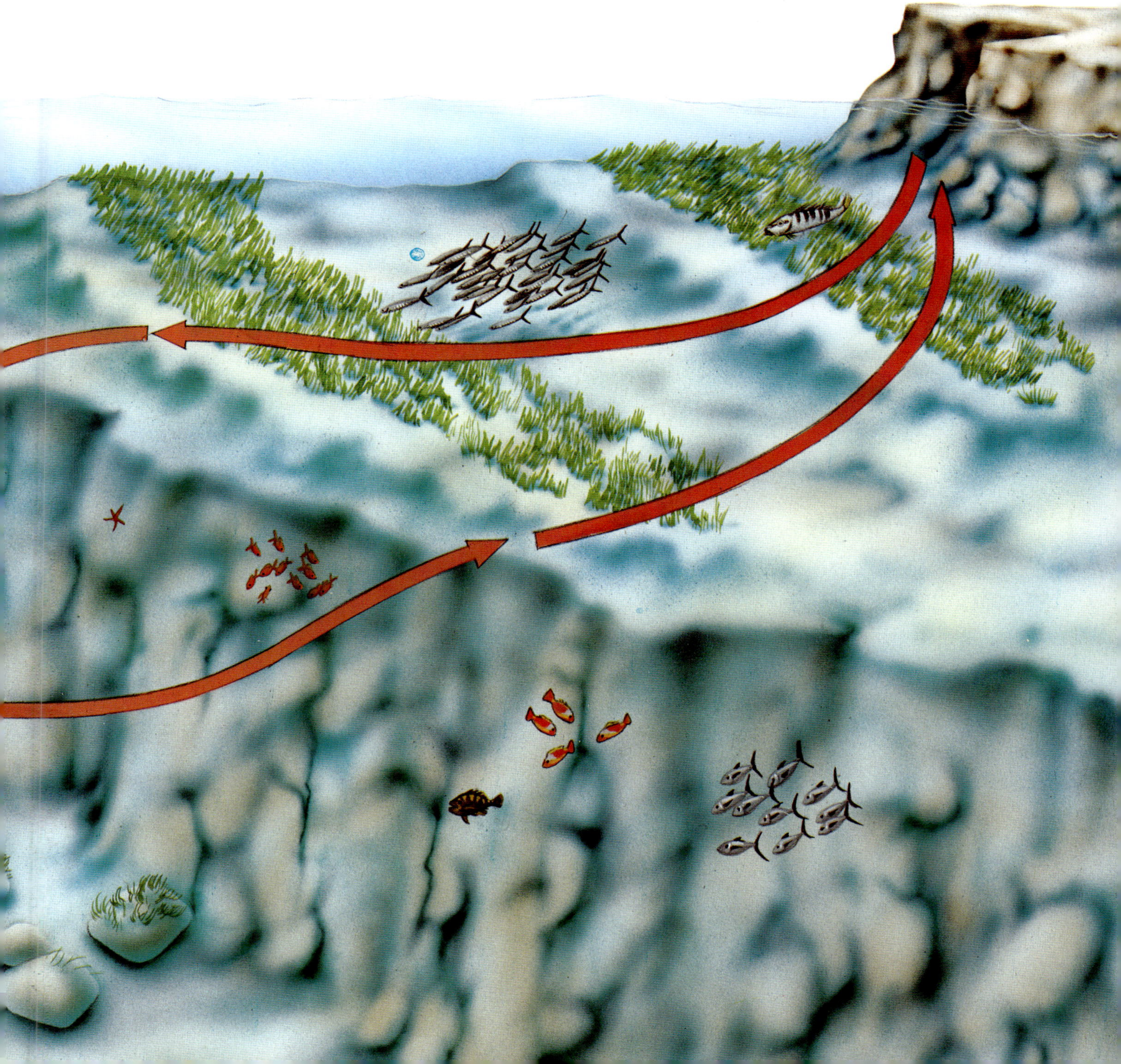

A - The point that gives this reef its name is characterized by a strange geologic formation, with an arch dividing two large openings in the rock.

B - The openings of the double arch are wide, and divers can enter with ease. This is one of the most characteristic diving areas.

C - At the start of the dive, you'll see large rocks where numerous sea urchins are grazing. Sea urchins have a complex mouth apparatus which they use to feed on algae.

D - At the start of the dive, the rock borders on a stretch of sand, very brightly illuminated due to its shallow depth. The ripple marks on the sediment indicate the presence of hydrodynamics.

E - A small brown scorpionfish deserves this close-up. Its large eyes and mouth, typical of predators, are quite evident.

F - The first part of the dive contains Neptune grass meadows and other areas covered with algae. Cuttlefish are common in these surroundings.

G - A small yellow black-faced blenny (Trypterigon delaisi) *rests on the sea floor. This is a male exhibiting his reproductive colours, as can be seen by the blue-edged fins and dark black head.*

A

B

C

D

LOCATION

A short distance to the east of Xwieni Bay - on the north coast of Gozo - is a very small "U" shaped cut into the rock - only a short distance from the road. Entry into the water is relatively easy but, once again, the rocks are sharp and it is easy to slip - so be warned. From here the diver heads out to sea in a northerly direction where, after some 200 metres a drop-off is discovered. At this point the diver should turn to his right (facing east) and follow the ledge which will slowly turn right round to the left. As it does so, the diver will see the two distinctive holes through the vertical rock face that is Double Arch Reef.

THE DIVE

This dive requires a long swim and competent, though fairly basic, underwater navigation skills. The seabed is only a few metres deep at the point of entry, so care must be taken not to drop heavily onto the underwater rocks which contain many thousands of sea urchins. The diver then follows a bearing of due north and pays attention to the seabed. The rock quickly gives way to sand as the seabed levels out at a depth of 9 metres. After some 50 metres or so, this drops again to a fairly uniform depth of 11 metres and finally to 14 metres as the diver passes over vast areas of seagrass (sometimes called eel grass) which, amongst others, is inhabited by cuttlefish, octopus and even the seahorse! A large shoal (approximately 200-250 fish) of fairly immature barracuda (each about 0.5 metres in length) are often seen in this area.
After a distance of about 200 metres, the diver will suddenly encounter a steep rocky drop-off which falls away vertically to 36 metres and stretches away to the east and the west. Here the diver turns to the right (due east) and follows the wall until it juts out and becomes an underwater headland. This "headland" curves right back around to the divers left within which "Double Arch Reef" is

found. At the very end of this "headland" is an isolated rock with a just a narrow fissure separating it from the remainder. Immediately prior to this fissure the diver will find two separate holes right through the rock - one immediately above the other! This is the Double Arch. Whenever I am confronted with curious structures and natural formations underwater, I cannot help but think about how they might have been formed. With a single arch it is probably fair to say that, because of a fault-line in the rock, it suddenly gave way and there it is. But how on earth a large section of rock fell away to create the second, upper hole through particular rock we shall never know. The top of the rock is at a depth of 16 metres and the remainder stretches down to a depth of 36 metres at the very bottom with the lower arch being by far the larger of the two holes. All divers must pay attention to their air consumption when diving this site. The long swim out requires an equally long swim back - all of which adds to the overall dive time and decompression at the end of that dive. The outward leg should be undertaken in a business-like manner with no time unduly wasted on matters of comparative trivia. Nor should any diver seek to set underwater speed records - both of which unnecessarily use too much air. The entry/exit point is well sheltered and is also ideal for decompression.

PHOTOGRAPHY

The object of this particular dive is to record on film one of the strangest structures to be found in Maltese waters: Double Arch Reef. A wide-angle lens is essential combined with very good and powerful lighting. I would also recommend a faster film - at least 200 ASA. As I have said above, it is a difficult subject. From the landward side, the arches are in permanent shadow, so the photographer must find a way of getting his fellow divers onto the far side - which is always well lit.

E

F

G

XATT L-AHMAR

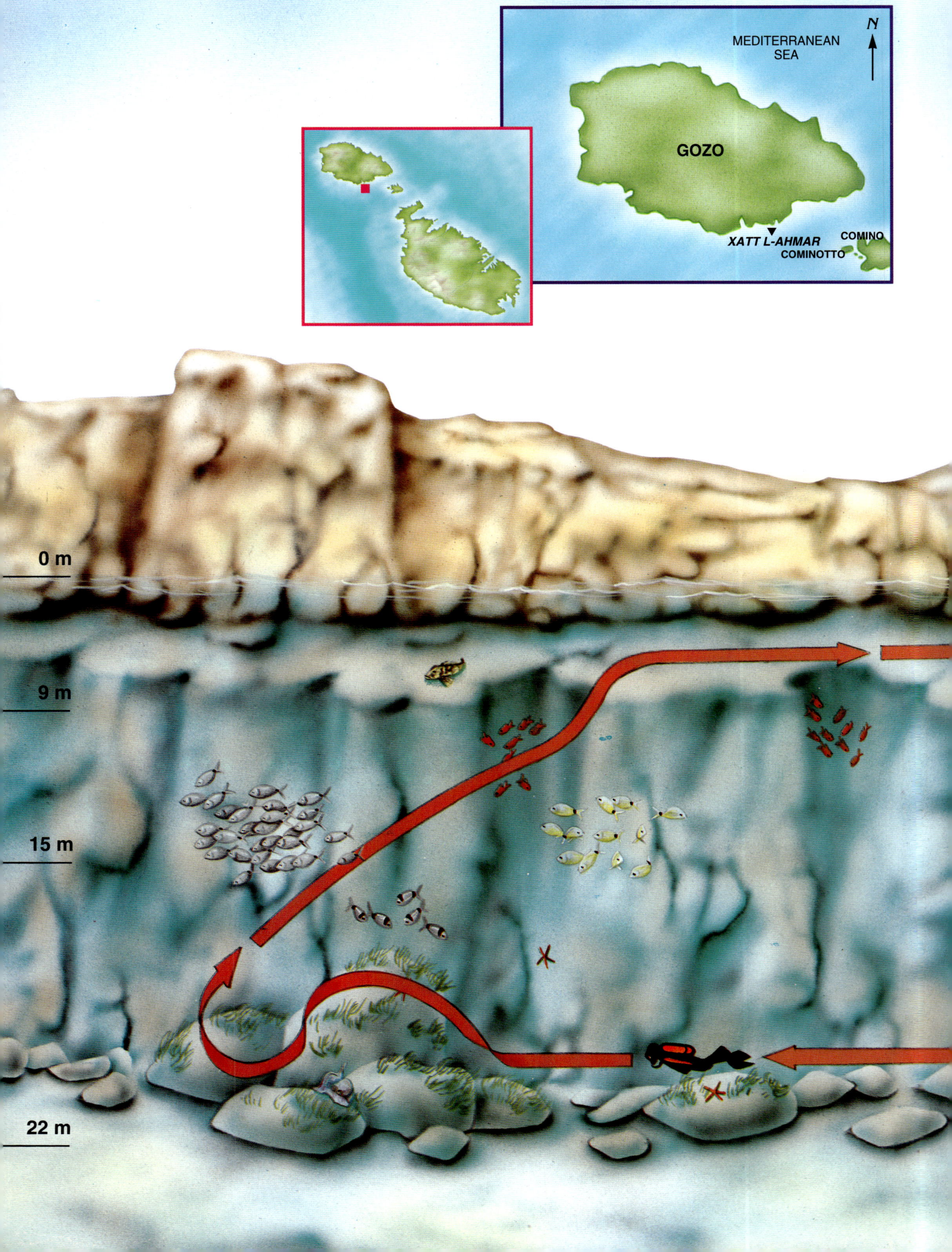

MEDITERRANEAN SEA
N
GOZO
XATT L-AHMAR
COMINO
COMINOTTO
0 m
9 m
15 m
22 m

N
XATT
L-AHMAR
MELLIEHA
POINT

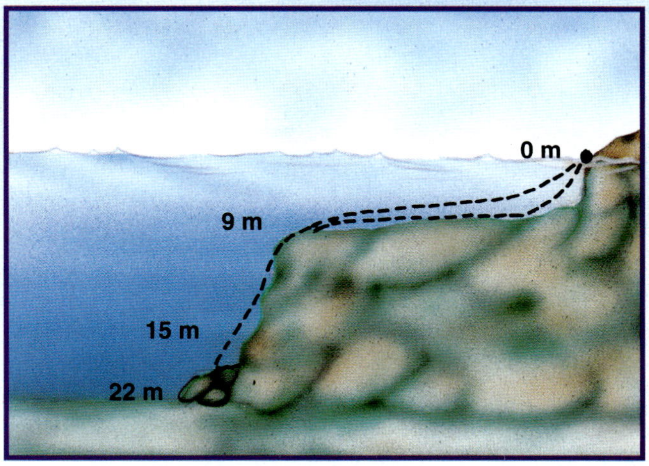
0 m
9 m
15 m
22 m

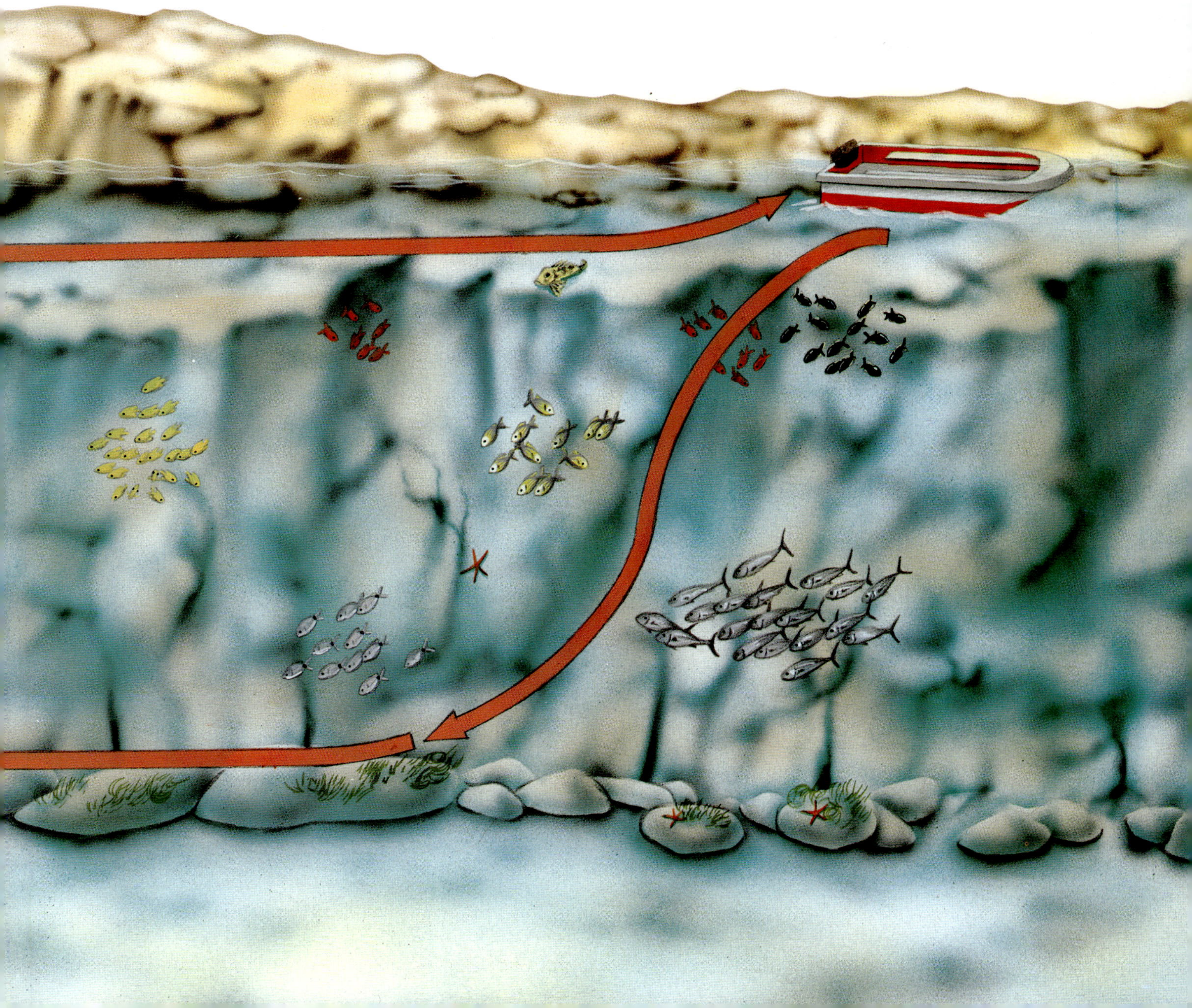

A - A little south of Mgarr is the small bay where the dive begins. You should ask a local how to reach the entry area, which is otherwise difficult to find.

B - When the sea is calm, the rocks on the coast in the diving area offer many convenient entry and exit points.

C - Large rocky masses alternate with slides of small rocks that shelter a large variety of fish and invertebrates: mullets, groupers, seabreams, octopuses and cuttlefish.

D - The route is varied, and after the initial shallows, you'll descend to the base of a wall 22 metres deep.

LOCATION

This is a small bay a short distance south-west of Mgarr and although clearly marked on the map, it is not an easy location to find. On leaving the main road many uncharted farm tracks criss-cross the area and, with the coast itself out of site, is very difficult to find the precise route. It is, however, well known to the local diving trade who will soon deliver the diver to the correct start point where there is a gentle slope across rocks and boulders to the water edge containing plenty of spots to accommodate an easy entry and exit to and from the water.

THE DIVE

This is a shore dive along a part of the coast which is often overlooked. Immediately below the surface the divers swim across a long and fairly wide horizontal ledge that is no more than 9 metres deep. This is covered with seaweed of an almost golden colour where large numbers of sprats and sardines are found feeding.
At first they seem almost oblivious to the presence of divers whilst always managing to keep a respectful distance. At the very edge, the divers drop down an uneven wall to a maximum depth of 22 metres before turning to the right and following the vase of this wall in a south-westerly direction.
Although, once again, the seabed is littered with rocks and boulders here they are slightly different with areas of very small rocks followed by areas where they are extremely large.
As strange as it may seem, it is almost as though they have been deliberately arranged solely to benefit divers!
Of course, they have not, but they do provide different habitats for different creatures, and this series of rocks stands out because of its inhabitants which include octopus, goatfish, small groupers, cuttlefish, seabreams and many others. Beyond these

A

B

C

D

E - The dive follows a part of the coast which is usually neglected. The first part of the route crosses a zone covered with algae, where schools of sprats and sardines can be seen.

F - A large grouper (Epinephelus marginatus) *hovers on the summit of a rock covered with algae. Groupers are territorial fish, and they stay within limited areas.*

G - The glint of the salemas reflected in the light of the camera flash contrasts with the azure blue of the open sea. Salemas are a quite common gregarious fish.

rocks, a sandy seabed provides excellent hunting territory for lizardfish, thornback rays and anglerfish and common stingray - although you should not expect to encounter all of these on a single dive.

After a distance of approximately 200 metres some large boulders, in which there are one or two interesting swim-throughs, signal the turning point of the dive. This usually means an ascent to the top of the wall which is then followed back to the start point. All along this area the diver will see small groups of two-banded and saddled seabreams in addition to much larger shoals of bogues and damselfish. Both above and below the edge of the reef there are also many other individual fish such as parrotfish, saupes, wrasses and scorpionfish - to name but a very few.

In fact the sheer variety of fish have marked this area for special attention and it is intended that a large wreck will be sunk close-by in the near future.

G

H

E

I

F

Photography:

This site is, therefore, ideal for close-up and macro photography of fish and other marine creatures.

The macro lens is particularly essential because there is every opportunity of finding something small and exciting in amongst the seaweed or the many nooks and crannies that make this dive so very interesting.

H - At night white-spotted octopuses are common. They are a different species from the common octopus (Octopus macropus).

I - A painted comber swims peacefully on the sea floor. This is one of the most common and easily identifiable fish in the area.

FESSEJ ROCK

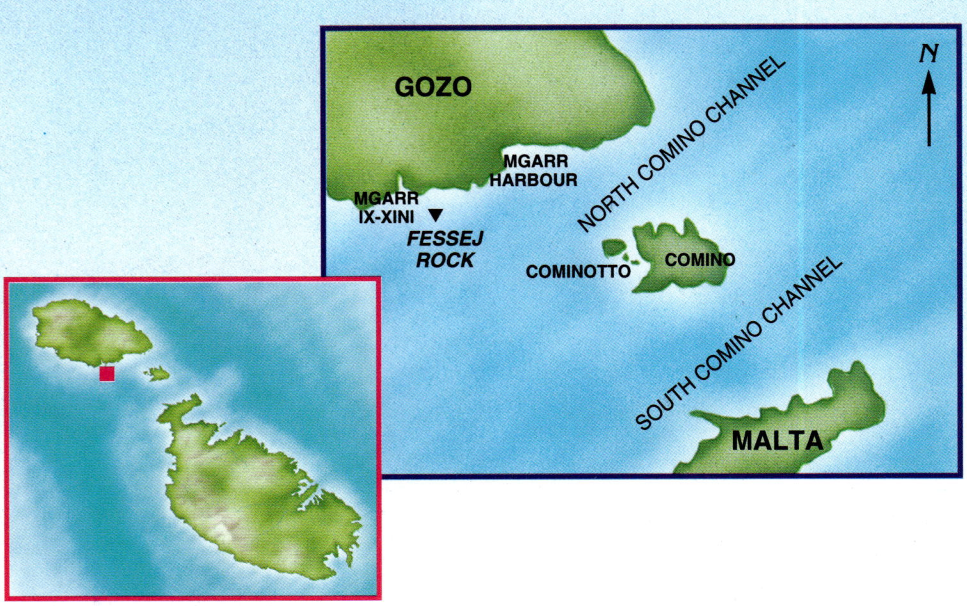
GOZO
MGARR HARBOUR
MGARR IX-XINI
FESSEJ ROCK
NORTH COMINO CHANNEL
N
COMINOTTO
COMINO
SOUTH COMINO CHANNEL
MALTA

0 m
10 m
20 m
45 m
50 m

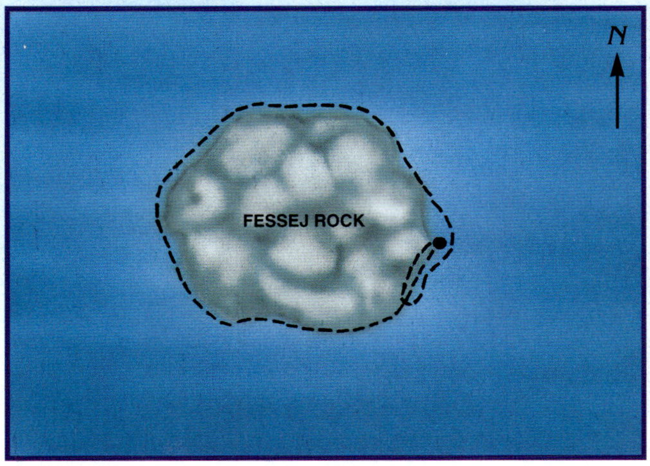
N
FESSEJ ROCK

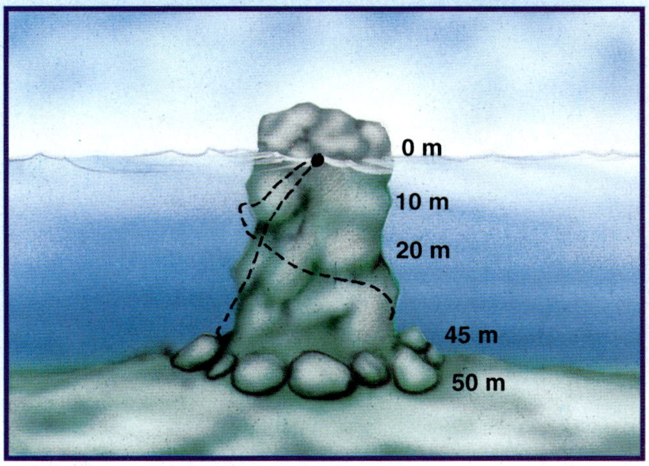
0 m
10 m
20 m
45 m
50 m

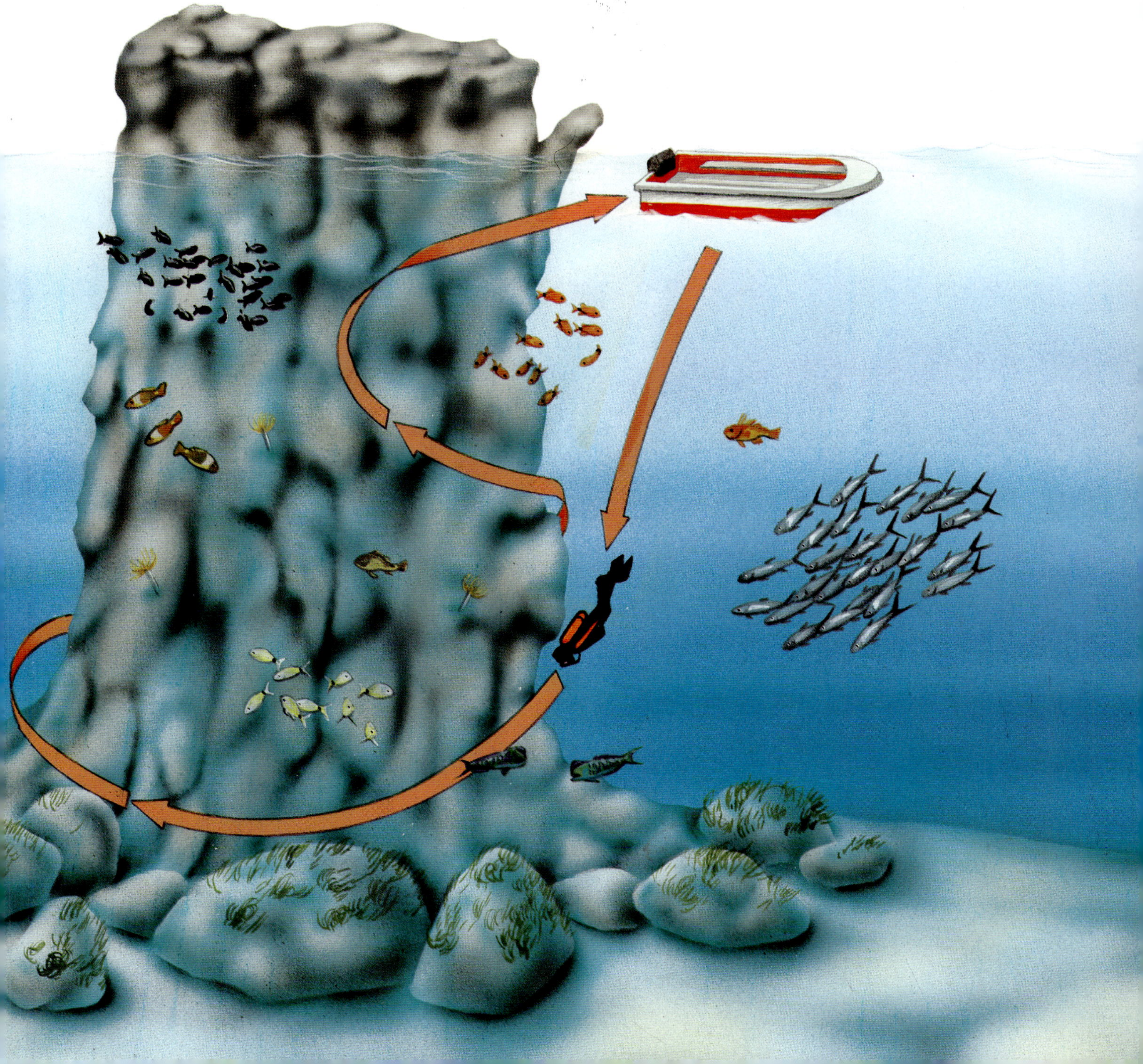

A

B

C

D

LOCATION

A very dark and very prominent rock is found in the sea close to the entrance of the inlet called Mgarr ix-Xini approximately 2.5 kilometres south-west of Mgarr harbour. This is a boat dive only with the rock itself providing adequate mooring.

THE DIVE

Fessej Rock is a tall, circular and vertical column of rock reaching up from very deep water. On its south-eastern side - just above the surface, is a hook of rock on which the dive boat is quite able to attach a mooring line. From here the divers enter the water and find themselves about to embark on one of the deepest dives in the country - making the site extremely popular with those who seek depths well beyond 50 metres. Of course, all dives are as limited to the depth the diver is seeking and I have limited this dive to 50 metres - which, in any event, is where the rock comes to an abrupt end.

Almost as soon as the divers begin the descent they also begin a circumnavigation of the rock. At first, the common fishes such as cardinalfish, scorpionfish and painted combers are quite plentiful but quickly become scarce as the divers get even deeper. At 30 metres it is the smaller groups of very large sheepshead breams and dentex that first catch the eye before these are replaced by much larger shoals of tuna and greater amberjacks, which often seem almost motionless in the water. Below these, the largest parrotfish are encountered - though quite what they find to chew at these depths is a mystery. On the rock itself there are also a number of large tube worms. At 50 metres, the steep sides of Fessej Rock suddenly give way to some very large boulders containing some excellent specimens of groupers and even some of the largest octopus I have ever seen. Below, the seabed continues ever deeper - although this is now at an angle

A - Fessey Rock is a steep, vertical column of rock that rises up from great depths on the southeast side, right across from the Mgarr ix-Xini inlet.

B - The wall in the deeper zones descends down to 50 metres and beyond. This is one of the most popular dives for those who like deep water.

C - The dive begins as you swim around a rocky tower that rises up from great depths. Less expert divers should refrain from following the rock down its vertical descent.

D - A gilt-head bream and a number of striped seabreams swim in the blue depths. These fish often patrol sandy areas in search of food.

of something in the region of 45 degrees. All around the base of the rock the boulders continue to reveal their inhabitants - which are not as used to divers as elsewhere and thus occasionally allow themselves to be approached.
At this depth, however, there is only a short time before the ascent must be commenced and this is usually achieved whilst still completing the circumnavigation of the entire rock. Once the shallower water is reached, the rock provides the ideal datum point for decompression whilst always providing the diver with much to see and explore at the same time.
Fessej Rock has much to offer divers of all grades and experience - except that novice divers do not have to go to 50 metres at the base of the rock just because it is there! Clearly, therefore, the deeper diving is for the more experienced diver who must plan the dive carefully and take note of air consumption and decompression times.

PHOTOGRAPHY

This is a deep dive with much to occupy the mind of the serious photographer. It is ideal for wide-angle photography. All around the rock, from near the surface down to 50 metres, there are spectacular vertical cliffs and obscure little outcrops and niches to provide excellent back-drops for those pictures of your fellow divers. In the deeper half of the dive large groupers are always encountered - though they often prove to be too wary of human beings to allow the photographer to get close enough for a good shot - perhaps that is why they have survived to become so very big!
There is also much to satisfy the macro photographer - especially in the shallows. Once again we find every little hole and fissure in the rock face occupied by those ever beautiful red cardinalfish - often with a bright yellow or red background or cup corals or sponges.

E

F

G

H

E - An ornate wrasse (Thalassoma pavo) *swims in the open water among a swarm of damselfish. This brightly coloured fish is the most "tropical" fish of the Mediterranean.*

F - Golden zoanthids (Parazoanthus axinellae) *are cnidarians, animals similar to corals, which feed on particles and organisms transported by the currents.*

G - A tiny, bright red blenny heads for its lair.

H - Many wreathy tuft tube worms (Sabella spallanzani) *can be seen on the wall. These are annelids that live within a long tube from which their elegant, spiral-shaped branchial tuft emerges.*

IL-KANTRA

N
MEDITERRANEAN
SEA
GOZO
MGARR IX-XINI
IL-KANTRA
COMINOTTO
COMINO

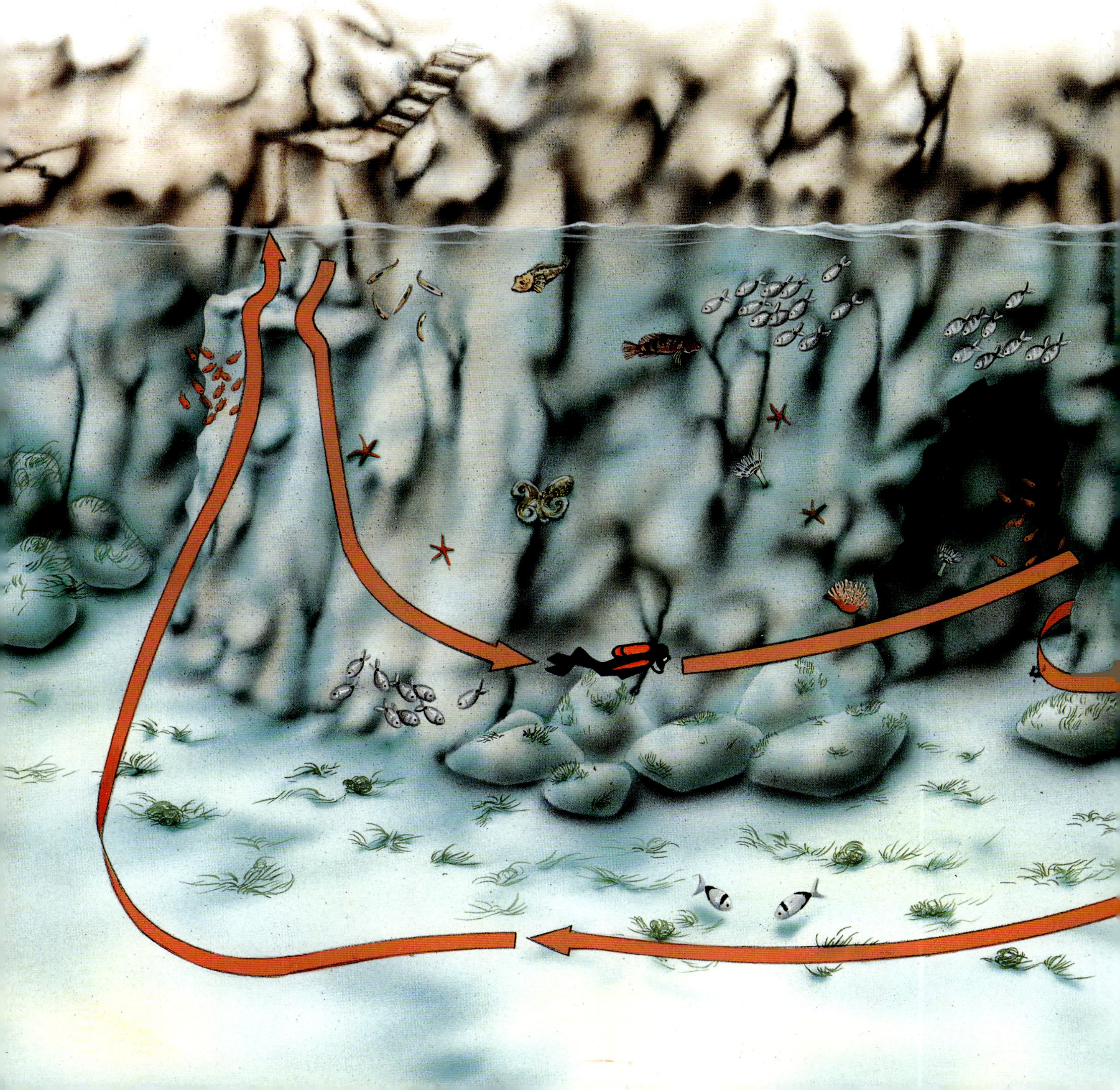

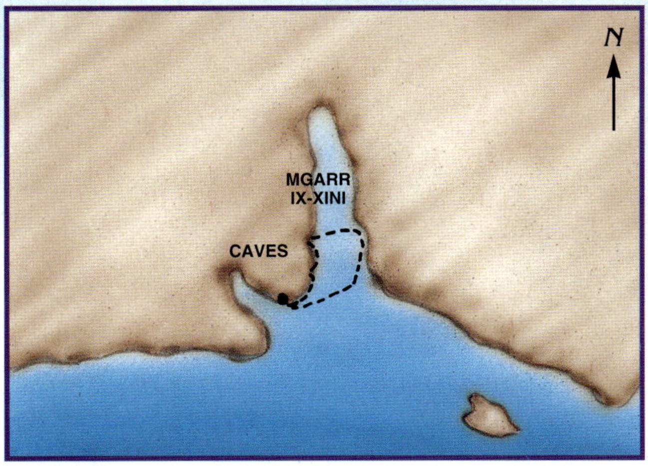
N
MGARR
IX-XINI
CAVES

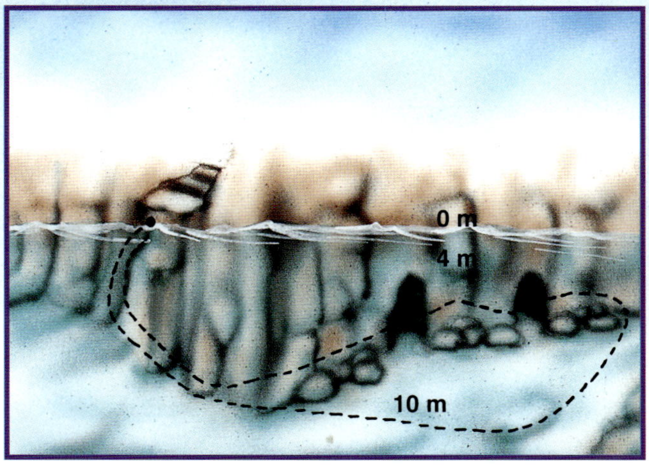
0 m
4 m
10 m

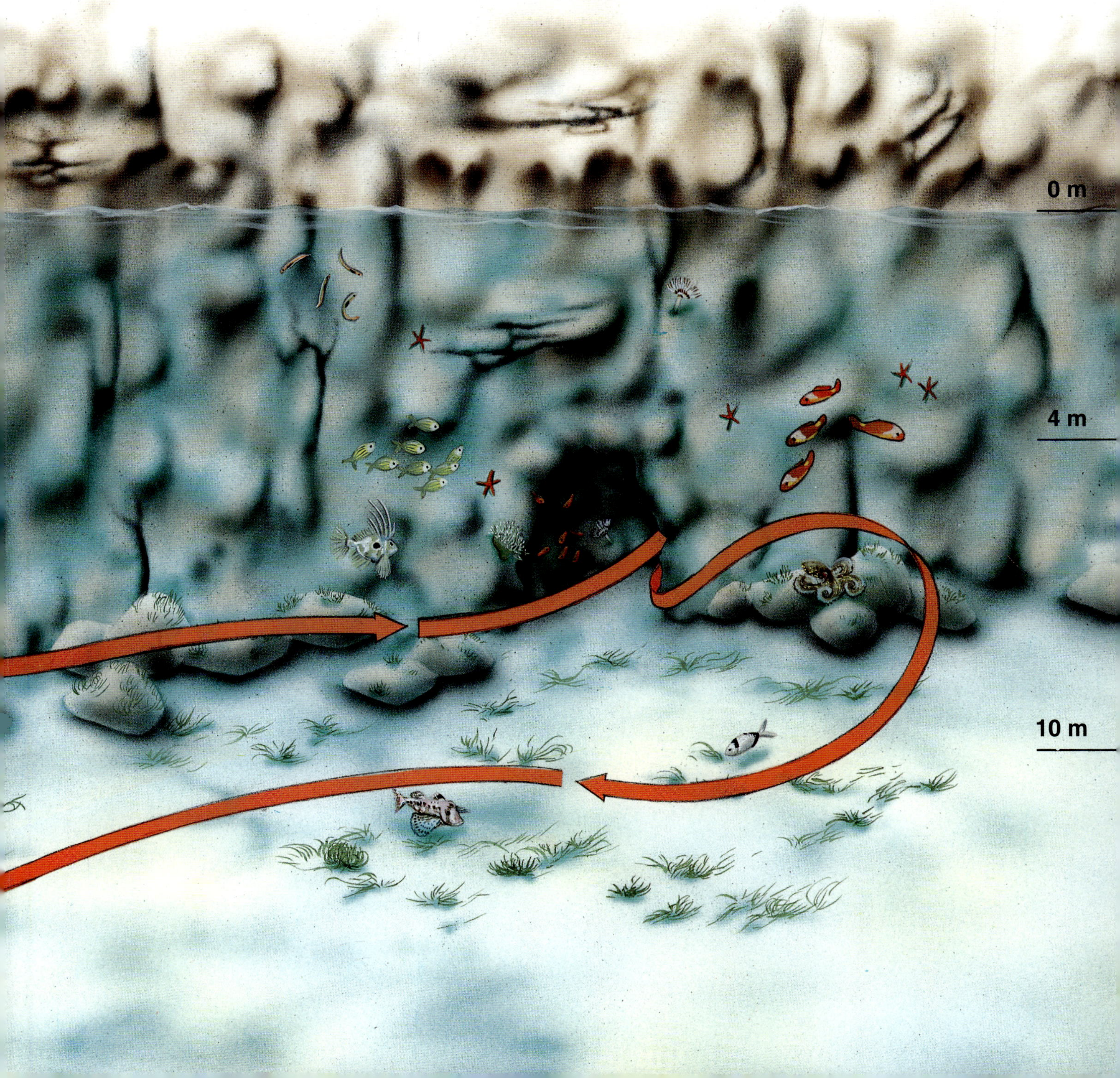
0 m
4 m
10 m

A - It is necessary to descend one hundred and three steps to reach the small concrete platform from which the divers enter the water, on the western side of the Mgarr ix-Xini inlet.

B - Sometimes visibility in the bay is poor, but even on these occasions the dive is extremely interesting, due to the variety of organisms you may encounter.

LOCATION

Just inside the western entrance to an inlet called Mgarr ix-Xini are no fewer than 103 steps leading right down to the water edge where a small concrete platform provides an excellent entry and exit point. Finding these steps amongst the many farm tracks can be difficult but the route is well known to the local diving trade. On entering the water the diver can swim around to his left and into the inlet where he will eventually discover two large caves or, alternatively, there is another site if the diver chooses to swim out towards the sea where there is improved underwater visibility.

THE DIVE

On entering the water the divers find themselves above a small ledge where seahorses are often found. They are, however, well camouflaged so they do take some finding. Below this ledge the seabed is at a depth of 8 metres. Here, the contours of the base of the cliff face are followed right round to the left where the diver enters the inlet almost immediately. The western side of the inlet is undoubtedly the more interesting side with a number of fish seen here - and nowhere else. These include flying gurnard, red gurnard, star-gazer and, on one occasion the John Dory! Other species include some excellent examples of goatfish, seabream, painted comber, scorpionfish, small octopus and large cuttlefish. A short distance along the side of the inlet the diver will also discover the first of two caves. This has a large entrance - 10 metres at the seabed and 3 metres at its top. Well inside this cave there is a very interesting ceiling where the diver is able to surface. For me, however, the best view is to look back at one's fellow divers as they approach the surface. Approximately 50 metres from the first cave, there is a second, much smaller cave.

C

D

A

B

C - Another typical resident of the sandy sea floor is the star-gazer (Uranoscopus scaber). *Its black dorsal fin has poisonous spines that can inflict painful wounds.*

D - Exciting encounters are possible on the sandy sea floor: here a streaked gurnard (Trygloporus lastoviza) *unfolds its "wings" as if it were gliding. Its broad pectoral fins are edged and dotted with blue.*

E - *You can see elegant narval shrimp with their long rostrum and antennae in the caves at the start of the dive.*

F - *A black-faced blenny rests among the algae. It feeds on tiny crustaceans, and when it is not the reproductive season it is difficult to tell males from females.*

G - *A red scorpionfish shows how varied the colours of this predator can be. Here it has perfectly adapted to the colour of the sea floor, with streaks that break up the image of the fish.*

Within the immediate entrances to both caves there are some very interesting anemones, sea squirts and even some shrimps carefully hidden amongst the curiously shaped walls.
Away from the cliff face, the seabed within the inlet comprises coarse sand with periodic growths of seaweed and seagrass and it is above these that those rarer fish are found. In addition there are many goatfish digging for their dinners and, interestingly, each of these fish will be found working with a single two-banded seabream - apparently waiting for something the goatfish overlooks.

PHOTOGRAPHY

The bay itself suffers from rather poor visibility and wide-angle photography tends, therefore, to be limited to the entrances and inside the two caves. That said, inside the first cave is particularly interesting with dramatic features stretching down from the roof at the far right-hand, upper corner.

G

H

E

I

F

If I were to select a single site ideally suited for macro and close-up photography it would have to be Il-Kantra. It is here that the diver will encounter numerous species of fish that are rarely seen elsewhere. Indeed it was at this site that I saw the very rare John Dory, red gurnard and star-gazer for the very first time ever. Fish life is so prolific that you can almost guarantee you will find something unusual - once we deliberately went looking for a flying gurnard - and found one!

H - *A cuttlefish becomes almost unrecognizable as it curls its tentacles and wrinkles the surface of its body. This is a common sight at Il-Kantra.*

I - *Camouflaged among the algae, a tiny blenny seeks refuge from the attack of predators.*

COMINO CAVES

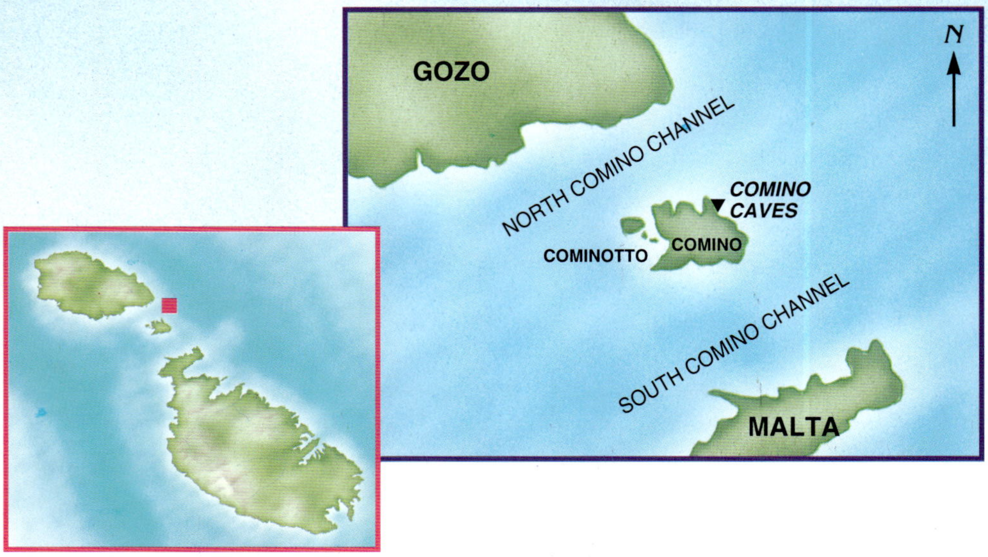

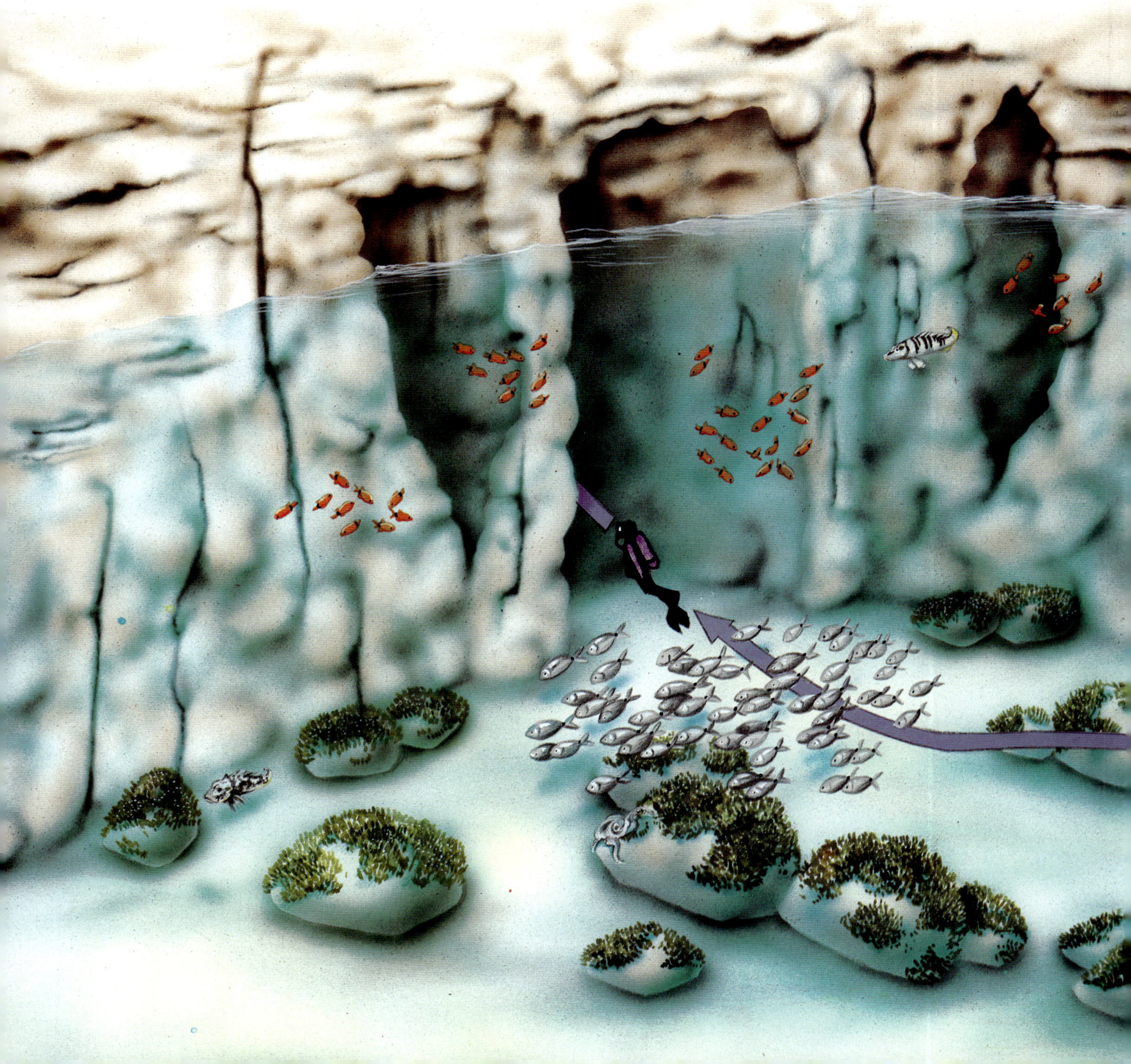

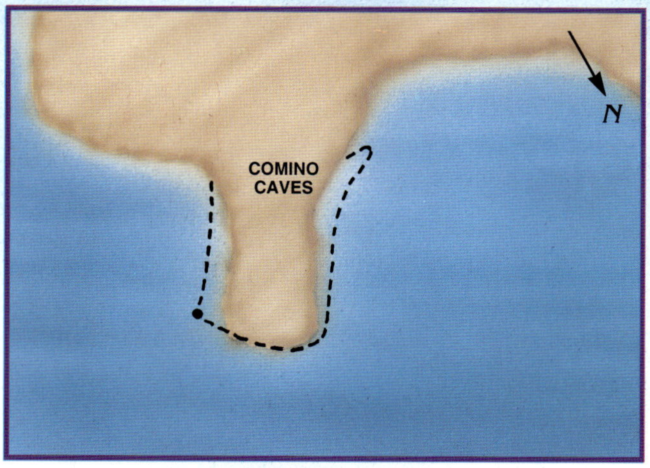
COMINO
CAVES
N

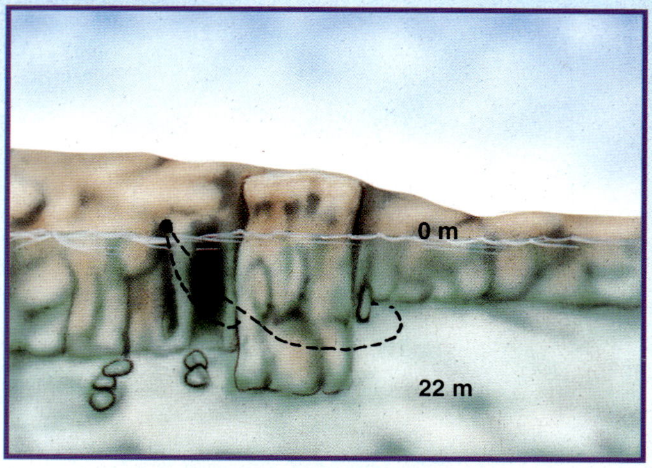
0 m
22 m

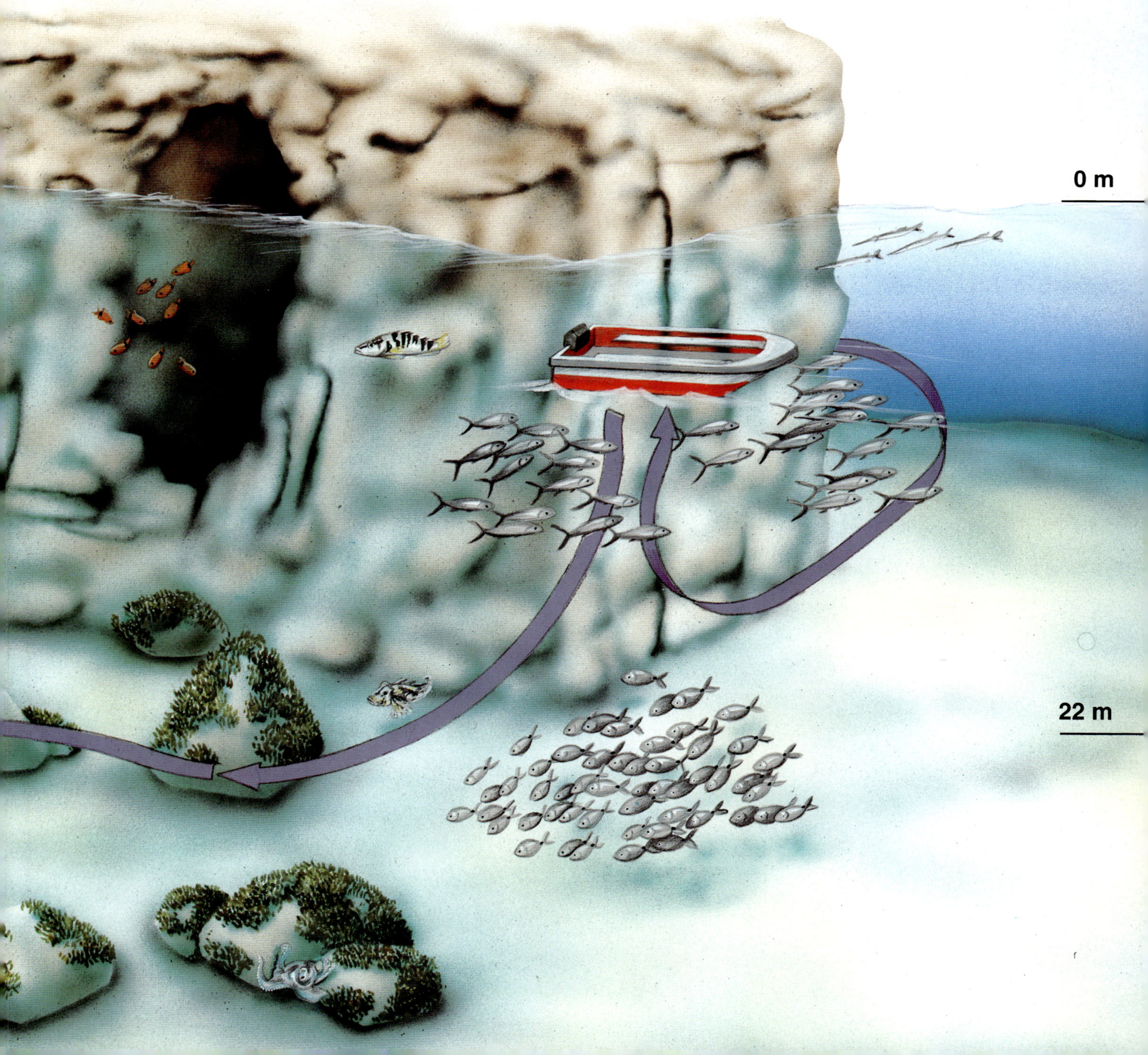
0 m
22 m

A

B

C

D

A - The island of Comino, between Malta and Gozo, is famous for its underwater caves, which can be seen on the north coast. An L-shaped inlet near the Ghemieri area has become one of the most popular sites for cave dives.

B - When they are offered food, saddled seabreams throng around divers in a sort of feeding frenzy; this has become a common sight.

C - Saddled seabreams are quite common in all dives in the Maltese archipelago. These members of the Sparidae family are always gregarious.

D - The light diminishes rapidly after the first few metres down, and a flashlight is always important to make the dive pleasant.

E - The habit of taking food from divers has resulted in an extraordinary concentration of saddled seabreams at the Comino Caves.

LOCATION

Between the islands of Malta and Gozo there is the island of Comino which has become extremely well known for its profusion of delightful underwater caves. These are situated on the north coast - just to the east of a headland called Ghemieri. Here there is an "L" shaped inlet where a number of caves can be seen from the surface. Right in the corner of this inlet is one of the most popular dives in the country which is usually visited as the second (shallower) dive of the day.

E

THE DIVE

This is a boat dive with plenty of good anchorage provided close inshore with a depth of 15 metres. On reaching the seabed the divers are immediately mobbed by many thousands of saddled seabreams. These fish are found throughout the Maltese Islands but, for some reason, it is here that they are regularly fed and, therefore amass in much greater numbers. When feeding these fish, the diver is temporarily lost to view and all divers seem to enjoy the spectacle.
Eventually, however, the divers head towards the cave entrance which is found right in the corner. This is only 10 metres deep at the entrance and immediately begins to get progressively shallower. At first, the cave appears as though it will end abruptly but, just as it turns to the right, two exits come into view. The first is on the right hand side

F - Forkbeards (Phycis phycis) *are typical cave fish which are easily identifiable by the two forked barbels under the jaw and the dorsal and ventral fins that extend to the tail.*

G - A tube worm (Bispira volutacornis) *shows off its branchial tuft, while another individual on the left has completely retracted it into the tube in which it lives.*

H - The giant sea lemons (Hypselodoris valenciennesi) *are among the largest nudibranchs of the Mediterranean. Their branchial tuft is quite evident, but can be fully retracted.*

I - A dotted sea slug (Discodoris atromaculata) *grazes on a sponge. The colour of this small nudibranch, which seem quite evident to us, is actually mimetic, as the spots break up the image of the animal.*

and is a tight squeeze. The dive leader will normally carry on to the second exit a little further on - which has much more room.
Whichever route is taken, the diver now enters a much larger cavern with a magnificent exit to the open sea. This cave is well worth closer inspection with its beautiful ceiling of bright yellow soft corals and deep red sponges. As the divers emerge from this cave they head round to the left where they are confronted with a very distinctive rock - which I have called "George Washington" because it is almost identical to his famous profile - perhaps the name will catch on!
The route now takes the diver through a narrow gap right behind "George Washington's neck" where the divers emerge above a very beautiful reef. This is alive with tube worms, seabreams, wrasses and many other species - both large and small. Here, the diver turns to the right and follows the contours of the headland all the way around to where the boat is anchored - and as they approach the saddled seabreams swim round to meet them.
Within the two caves, depths vary from 10-15 metres - but most of the journey is in much shallower water. This site, therefore, offers countless opportunities for photography as well as safe, yet adventurous cave diving. In addition, the vast numbers of seemingly tame fish has made this site a firm favourite with all divers.

PHOTOGRAPHY

The caves and the large shoals of saddled seabreams surrounding the divers are both subjects which are ideal for wide-angle photography. The inner features and the entrances of both caves should be included - as should George Washington - from the right angle! As for the fish, I found the best results were just as the diver had finished feeding and was swimming away with a few fish in pursuit.
There are also many ideal subjects for macro photography - the delicate sponges and corals within the caves as well as the many fish and other items found on the reef - to name but a few.

F

G

H

I

LANTERN POINT

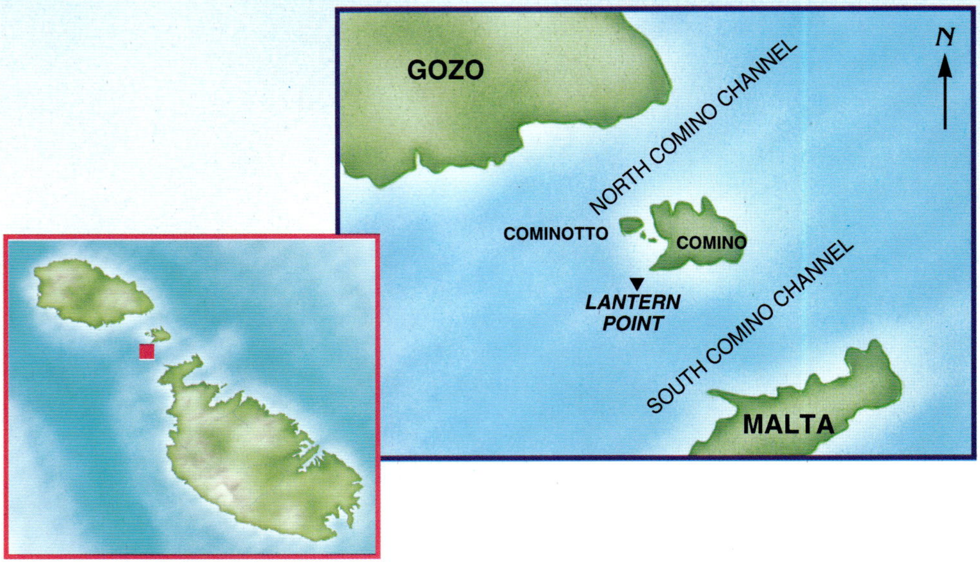

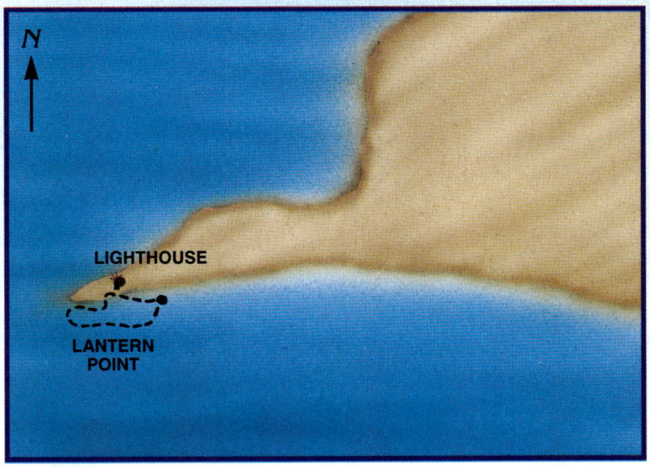
N
LIGHTHOUSE
LANTERN POINT

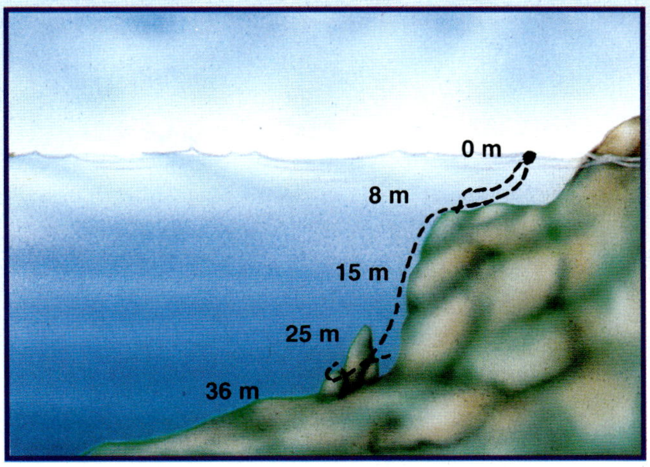
0 m
8 m
15 m
25 m
36 m

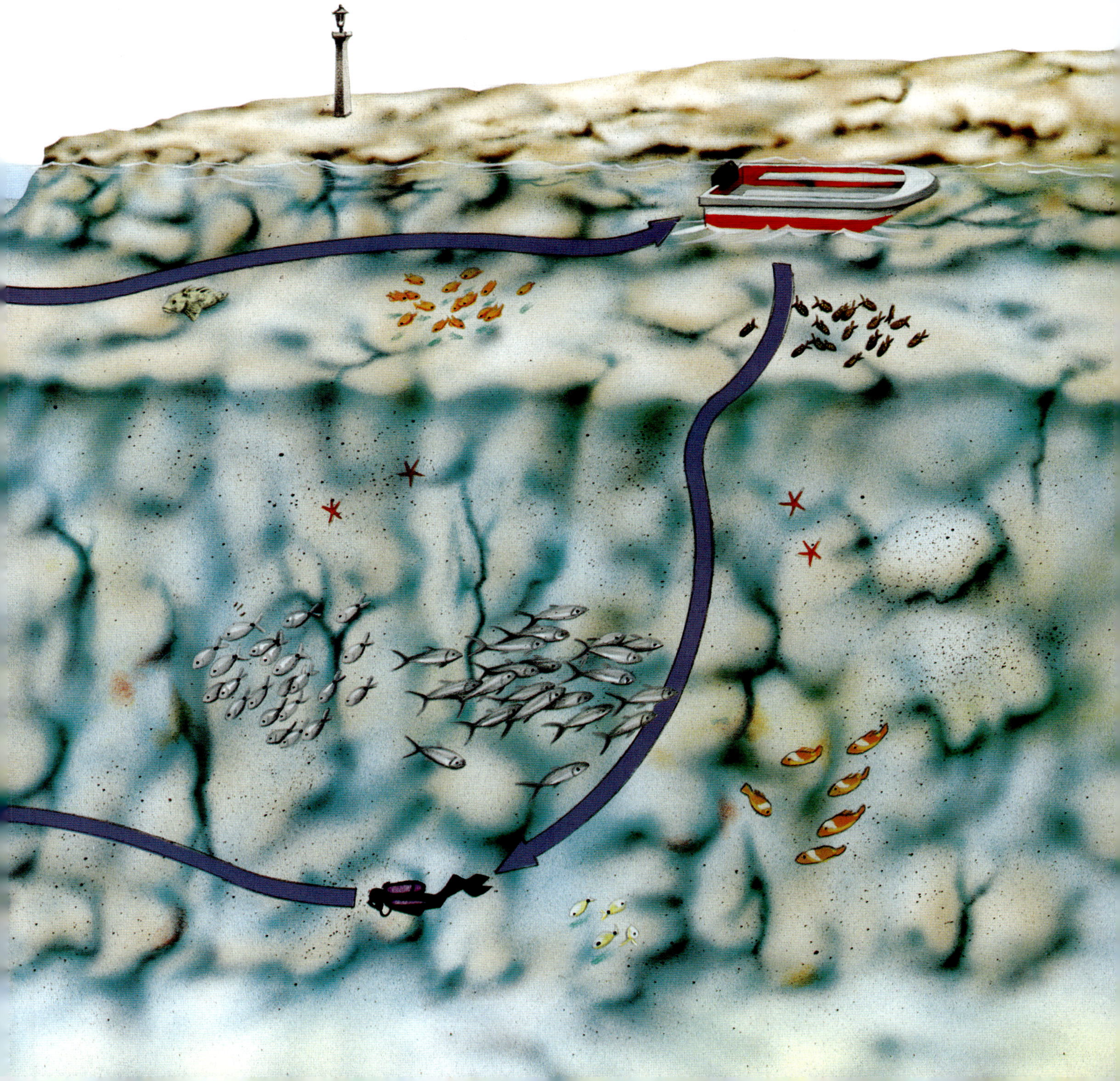

A - The southwest side of Comino is called Ras-i-Irqieqa, and its tip is marked by a small lantern. The dive begins right under this miniature lighthouse.

B - Descend to a wide, level, shallow area that leads straight south to a drop-off that plunges down to 36 metres, where large boulders rest.

LOCATION

The very "pointed" south-west corner of Comino is called Ras-I-Irqieqa - and is clearly marked on tourist maps. Almost at the very end of this rocky promontory is a hazard light - a lantern, from where the site derives its name. This light is about 2 metres tall and is a miniature lighthouse to warn shipping. Directly below this light is where the dive commences. This is another boat dive with adequate anchorage provided by the relatively shallow waters close inshore.

THE DIVE

Immediately below the boat - at depths of 6-8 metres, the divers descend to a wide underwater plateau. Swimming almost due south, they will soon discover the drop-off which marks the start of a descent down a vertical wall to about 36 metres. Along the entire length of the wall there is a lot to see with much of the fish life being different from anything else so far encountered. Conger eels, spiny lobsters and even small shoals of parrotfish are often reported.

At the base of the cliff, the divers turn to their right where they will soon encounter some very large boulders at 36 metres. These boulders are literally teeming with fish life - groupers, octopus, cuttlefish and some of the largest goatfish I have ever seen.

Looking away from the wall the diver may well encounter amberjacks, tuna and even barracudas.

Hidden from view, behind these boulders is an interesting cave. Being permanently in the shade, it has developed some really magnificent soft, orange and virgin lace corals in addition to large areas of red sponge. There are also many cardinalfish and sometimes the diver can be quite overwhelmed by the quantity and brightness of the colours revealed in torchlight.

A short distance away the diver

C

D

A

B

C - If we observe this apparently barren seabed carefully we discover a rich fauna. In this image a diver has "discovered" a scorpionfish hidden among the algae.

D - The rocks that end on a sandy seabed are covered with lush vegetation. If you wander among the rocks you will discover eels, lobsters and large parrotfish.

E - A detail of the golden zoanthids shows the structure of these animals that look like flowers. Here the column and tentacles around the mouth are quite evident.

F - This rocky wall, covered by algae and encrusting organisms, almost reaches the water surface.

will discover a second cave entrance at 16 metres. This should be entered when the diver is ready to commence the final ascent because, inside, the ceiling becomes a tunnel which leads upwards allowing the diver to exit on top of the plateau at 8 metres. This tunnel is also called the Chimney but is very distinct from others because a moray eel and a conger eel are known to occupy the same small crevice in the rock - where they, apparently live in complete harmony.

H

E

F

G

PHOTOGRAPHY

This is another of those sites that cater for different photographic requirements. A wide angle lens is essential for capturing divers as they inspect and enjoy the many features below the drop-off. Here the over-hangs and curious crevices are ideal for framing distant divers. In addition, this site provides yet another excellent opportunity for macro photography with a wide variety of marine life - some of which are more common here than elsewhere.

G - A small moray is hidden among the dense carpet of algae (Dictyopteris membranacea) *that covers the rocks near the surface.*

H - In the shady area the wall is covered by a carpet of orange corals and golden zoanthids. The light of the camera flash shows off the vivid colours of these cnidarians.

COMINOTTO REEF

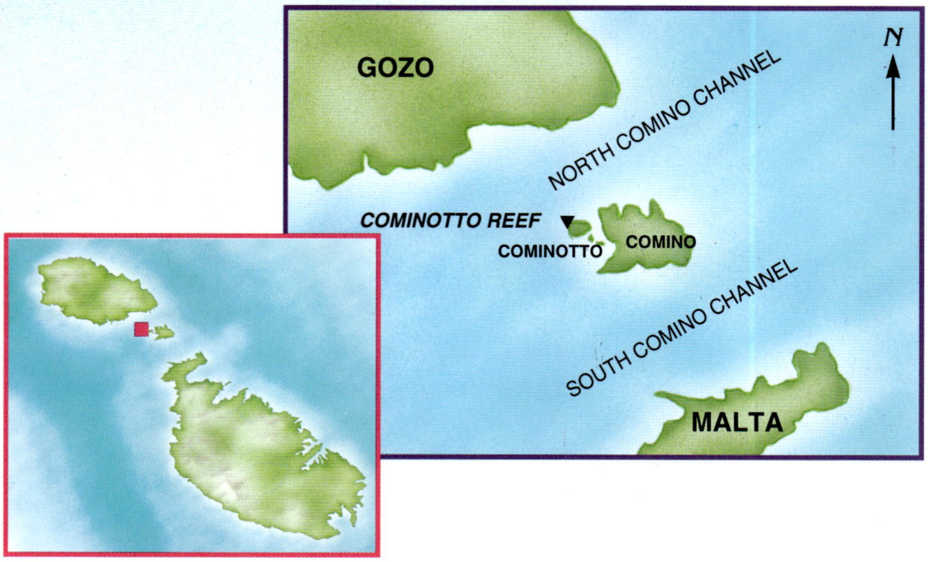

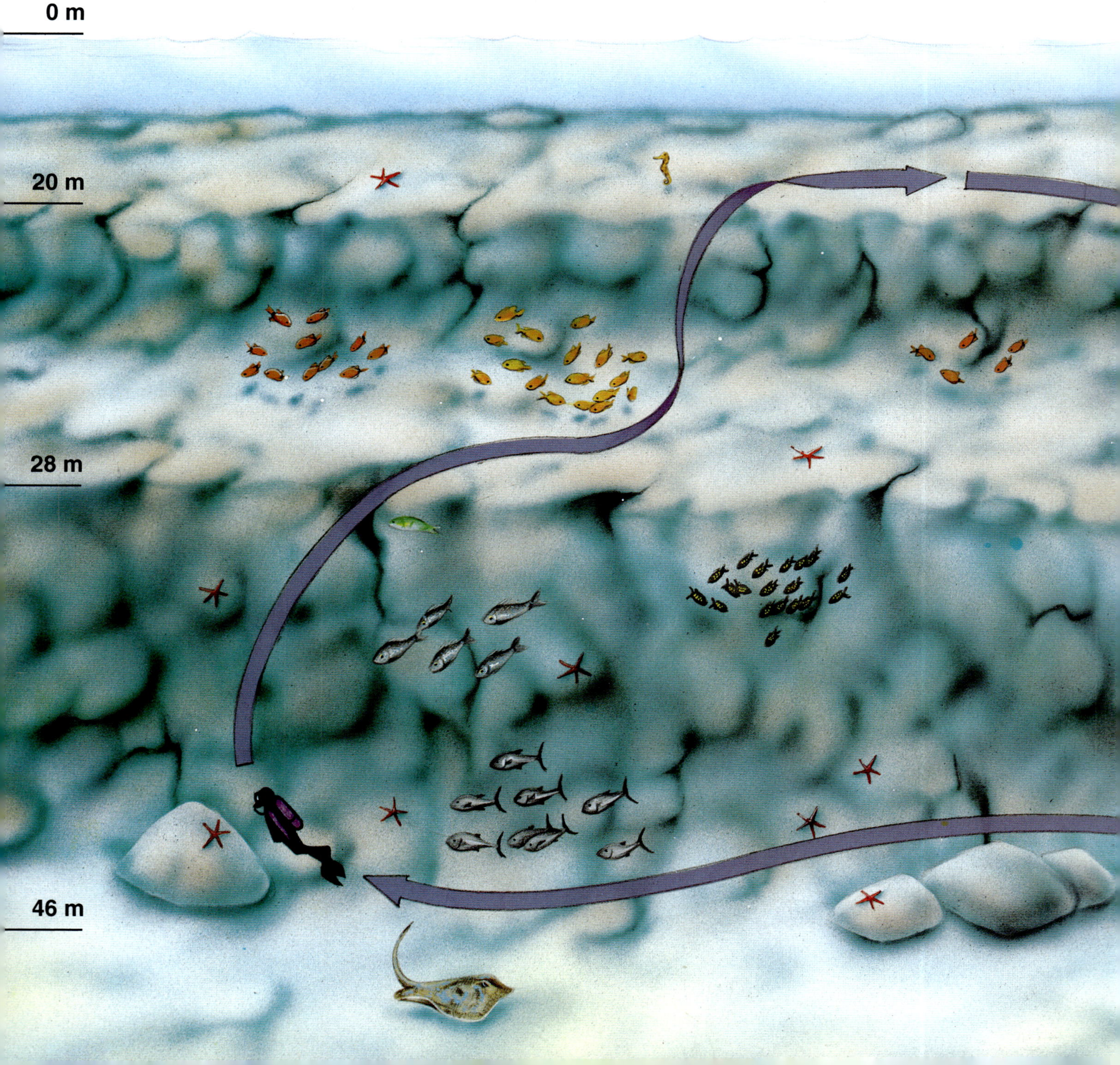

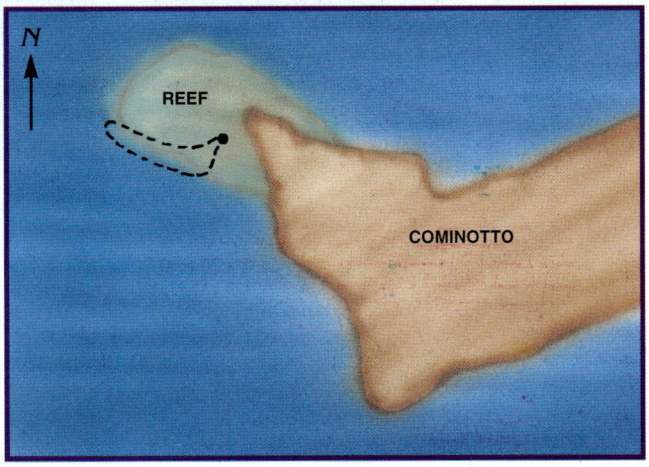
N
REEF
COMINOTTO

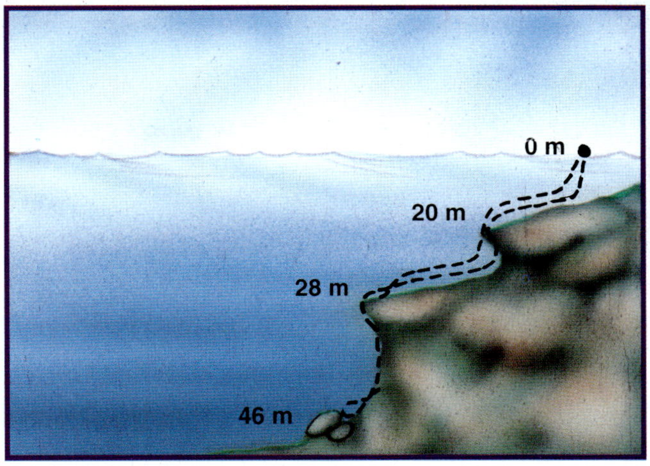
0 m
20 m
28 m
46 m

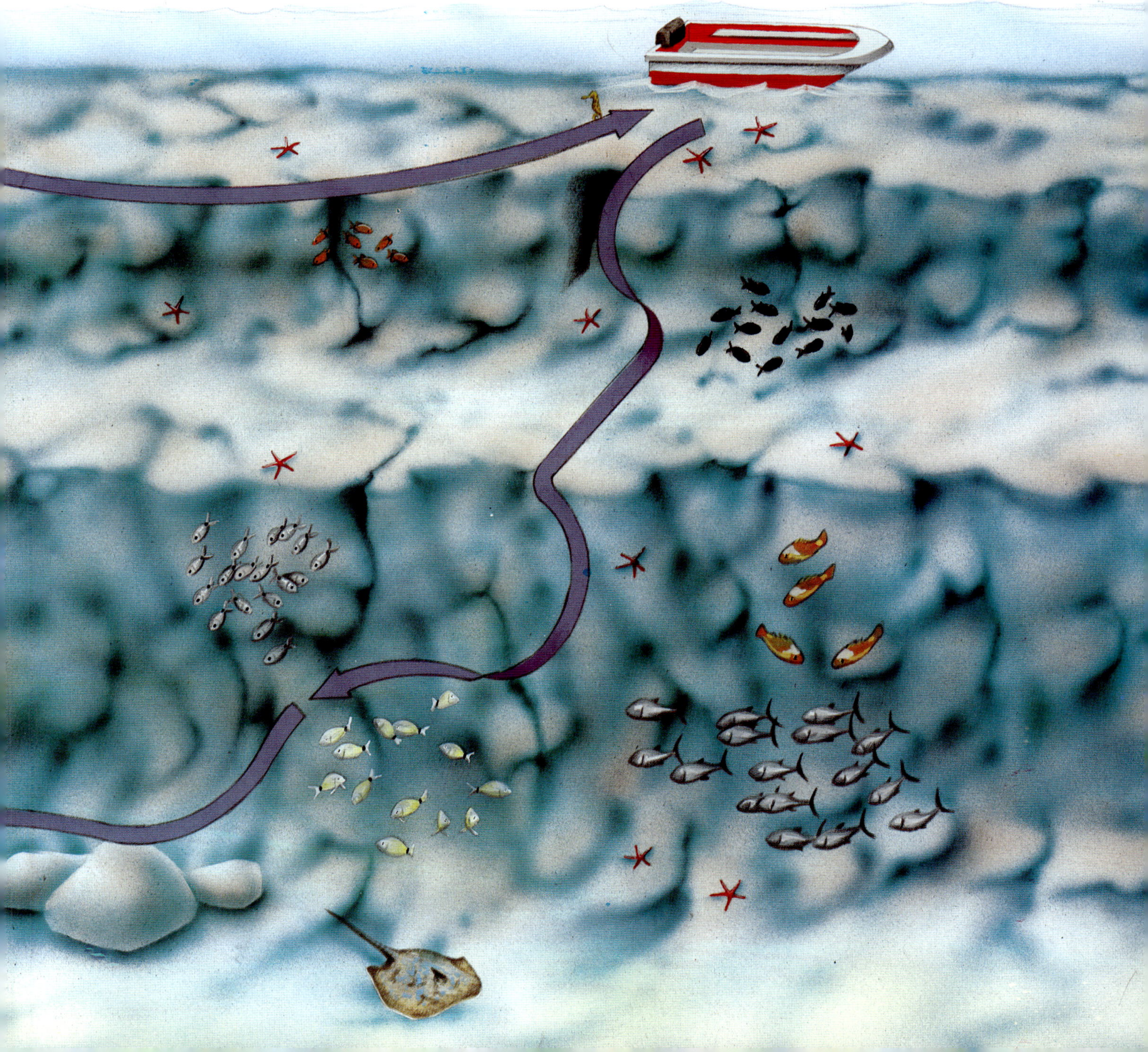

LOCATION

Off the north-west corner of Comino lies the much smaller island of Cominotto and off its north-west point the coast points to an underwater reef that is the subject of this particular dive. Due to the presence of surface traffic - including large vehicle ferries, the reef is clearly marked by a West Sector Cardinal Buoy This is a boat dive with plenty of good anchorage between Buoy and shore.

C

THE DIVE

This dive is often overlooked - which is all the more surprising

A

D

B

because the underwater terrain is slightly different, varied and often exciting. The top of the reef forms a large flat plateau which stretches from 8 metres to 20 metres at its deepest before giving way to a drop-off. On the southern side there are distinct phases to the drop-off with a further horizontal ledge encountered at 28 metres.
The vertical wall above this ledge is curved with many little cuts, cracks and fissures providing excellent refuge for many of the smaller species of fish one expects to find in these waters. There is also an abundance of tube worms, soft corals and red sponge to add considerable colour to these shaded areas. Immediately below this ledge the drop-off continues straight down to 46 metres where the diver will once again discover fallen rocks and small boulders. This lower part of the reef wall is also curved - a larger version of the one found above the ledge. Here, there are also numerous cracks and fissures in the surface of the rock - except that these are much larger and, therefore, are inhabited by larger specimens. The most common fishes here are painted combers, parrotfish, scorpionfish, rainbow and turkish wrasses and the very common octopus with very large starfish and spiny starfish found all over

A - Across from the northwest corner of Comino is Cominotto; the southwest coast of this little flat island is a good place to start your dive, which begins on a rocky underwater ridge.

B - This often neglected dive offers quite varied seascapes, both on the flat area and on the drop-off that leads to a platform 28m deep.

C - From the flat area at a depth of 28m, another vertical drop-off plunges down to a depth of 46m. Look around as you swim along the wall, and you may even spot tunas and swordfish.

D - A rainbow wrasse (Coris julis) swims along the wall. This is a male, easily distinguishable by his green, orange and black horizontal stripes.

the wall.
As the divers progress in a north-westerly direction at the base of the wall they should always remember to pause and look away from the reef in two directions. Firstly, above, where large shoals of bogues and two-banded seabreams dominate the scenery. Secondly, out to sea where there is every chance of spotting tuna and the occasional swordfish.
On this site the rocks at the base of the reef are not as numerous as elsewhere and there are large gaps where there are none at all. Here the seabed comprises of a coarse sand where very large goatfish, red mullets and common stingrays continue their never-ending hunt for food. Reaching a second, and quite distinctive, clump of rocks is the signal to commence the journey back to the surface.
Almost as soon as the diver reached the ledge at 28 metres, he will be almost surrounded by vast numbers of damselfish whilst just above these, on the main plateau, large shoals of sprats are often encountered.
Once again, the upper reaches of the reef are shallow enough for decompression whilst the abundant fish life is more than enough to sustain interest until it is time to surface.

G

H

E

F

PHOTOGRAPHY

The continual passing of maritime traffic does have an adverse affect on underwater visibility. This will affect wide-angle photographs more than others although the reef wall can provide some excellent background material for photographs of divers.
If I were limited to a single lens, however, it would have to be my 55mm Micro-NIKKOR. This allows close-up photographs of some of the larger fish such as amberjacks and groupers as well as the medium-sized octopus, scorpionfish and cuttlefish - found on almost every dive. In addition, the macro facility would always be available for the ever-present smaller species.

E - Golden zoanthids get their scientific name, Parazonathus axinellae, from the frequency with which they colonize sponges from the genus Axinella, as shown in this photo.

F - A brown algae seems to be resting its branches on the long arms of a red star.

G - In addition to being an endemic species, the dotted sea slug is also one of the most common nudibranchs in the Mediterranean. To protect itself, it can retract its rhinophores and its branchial tuft, as seen in the photo.

H - The long tentacles of a sea anemone (Anemonia sulcata) protrude from the rock. The animal's column is completely hidden, and it is always difficult to spot.

THE FAUNA AND FLORA OF THE MALTESE WATERS

The archipelago of Malta, three islands and some islets covering just above three hundred square kilometres of surface, lies less than a hundred kilometres south of the southern tip of Sicily, which it was still part of during the last ice age, when the Mediterranean was some hundred metres lower than today. The isolation of Malta is therefore the result of the changing sea level, but the sea has also contributed to the formation of the island, where one finds immense natural deposits of *globigerinae*, small foraminiferal protozoans with globular calcareous shells that have been transformed into a yellow building stone, soft to cut but resistant.
The force of the sea has left its mark on the variegated coast of the archipelago. Malta, Gozo and Comino are dominated by jagged coastlines interrupted by coves, bays and natural arches and grottoes, excavated by the sea or eroded by atmospheric agents after the islands emerged. Only this combination of forces could have created the underwater tunnels of Dweira Point on Gozo and the area covered by stalactites of the internal sea (the Qawra) of Gozo.
The entire archipelago is characterized by the very clear water, with an average visibility of about thirty metres thanks to the distance from the continental coasts and the currents that continuously renew the waters. The water temperature, which never drops below 13° C, is another important factor, and makes these islands one of the main stages of the by now regular invasion of tropical species originating from the Red Sea, which are conquering the Eastern Mediterranean.
After this brief analysis of the relationship between the sea and the Maltese islands, we proceed to discover the underwater life, which is extremely rich due to the varied nature of the seabeds. The rugged coastline above the surface is equalled by these sceneries below, with countless grottoes and crevices and cliffs that continue for dozens of metres below the surface and landslides that testify how violent the sea can be. The fauna and flora feature the characteristic Mediterranean species. The numerous shallows that sometimes arrive at one or two metres from the surface are rich with fish of passage: herrings, pilchards, tunas, sea urchins live in these waters some part of the year, along with carangids and mackerel that form part of rich and complex food chains.
In sheltered bays we find luxurious meadows of neptune grass which, due to the clear water, venture beyond 30 metres and represent the ideal habitat of pipe-fish and seahorses as well as numerous other species living in the very different microhabitats created in the tangle of leaves and rootstocks, or in the area bordering on the sand where one may also encounter the Red Sea mullet.
This fish, recognized by its pink body and long dark lateral streaks, has colonized these waters, warm enough for this tropical species. At greater depths the light gets too scarce for the neptune grass, which is replaced by another flora and fauna. The walls become a palette of colours: the sponges cover the rock

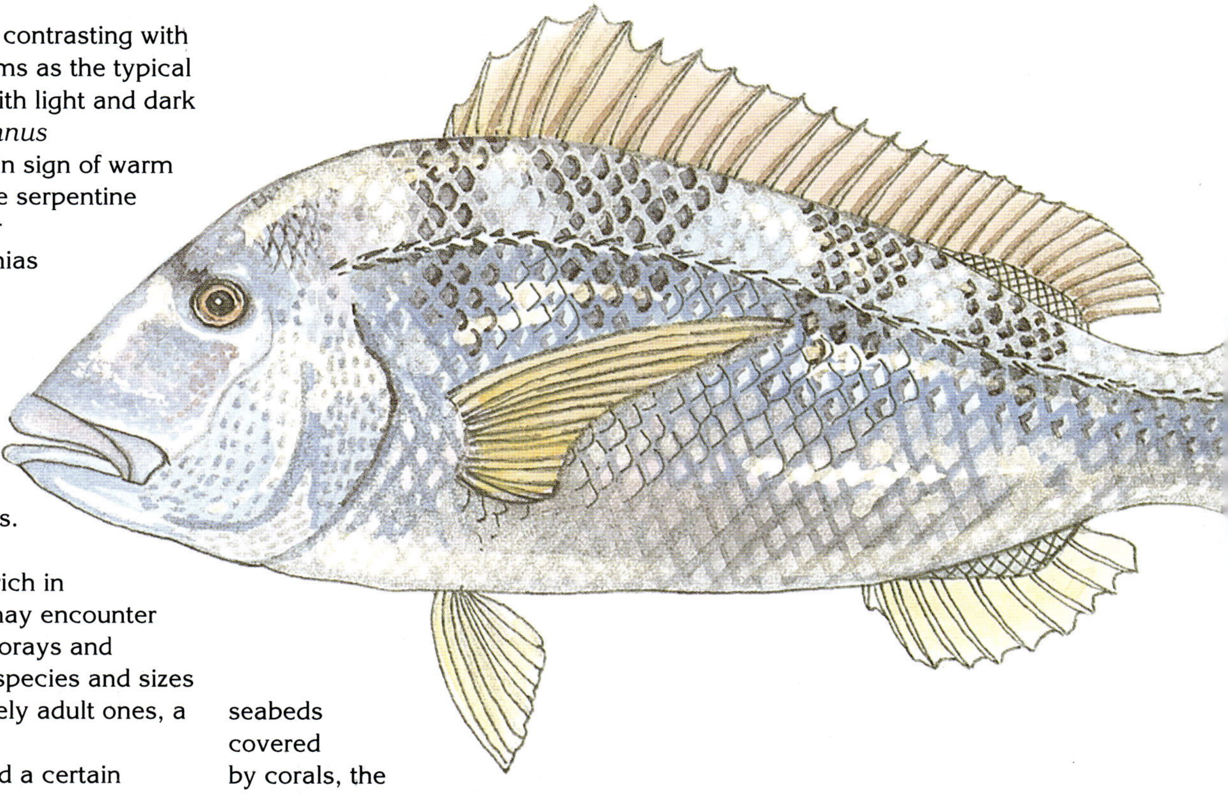

lavishly, blending or contrasting with all the other organisms as the typical crown sea urchins with light and dark bands (*Centrostephanus longispinus*) a certain sign of warm waters, as well as the serpentine starfish (*Ophidiaster ophidianus*). Gorgonias are abundant, both yellow (*Eunicella cavolini*) and red ones (*Paramuricea clavata*); these seabeds represent one of their easternmost outposts.
The soft rock of the seabed is generally rich in crevices where we may encounter octopus, lobsters, morays and groupers of various species and sizes from small to definitely adult ones, a certain sign of the rich waters and a certain attention for the conservation of the habitats.
The great variety of forms, colours, behaviours of the marine organisms never fail to leave the diver speechless, even if Malta is not his first destination. One cannot speak of the rich crown sea urchin as symbol of the high temperatures of the Maltese waters without also mentioning the large meadow sea urchin (*Sphaerechinus granularis*) with its violet and white spines that are generally associated with wrasses, both the common species and the rainbow wrasse. Large schools of *chromis* often swim above, along rock walls and near shallows. Where the algae is abundant it is not unusual to encounter salemas which, if lit by the sun in a few metres depth, flaunt all the gloss of their characteristic golden and blue streaks.
Also the seambream is silvery, with more or numerous dark bands depending on the species; the behaviour of this fish can be considered as an indicator of the respect shown by Man for the environment in a given area.
In fact, the more trustful and easy to approach these fish, the greater is the attention paid by divers and humans in general to the sea and its defence.
From the area of the seabreams a few strokes bring us towards deeper seabeds covered by corals, the most interesting area, especially due to its variety. Also here algae, sponges, ascidians, briozoans and anellids share the rocky substratum, sometimes growing on top of, or eliminating, one another in a continuous quest for the space best suited to their vital requirements.
Brown meagres and conger eels can be glimpsed in the crevices, while shady areas host schools of red *chromis* or *canari* (*Callanthias ruber*); this species, similar to the former, is more rare and characterized by a tail formed like a falciform half-moon. Scorpionfish and octopuses stud the walls, only revealing themselves at the last moment, when they feel discovered even though they are perfectly camouflaged.
The Maltese archipelago therefore vaunts a cross-section of the best the Mediterranean can offer, favoured by its central position and the structure of its coastline, which presents, in a limited space, fascinating sights of incomparable beauty, especially for those who love grottoes, the perhaps most characteristic element of everything that Malta, Gozo and Comino conceal under the surface.

Sea cactus - *Halimeda tuna*

Alga made up of a series of discoid articles, connected together and looking like a miniature prickly pear. Green or yellowy-green, with white stripes caused by limestone encrustations. Grows on rocky substrates, from the surface to a depth of 75 metres. Grows to 10-20 centimetres. ▶

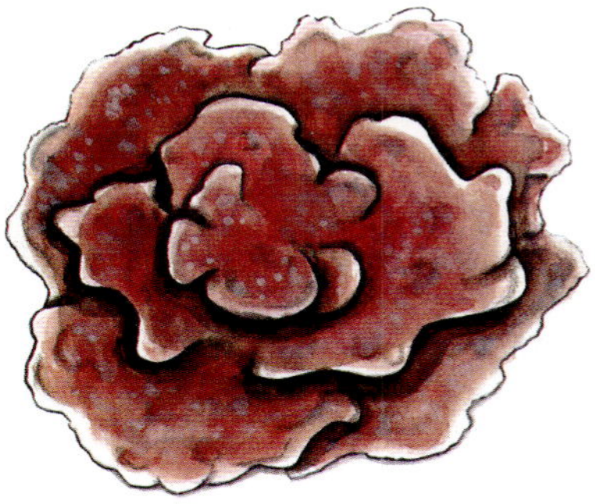

Pseudolithophyllum expansum

◀ Completely calcified red seaweed, purplish-pink in colour, which encrusts hard, poorly-illuminated substrates from 3-5 metres to over 60 metres deep. This seaweed are some of the main constituents of the coral environment, where it cements detritus, pieces of rock and algae together. Maximum size 25-30 centimetres diameter.

Neptune grass - *Posidonia oceanica* ▶

The most characteristic of all marine plants, the true symbol of the mediterranean. Grows on sandy and detrital bottoms, from the surface to 30-35 metres depth. Has true roots, stem, leaves, flowers and fruits. The flowers are yellow and the fruits are similar to small olives. The leaves are around one centimetre wide and up to 100 centimetres long.

Axinella cannabina

◀ Columnar sponge with axes from which grow protuberance-like branches having the oscula at the tips. Yellow or orange. Grows on rocky bottoms from 20 to 100 metres deep. Maximum size 50-60 centimetres.

Greek bating sponge
Spongia officinalis

This is the sponge which has been fished for centuries in the Mediterranean. Solid, rounded shape with irregular lobes. Whitish or black. Grows on rocky bottoms up to 40 metres deep. Measures up to 35-40 centimetres diameter. ▶

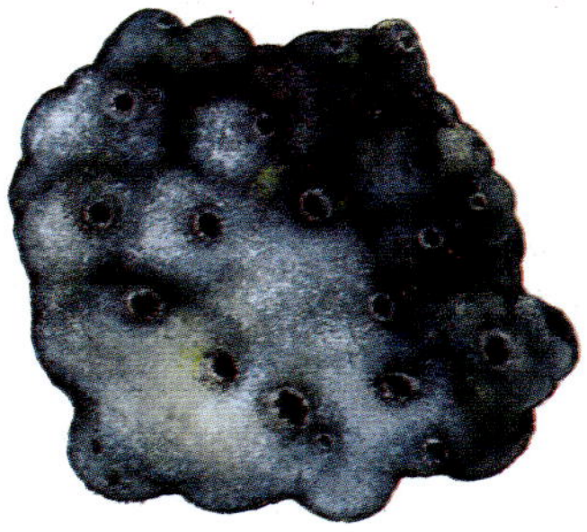

Red sea fan - *Paramuricea clavata*

Red gorgonian with huge fans made up of dense irregular ramifications, often merged into each other. The branches are thin and flexible and the presence of defensive spicules give them their rough surface. Although it is dark red in colour there are specimens with yellow tipped branches. Grows on rocky bottoms below depths of 30-35 metres. Maximum height 1 metre.

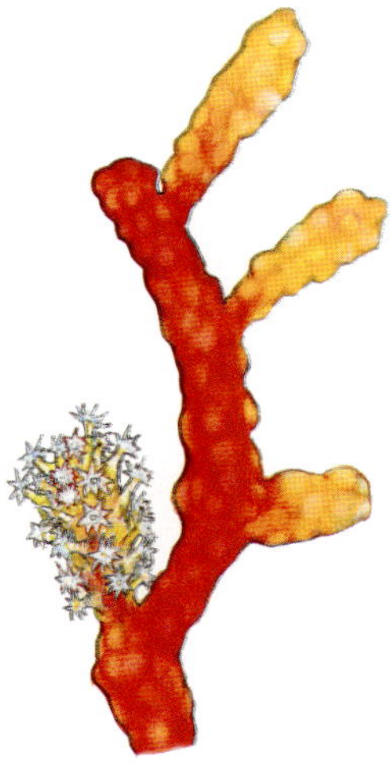

Yellow sea fan - *Eunicella cavolinii*

Gorgonian with fan-shaped colonies which are highly ramified, often dichotomically. The branches are flexible and rough in correspondence with the polyps. Yellow. Grows on rocky bottoms from 10 to 150 metres deep. Maximum size 30-40 centimetres.

Golden zoanthid - *Parazoanthus axinellae*

Colonial anthozoan consisting of elongated retractile polyps which all start from a common encrusting base. Their are 24-36 long, slim tentacles around the mouth. Yellow. Lives on rocky bottoms and on other organisms (e.g. sponges) from depths of 5-10 metres to over 100. Colonies can cover broad surfaces.

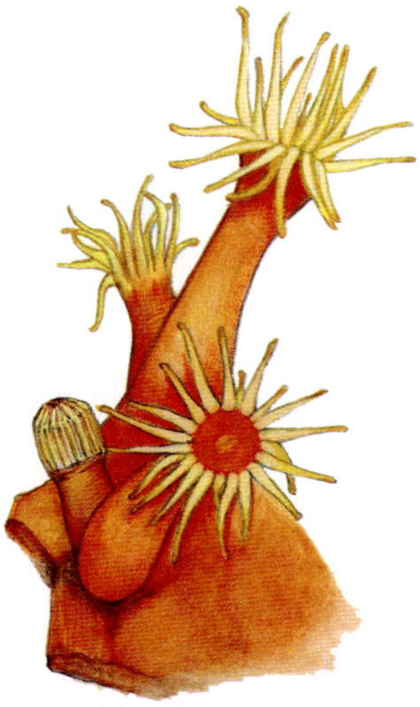

Tube dwelling anemone - *Cerianthus membranaceus*

Anthozoan with elongated body protected by a large tube much of which is buried in sediment. The exposed part has a double crown of long tentacles (more than 200). Colour varies from purple to brown. Lives on sandy or muddy bottoms from 5-6 metres to below 40. Maximum size 40 centimetres.

Lamellated haliotis - *Haliotis lamellosa*

Highly mimetic mollusc with a, ear-shaped shell with a row of holes for the sensory filaments of the mantle. Very pearly inside. Found on rocky substrates from 1-2 metres to 15-20 metres deep, to which it clings tenaciously. Maximum size 7 centimetres.

Cowrie - *Luria lurida*

One of the few cowries found in the Mediterranean and is immediately recognisable by its oval shape and its shiny mantle. Brownish with dark blotches on both extremities. Found on rocky and sandy beds with poor illumination and in caves, from 4-5 metres down to 40-45 metres deep. Maximum size 5 centimetres.

Knobbed triton - *Charonia rubicunda*

Large gastropod mollusc with a spindle-shaped spiral shell, with a very wide final whorl. Feeds on echinoderms, particularly red stars. Greyish-pink with white and brownish stripes and blotches. Porcelain-like inside. Found on rocky and detrital beds from 15-20 to over 40 metres deep. Maximum size 40 centimetres.

Hypselodoris valenciennesi

Nudibranch gastropod mollusc with a body similar to a snail's, very elongated and with undulated edges. It has a pair of lamellar tentacles on its head and a prominent branchial tuft. Violet to yelowish-green with numerous yellow blotches. Found on rocky and detritus beds from 3-4 to over 40 metres deep. Maximum size approx. 20 centimetres.

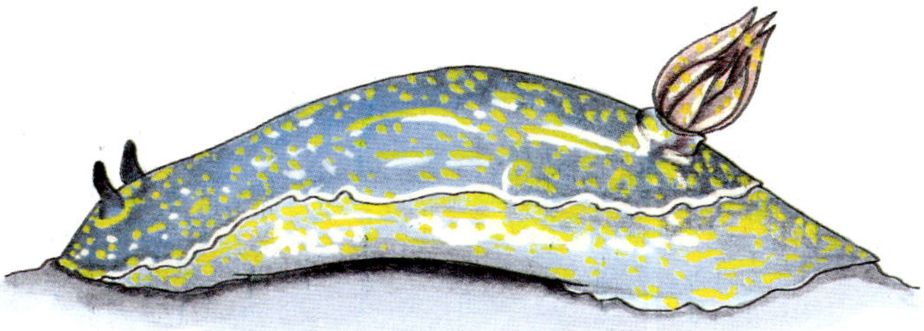

Discodoris atromaculata

Nudibranch gastropod mollusc with rounded, flat, body. Easily recognised by its whitish colour with dark blotches and because it is nearly always found on the sponge *Petrosia ficiformis*, on which it feeds. Found on rocky beds from 5 metres down to 40-50. Measures up to 15 centimetres.

Flabellina affinis

Nudibranch gastropod mollusc with slim, elongated body, marked by numerous elongated lateral papillae grouped in tufts. Varying shades of pink. Found on rocky beds from 5 to 50 metres, and is usually found in the company of the hydroids on which it feeds. Maximum 4 centimetres.

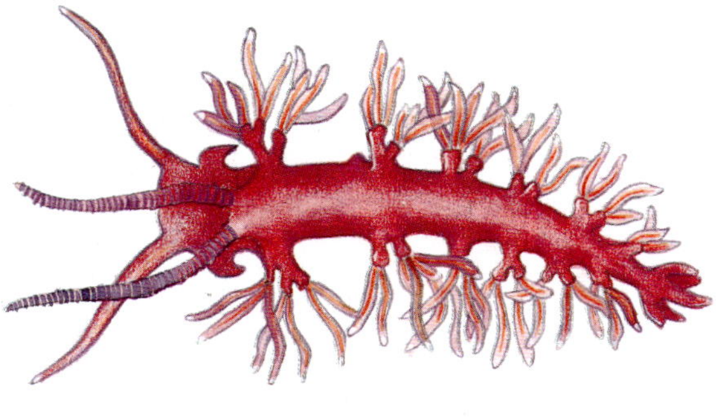

Fan mussel - *Pinna nobilis*

The biggest of the bivalve molluscs in the Mediterranean. It has symmetrical, triangular valves, red mother-of-pearl inside and strongly encrusted on the outside. Lives stuck vertically into the sand or in the posidonia meadows, from 3-4 metres to over 30. Maximum size 90 metres.

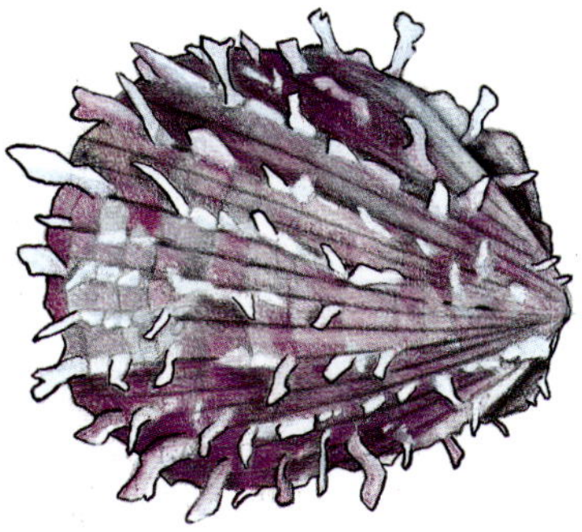

Thorny oyster - *Spondylus gaederopus*

Bivalve mollusc with strong, asymmetrical shell with a convex valve and a flat one. Characteristic long, robust spines decorate the shell. Often covered sand hidden by the red sponge *Crambe crambe*, which hides it. Found on rocky substrates to which it encrusted. Maximum size 15 centimetres.

Common octopus - *Octopus vulgaris*

Cephalopod mollusc belonging to the *Octopod* order. Easily recognised by its large, globular head which is distinct from the rest of its body, formed by eight tentacles with double rows of suckers. Colouring is variable due to its mimetic abilities. Found on rocky or detrital beds with crevices, from a few metres to over 100. Maximum size 60 centimetres.

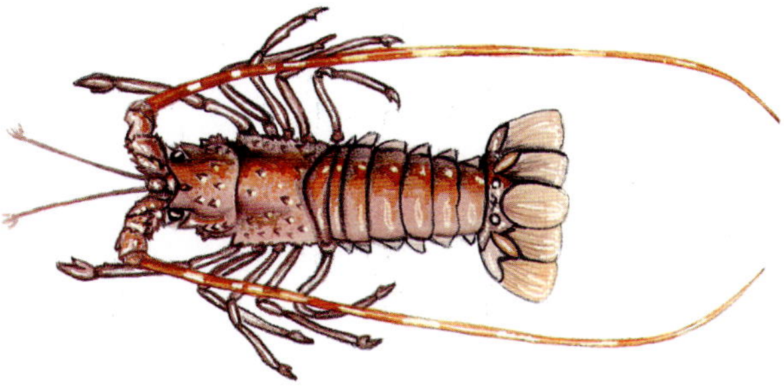

Spiny lobster - *Palinurus elephas*

Large crustacean with convex carapace covered with spines and tubercles. Antennae longer than the body. Dark red with a few white blotches all over the body. White-striped feet. Found on rocky bottoms inside crevices, from 10-15 metres down to 70. Maximum size 50 centimetres.

Locust lobster - *Scyllarides latus*

Crustacean with squashed, rectangular body, wider at the front end than the rear. Typical, flattened lamellar antennae with a wavy front edge. Reddish brown with violet antennules. Lives on rocky sea-beds from 10 to 100 metres. Maximum size 45 centimetres.

Spinous spider crab - *Maja squinado*

Crab with ovoid carapace, very convex, covered with a large number of spines. Forked rostrum. Very long limbs. Yellowish or reddish brown in colour. Found on rocky, algae-rich sea-beds, from depths of 3-5 metres down to 70 metres. Maximum size 18 centimetres.

▶

◀

Sea lace bryozoan - *Sertella septentrionalis*

Lacy colony made up of expanded, erect laminae with fluted edges. Colour varies from bright pink to whitish. Found on rocky, poorly-illuminated bottoms and inside caves, from 10 to 35 metres deep. Measures up to 10 centimetres.

ECHINODERMS

Crinoid - *Antedon mediterranea*

Characteristically-shaped echinoderm, consisting of a small central body with ten thin arms which look feathery due to the lateral pinnules. Colour varies from red to yellow to white to pink. Found on rocky or sandy and detrital floors, from 10-15 metres to over 80. Maximum size 25 centimetres.

▶

◀

Sea cucumber - *Holothuria tubulosa*

Cylindrically-bodied animal covered in a thick, leathery integument. The upper part is covered with papillae and the belly is covered with bands of tube-feet. Brownish sometimes with reddish reflections. Found on rocky, muddy and sandy bottoms from 3-5 metres down to 100. Maximum size 30 centimetres.

Ophidiaster ophidianus

Red star with long, flexible, cylindrical arms attached to a small central disc. Crimson or orange-red with dark markings. Found on rocky bottoms from 7-10 metres down to 100. Measures up to 35 centimetres.

▶

Red star - *Echinaster sepositus*

The commonest red star in the Mediterranean. The central disc is small and has five circular-sectioned, pointed arms attached to it. Granulous surface. Colour varies from dark red to orangy-red. Found on rocky, detrital bottoms and amongst Neptune grass, from 2-3 metres down to 250 metres. Measures up to 30 centimetres.

Long-spined urchin - *Centrostephanus longispinus*

Round-bodied urchin with numerous, very long and highly mobile, spines. Purply-brown ; the spines have alternate light and dark hoops. Found on rocky, poorly-illuminated bottoms, from 10-15 metres down to 200. Shell diameter up to 4 centimetres.

White tip sea urchin - *Sphaerechinus granularis*

Round shape, easily recognised by its blue-purple spines with white tips. Found on rocky bottoms and amongst Neptune grass, from 3-5 metres to 100. Maximum shell diameter 13 centimetres.

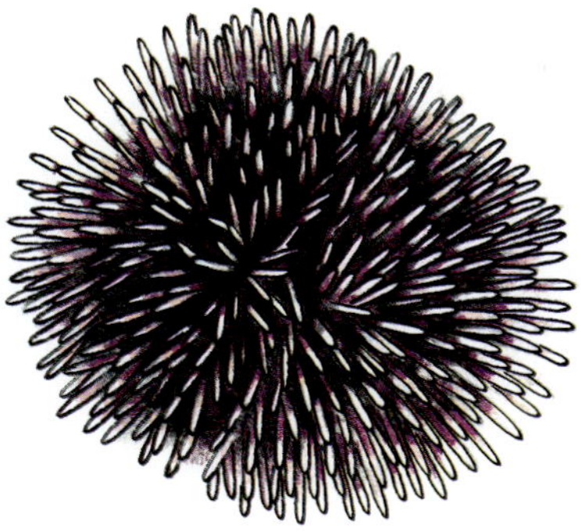

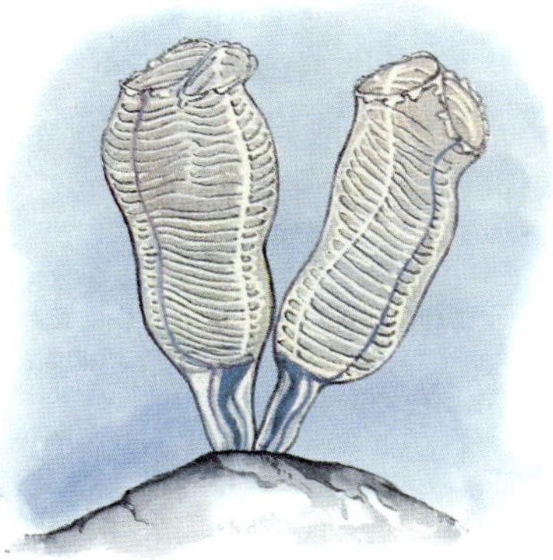

ASCIDIANS
Glass bell tunicate - *Clavelina lepadiformis*

Colonial ascidians, consisting of transparent individuals attached to a single stolon. The individuals are club-shaped and transparent, showing the internal organs. Found on rocky floors, sometimes attached to other organisms, from 3-5 metres deep to 50. Maximum size 6 centimetres.

Sea potato - *Halocinthya papillosa*

One of the common ascidians, shaped like a little barrel from which the mouth and cloacal siphons emerge. Its tunic is rough to the touch. Red and yellow or white. Found on rocky bottoms and amongst Neptune grass from 10-15 metres to over 100. Maximum size up to 12 centimetres.

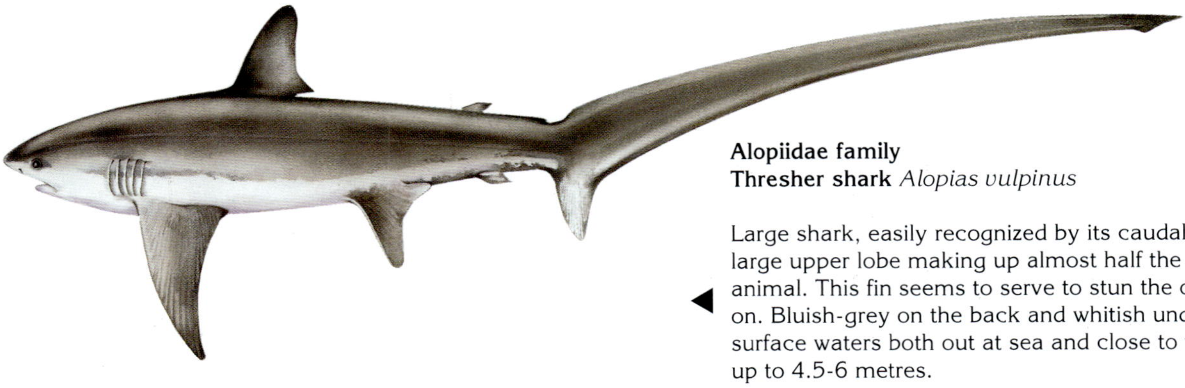

Alopiidae family
Thresher shark *Alopias vulpinus*

Large shark, easily recognized by its caudal fin, with a very large upper lobe making up almost half the total length of the animal. This fin seems to serve to stun the oceanic fish it feeds on. Bluish-grey on the back and whitish underneath. Lives in surface waters both out at sea and close to the coast. Measures up to 4.5-6 metres.

Lamnidae family
White shark - *Carcharodon carcharias*

Large shark with short, pointed snout with wide mouth equipped with big triangular teeth with saw-toothed edges. The first dorsal fin is tall and developed. The caudal is characteristically sickle-shaped with almost identical lobes. The colouration is dark grey on the back and white underneath. Predator on top of the food chain, it feeds mainly on tuna and small cetaceans. Reaches lengths of over 7 metres.

Shortfin mako - *Isurus oxyrhinchus*

Large shark with tapering body, pointed snout and thin, carinate caudal peduncle that supports a crescent-shaped caudal fin of which upper lobe is slightly more developed. The teeth are elongated and smooth. The colouration is more or less dark blue on the back and white underneath. It feeds mainly on fish (small tuna, mackerel, trevallys). Prefers temperate waters and migrates with the changing temperature. It measures up to 4 metres.

Scyliorhinidae family
Lesser spotted dogfish - *Scylliorhynus canicula*

Small, streamlined shark with short, rounded snout. The nostrils are large and partly cover the mouth. The first dorsal starts behind the base of the pelvis. Light brown with numerous dark spots. Lays characteristic eggs with rectangular shells equipped with tentacles that attach to the gorgonians. Feeds on invertebrates. Lives in coastal waters close to sand and mud or gravel bottoms from 35-40 to more than 150 metres depth. Measures up to 80 centimetres.

Nurse hound - *Scylliorhynus stellaris*

Small, streamlined shark with short, rounded snout. The nostrils are smaller than the previous species. The first dorsal fin starts in front of the base of the pelvis. The colouration is greyish brown on the back and light underneath with many large, rounded light brown and white spots. Lays rectangular eggs. Lives near rocky or muddy bottoms from 20 to more than 150 metres. Feed on crustaceans, cephalopods and benthic fish. Measures up to 150 centimetres.

Carcharhinidae family
Blue shark - *Prionace glauca*

Streamlined shark with dorsal slightly set back and very developed, sickle-shaped pectorals. The teeth are quite narrow, triangular and saw-tooth edged. The upper lobe of the caudal is well developed and pointed. Feeds on fish, squid and benthic organisms. Typical blue colour on the back. Lives in coastal and oceanic waters between the surface and a depth of 150 metres. Measures up to 3.8 metres.

Torpedinidae family
Marbled electric ray - *Torpedo marmorata*

Ray-shaped, with a flattened body in which the head, trunk and pectoral fins are widened to form a more or less circular disk. The front edge is waved. There are two transparent electric organs on either side of the head. The colouration is solid brown with five ocellar, bluish spots bordered by concentric light and dark rings. Mainly feeds on benthic fish. It lives on gravel, sand and mud seabeds from 20 to 150 metres. Measures up to 60 centimetres.

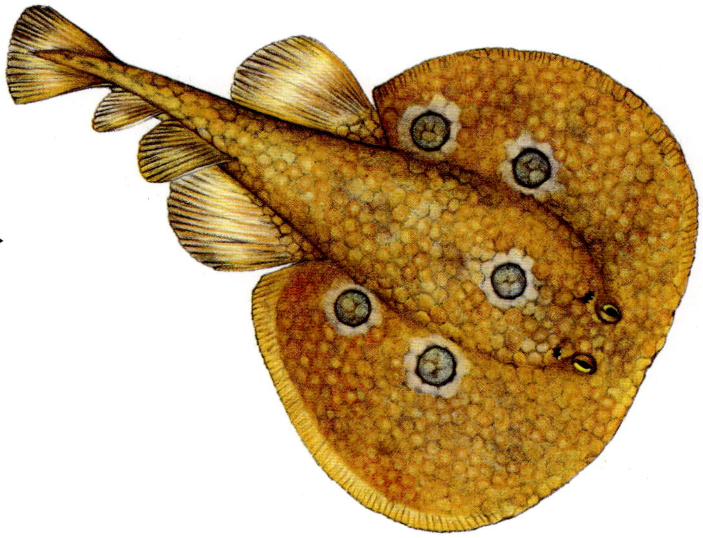

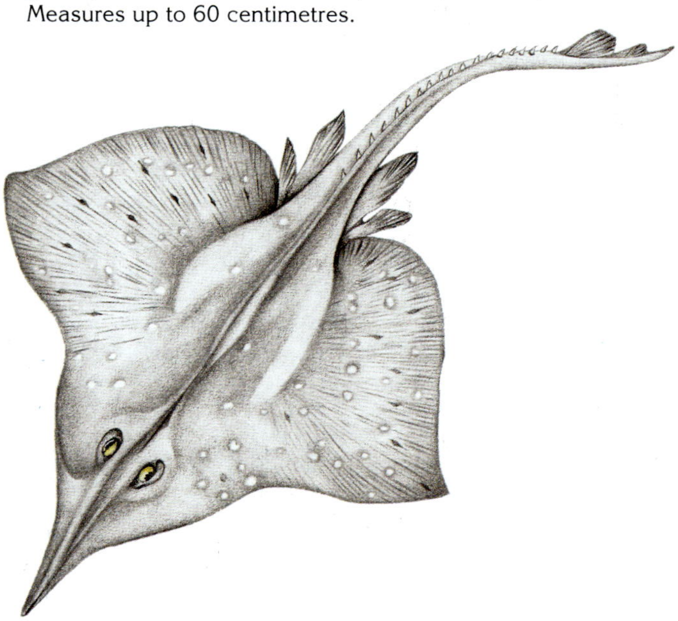

Rajidae family
Longnosed skate - Raja oxyrhinchus

Ray with typically elongated snout; the front edges of the disc are concave. The edge of the fins is sharp. The back and belly are characterized by a large number of spines that are absent around the eyes. The colouration is greyish brown with white and black points on the back, and light underneath. Feeds on benthic invertebrates. Lives on sandy and sandy-muddy seabeds to a depth of 900 metres. Measures up to 150 centimetres.

Starry ray - *Raja asterias*

Ray with strongly depressed body, forming a disc joining the head, trunk and pectorals. The front edges of the disc are slightly sinuous. The tail is quite distinct from the body. The centre of the back has a row of raised notches that continue on the tail. Brownish with numerous dark and yellowish circular blotches, with white belly. Lives on sandy-muddy seabeds from 10 to 300 metres. Measures up to 80 centimetres.

Thornback ray - *Raja clavata*

Flattened front to back, forming a disc joining head, trunk and pectorals, which have sharp points. There are numerous spines on the back and a series of large notches in a row down the middle of the body. Also the tail has well-developed spines along the middle. In female specimens also the belly is spined. Brownish, with numerous marks on the tail. Feeds on crustaceans, cephalopods and fish. It lives on sandy-muddy and sandy seabeds from 10 to 200 metres depth. Measures up to 110 centimetres.

Dasyatidae family
Stingray - *Dasyatis pastinaca*

Ray with disc-shaped body, slightly wider than long. The snout is pointed. No dorsal fin, and the tail is 1.5 times as long as the disc. Just before the middle of the tail there is a well-developed spine. Olive-coloured with reddish nuances. Feeds on crustaceans, cephalopods and bivalve molluscs. Reproduction seems to occur twice a year. Lives on sandy-muddy and detrital seabeds from a few metres to 200 metres depth. Measures up to 2.5 metres.

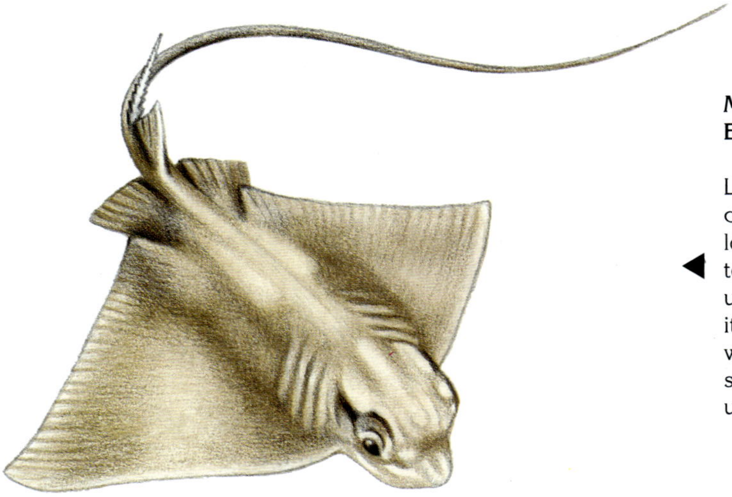

Myliobatidae family
Eagle ray - *Myliobatis aquila*

Large ray with rhomboid disc, wider than long. The stocky, convex head is quite distinct from the disc. The tail is much longer than the body and has a small dorsal fin before the saw-toothed spine. The colouration is dark on the back and white underneath. Feeds on a large variety of invertebrates which it uncovers by moving the sediments of the seabed with the wings and the body. Lives close to sandy and sandy-muddy seabeds in coastal waters to a depth of 200 metres. Measures up to 2.6 metres length.

Muraenidae family
Moray eel - *Muraena helena*

Eel-shaped body, robust and slightly compressed at the rear end. The head is short with a well-developed mouth that is almost always held open. No pectoral fins. The colouration is marbled, yellow and brown with whitish streaks, but very dark or black specimens are sometimes found. Most active by night. Feeds on octopus and fish. Lives on rocky seabeds from a few metres to 80 metres. Measures up to 1.3 metres.

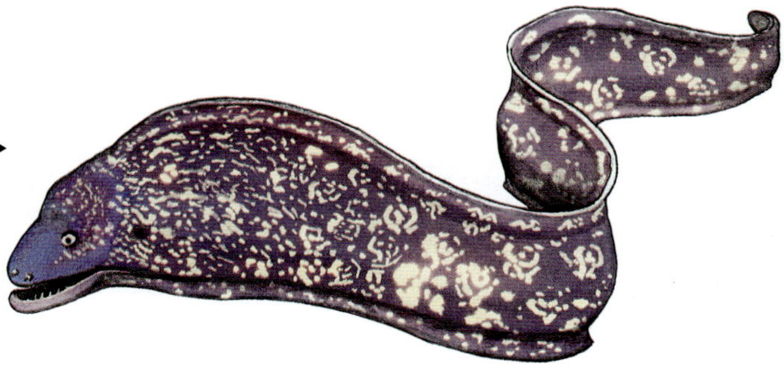

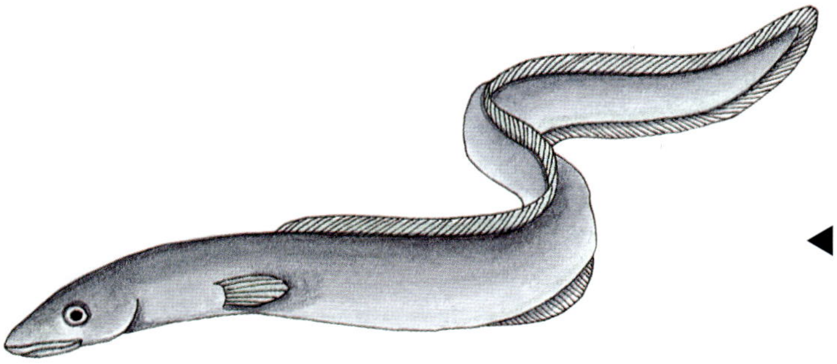

Congridae family
Conger eel - *Conger conger*

Eel-shaped body with a subcylindrical front end. Elongated snout with wide mouth and big lips. It can easily be distinguished from the moray by the well-developed pectorals. The teeth are placed so close as to form a continuous, very cutting edge. The colouration varies from blackish to whitish. Feeds on fish, crustaceans and cephalopods. Lives on rocky and sandy-muddy seabeds from 3-5 to more than 100 metres. Measures up to 2 metres.

Clupeidae family
Pilchard - *Sardina pilchardus*

Fish with oval-sectioned, tapering, somewhat compressed body. Ventral profile is characterized by a series of small projecting, toothed scales. The tail is clearly forked. Greenish back, golden white sides with dark marks. Feeds on planktonic organisms. Lives in large shoals in oceanic and coastal waters from 10-15 to 180 metres depth. Measures up to 25 centimetres.

Engraulidae family
Anchovy - *Engraulis encrasicolus*

Very slim, tapered body that ends in a conical, pointed snout. The upper jaw is more developed than the lower and the mouth is thus placed low. The scales tend to fall off if the animal is handled. The colouration is bluish green on the back and silvery on the flanks. Mainly feeds on small planktonic crustaceans. Lives in shoals in oceanic and coastal waters near the surface in summer and to 100-180 metres depth in winter. Measures up to 20 centimetres.

Gadidae family
Forkbeard - *Phycis phycis*

Fish with tapered, deep body, compressed back section. One barbel on the jaw. The ventral fins are thread-like and forked. The second dorsal and the anal fins are similar and symmetric. The colouration is dark brown or reddish brown. Feeds on small fish and invertebrates. Lives on rocky and sandy-muddy seabeds from 10-20 to 650 metres. Measures up to 65 centimetres.

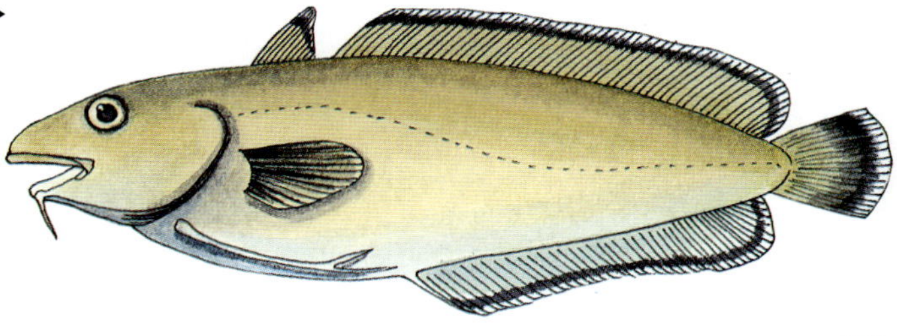

Gobiesocidae family
Cling fish - *Lepadogaster candollei*

Small fish with a compressed front end and elongated head. The mouth is on the underside and there are two suckers between the pelvic fins, which the fish uses to fix itself to the seabed and resist the force of the waves. The colouration is reddish or greenish yellow. It lives in surface waters on rocky seabeds and reefs rich in alga. Measures up to 7 centimetres.

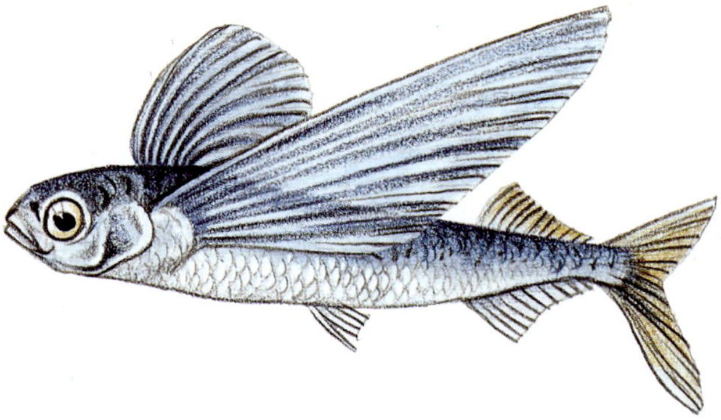

Exocoetidae family
Blackwing flying fish - *Hirundichthys rondeletii*

Fish with elongated body that flattens towards the belly. The pectorals are very developed and extend to the dorsal fin. The lower lobe of the caudal is more developed than the upper. The ventral fins are in a receded position. The colouration is bluish on the back and light underneath. Lives near the surface from which it emerges if scared, making long, planing leaps in the air. Measures up to 30 centimetres.

Belonidae family
Gar-fish - *Belone belone*

Elongated, subcylindrical body with pointed snout and jaws that are elongated into a kind of beak. The dorsal and anal fins are withdrawn and recede the caudal by a little. Bluish back and silvery white flanks and belly. Feeds mainly on small clupeids. Lives in coastal waters between the surface and 20-30 metres depth. Measures up to 90 centimetres.

Zeidae family
John Dory - Zeus faber

Oval shaped, deep and compressed body. Has characteristic long rays on the dorsal fin and occelar marking on the sides, which make it easy to recognize. Golden-grey with dark shading. The mouth is quite protractile and serves to catch small fish and invertebrates. Lives near sandy and muddy seabeds from 20-30 to 400 metres. Measures up to 60 centimetres.

Caproidae family
Drumfish - *Capros aper*

Fish with tall, compressed body. Convex area over the eyes. The mouth is small and very protractile and is converted into a tube when capturing prey. The fish is covered by small, rough scales. The colouration is red with yellow, transverse bands. Feeds on worms and molluscs. Lives near muddy seabeds from 25 to 600 metres. Measures up to 16 centimetres.

Macrorhamphosidae family
Longspine snipefish - *Macroramphosus scolopax*

Fish with tall, compressed body terminating in an elongated head. The snout is long and tube-shaped with a small, terminal mouth. Lateral, very big eyes. The surface of the body is rough to the touch. The colouration is pinkish red. Is gregarious and feeds on both oceanic and benthic invertebrates. Lives in waters near the seabed from 40-50 to more than 200 metres. Measures up to 20 centimetres.

Syngnathidae family
Common sea-horse - *Hippocampus hippocampus*

Unmistakable fish. The body is formed of a series of superimposed bony rings. The head is positioned at an angle to the body and the prehensile tail. The colouration is brownish or greenish black. The male keeps the fecundated eggs in a fold in his body until they open. Lives near neptune grass from 2-4 to 20-30 metres. Measures up to 15 centimetres.

Pipe-fish - *Syngnathus acus*

Fish with very long, thin body formed of bony polygonal rings welded to one another. The snout is thin with a terminal mouth. The males have an incubator pocket in front of the tail. The colouration varies from brown to greenish. Feeds on small invertebrates. Lives among neptune grass and algae or on detrital seabeds. Measures up to 35 centimetres.

Dactylopteridae family
Flying gurnard - *Dactylopterus volitans*

Fish with elongated body, very square at the front. The head is covered with strong dermic bones that become large spines towards the rear. Distinctive pectoral fins in two parts, the second being very ample and brightly coloured in blue with white blotches. Feeds mainly on crabs and bivalve molluscs. Lives on sandy and muddy seabeds and near neptune grass from 8-10 to 80 metres. Measures up to 50 centimetres.

Scorpaenidae family
Red scorpionfish - *Scorpaena scrofa*

This is the biggest scorpionfish in the Mediterranean, and can be recognized first and foremost by the large number of jagged appendices on the head, mouth and flanks. The head is covered by spines. The colouration is reddish with brownish and black spots. Feeds on fish and shellfish. Lives on rocky and detrital seabeds and among neptune grass from 3-4 to more than 300 metres. Can grow to be longer than 50 centimetres.

Black scorpionfish - *Scorpaena porcus*

Fish with the stocky body characteristic of scorpionfish, which can be recognized by the developed protuberances above the eyes and the numerous spines on the head and the operculi. The colouration is blackish brown with more or less dark spots. Feeds on small fish which it captures by lying in ambush on the seabed. Lives on rocky and detrital seabeds and among neptune grass from 3-4 to more than 100 metres. Measures up to 30 centimetres.

Small red scorpionfish - *Scorpaena notata*

The head of this scorpionfish is practically without cutaneous appendices, but has sturdy spines under the eyes and along the operculi. Can be recognized by its bright red colouration and the black spot in the middle of the dorsal fin. Lives on rocky, poorly illuminated seabeds from 5 to 700 metres. Measures up to 18 centimetres.

Rockfish - *Helicolenus dactylopterus*

Fish with stocky body and large head with small, scattered spines. The mouth is wide; the teeth are numerous, small and villiform. The colouration is yellowish red, white-marbled, with five or six transverse dark bands. Feeds on crustaceans, molluscs and cephalopods. Lives on rocky and detrital seabeds to a depth of 1,000 metres. Measures up to 45 centimetres.

Peristediidae family
African armoured searobin - *Peristedion cataphractum*

The body is elongated with octagonal section and entirely covered by large bony scales. The head is plated and terminates in two characteristic rostrum-shaped extensions. Two long ramified barbels can be observed under the snout. The colouration is red. Feeds on small benthic invertebrates. Lives on sandy-muddy and detrital seabeds from 30 to 700 metres. Measures up to 40 centimetres.

Triglidae family
Streaked gurnard - *Trygloporus lastoviza*

Fish with a streamlined body that tapers towards the tail. Large head covered with bony plates. Has characteristic wide pectoral fins with blue marks, the first three rays of which are separate and mobile, which enables it to make short movements on the seabed. The colouration is reddish on the back and bright underneath. Feeds on small crustaceans. Lives on detrital and sandy-muddy seabeds from 20 to over 200 metres. Measures up to 40 centimetres.

Gurnard - *Trigla lyra*

The body of this fish is elongated, with a subquadrangular profile. The head is big and covered by strong bony plates which are ridged and spiny. The first three rays of the pectorals are free. The colouration is reddish with bluish spots on the fins. Lives on muddy or detrital seabeds from 40-50 to more than 400 metres. Measures up to 60 centimetres.

Percichthyidae family
Sea bass - *Dicentrarchus labrax*

Streamlined, tapering body with powerful head and well-developed mouth. Sturdy, forward-facing spines on the preoperculum. Double dorsal fin. The colouration is silvery grey. Voracious predator, it feeds on small fish. Lives near sandy and rocky seabeds from 3-5 down to 100 metres. Measures up to 1 metre.

Serranidae family
Swallow tail seaperch - *Anthias anthias*

Fish with oval body, short snout and clearly sickle-shaped tail with elongated lobes. The ventral fins are also very developed. The colouration is red or intense pink with golden streaks on head and flanks. This species is territorial and lives in large groups near rocky, poorly-illuminated bottoms with plenty of crevices from 15-20 to 200 metres. Measures up to 25 centimeres.

Parrot seaperch - *Callanthias ruber*

Small fish with short head and tapered body. The eyes are quite large. The rear ray of the dorsal is extended in a filament. The tail has elongated, filamentous lobes. The colouration is red or pink. Feeds on small crustaceans. Lives on rocky seabeds and poorly-illuminated areas of the coral formations to 300 metres depth. Measures up to 27 centimetres.

Brown grouper - *Epinephelus marginatus*

Fish with stocky, oval body, powerful head and large mouth. The caudal is ample and rounded. The colouration is brownish with more or less dark spots. Lives on rocky and uneven seabeds from 3-5 metres to 100 metres where it generally chooses a fixed territory around a lair. Measures up to 1 metre.

Wreck fish - *Polyprion americanum*

Fish with deep, powerful body and large head with slight concavity on nape. A transverse bony crest can be observed on the operculum. The scales of the body are small and very rough. The colouration is brownish grey. Lives on rocky and sandy-muddy seabeds from 30-40 to 400 metres, often near wrecks. Young specimens can often be observed near the surface, in the shade of floating objects. Measures up to 2 metres.

Painted comber - *Serranus scriba*

Fish with tapering, somewhat compressed body and with pointed head. The colouration is reddish grey with dark vertical bands and a distinctive bluish blotch on the flanks. Has characteristic variegated patterns on snout and operculi. Voracious predator, it feeds on molluscs, crustaceans and fish. Lives on rocky seabeds near neptune grass from 4-5 to more than 100 metres. Measures up to 35 centimetres.

Apogonidae family
Cardinal fish - *Apogon imberbis*

Oval-bodied fish with short head and large eyes. The jaw is prominent. The first dorsal is less developed than the second one. The colouration is red or pink with white streaks across the eyes. After having fecundated the eggs the male incubates them in his mouth until they open. Found on rocky bottoms with plenty of crevices, from 2-3 to 200 metres. Measures up to 15 centimetres.

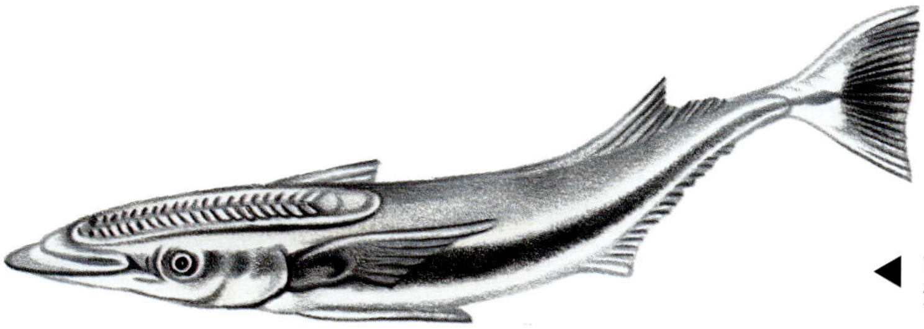

Echeneididae family
Shark-sucker - *Echeneis naucrates*

Elongated, tapering fish. Is easily recognized by the first dorsal fin which has evolved into a sucker (ventose) with transverse lamellae. The colouration is whitish with a wide dark longitudinal band from snout to tail. Lives in coastal waters, where it swims alone or attached to a large fish, usually a shark, with which it lives in symbiosis, freeing it from cutaneous parasites. Measures up to 1 metre.

Carangidae family
Leer-fish - *Lichia amia*

Fish with long, moderately deep body that terminates in a pointed snout. The mouth is developed and its opening extends past the eye. The lateral line is very irregular. The first dorsal fin is reduced to seven small spines united at the base by a membrane. The colouration is dark on the back and silvery white on the flanks and belly. Feeds on small oceanic fish. Lives in coastal waters between the surface and 50 metres. Measures up to 2 metres.

Amberjack - *Seriola dumerili*

Fish with tapering, stocky body that is compressed laterally. The head is well-developed. The caudal, supported by a slim peduncle, is well-defined and twin-lobed. The colouration is silvery grey. A dark streak extends from the eyes to the nape. It forms schools, sometimes of many dozens of specimens. Lives in oceanic waters, but arrives close to the coast, remaining ad depths from 10-15 to 70 metres. Measures up to 2 metres.

Blue runner - *Caranx crysos*

The body is tapering and laterally compressed. The snout is somewhat rounded, the mouth wide with canine-shaped teeth flanked by a second row of smaller teeth. The pectoral fins are sickle-shaped and elongated. The rear part of the lateral line is raised. The colouration is olive blue on the back and silvery on the flanks. Feeds on small oceanic fish and shrimp. Lives in schools near the coast up to 100 metres depth. Measures up to 70 centimetres.

Pilot fish - *Naucrates ductor*

The body is elongated and terminates abruptly in a blunt snout. The first dorsal consists of a few isolated rays. The caudal peduncle has a fleshy keel on either side. The colouration is silvery with large, dark transverse bands. Lives in oceanic waters where it follows sharks and other large fish, probably feeding on the rests of their prey. Measures up to 70 centimetres.

Pompano - *Trachinotus ovatus*

The body is elongated and compressed. The second dorsal and the anal are symmetric. The colouration is greenish grey on the back and silvery white with some spots on the flanks. The tips of the dorsal, anal and caudal fins are black. Lives in schools and feeds mainly on small invertebrates. Found in coastal waters near beaches and muddy and detrital seabeds to a depth of 200 metres. Measures up to 70 centimetres.

Horse mackerel - *Trachurus mediterraneus*

The body is elongated and somewhat compressed. The eyes are large and protected by a well-developed fatty eyelid. The lateral line is raised on bony shields. The colouration is bluish grey on the back and light on the belly. Feeds on pilchards, anchovies and small crustaceans. This species is migratory and lives in shoals in deep-sea and coastal waters from the surface to 600 metres. Measures up to 60 centimetres.

Sparidae family
Bogue - *Boops boops*

Tapering body, subcylindrical at the front. Short snout, large eyes. The colouration is bluish or greenish on the back and silvery with golden streaks on the flanks. This fish is gregarious and rises towards the surface by night. The adults are herbivorous. Lives on rocky, detrital and sandy-muddy seabeds and among neptune grass from 3-5 to 350 metres. Measures up to 36 centimetres.

Dentex - *Dentex dentex*

Robust, deep and compressed body. Large head and wide mouth with big, canine teeth. The colouration is bluish grey with dark blotches on the flanks. The fins are shaded with pink. This fish lives alone and is a voracious predator of fish and octopus. Found close to rocky, sandy seabeds and neptune grass from 15 to 150 metres. Measures up to 100 metres.

White seabream - *Diplodus sargus sargus*

Fish with oval, very tall and compressed body. The colouration is silvery grey, darker on the snout. Has 8-9 alternating light and dark stripes on the flanks. The rear edge of the caudal is black. Forms small groups that remain near the seabed. Lives on sandy and rocky seabeds near rocks from 2-3 to more than 50 metres. Measures up to 45 centimetres.

Sharpsnout seabream - *Diplodus puntazzo*

Fish with oval body and pointed snout. When slightly open, the mouth reveals large, dark incisors. The colouration is silvery grey. Has 5-7 alternating light and dark streaks on the flanks. The caudal peduncle is dark. Is gregarious, and the young may also venture in brackish water. Lives on rocky seabeds from 2-3 to 150 metres. Measures up to 60 centimetres.

Two-banded seabream - *Diplodus vulgaris*

Oval, deep and compressed body. The mouth is slightly protractile and has strong front incisors and lateral molars. The colouration is brownish or greenish grey. A distinctive dark band can be observed on the nape. The tail peduncle has a dark mark extending along the rays of the dorsal and anal fins. Lives on rocky and sandy seabeds and among neptune grass from 2-3 to 130 metres. Measures up to 45 centimetres.

Striped seabream - *Lithognathus mormyrus*

Elongated, compressed body which terminates in a long and pointed snout. The colouration is silvery grey, darker on the back. Has 14-15 dark vertical streaks on the flanks. This fish feeds on small benthic invertebrates which it drives out by digging in the sediments. Lives on sandy seabeds and near neptune grass from 2-3 to 80 metres. Measures up to 55 centimetres.

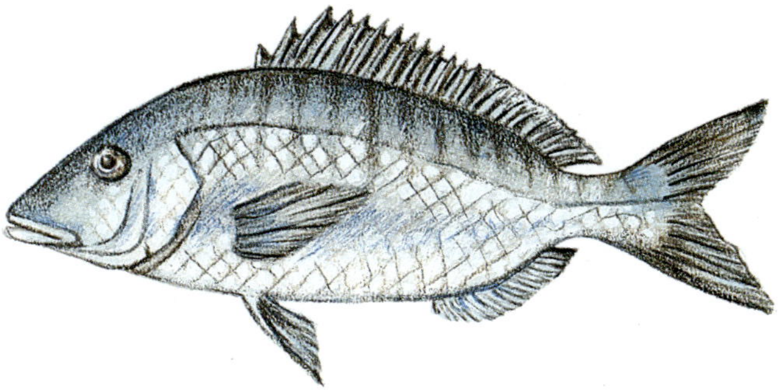

Saddled Seabream - *Oblada melanura*

Fish with elongated, not very compressed body. The snout is short, the eyes large, the colouration is silvery grey with bluish reflexes on the back. Has a distinctive large black saddle-shaped spot with white edges on the caudal peduncle. Found on rocky seabeds and near neptune grass from 3-5 to 40 metres. Measures up to 30 centimetres.

Pandora - *Pagellus erythrinus*

The body is oval and compressed and terminates in a pointed snout; the profile of the head is straight. The eyes are small. The colouration is bright pink with small bluish spots on the upper part of the flanks. The rear margin of the operculum is reddish. Feeds mainly on small benthic fish and invertebrates and alga. Lives on rocky, detrital and sandy-muddy seabed from 15-20 to 300 metres. Measures up to 60 centimetres.

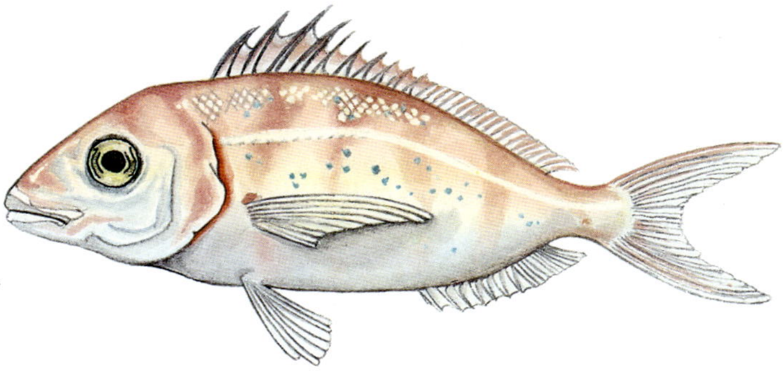

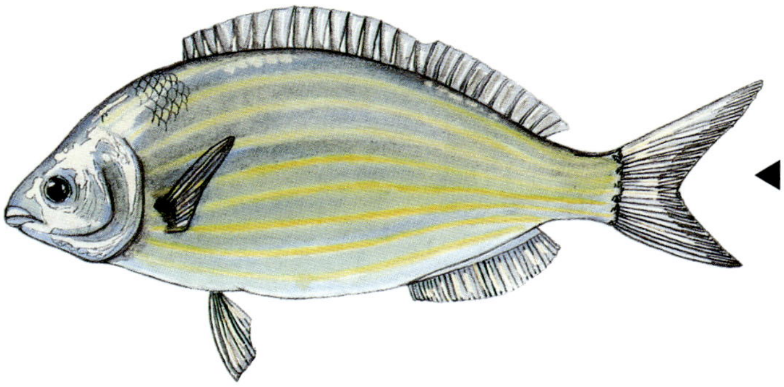

Salema - *Sarpa salpa*

Elongated, compressed body. Small head and rounded snout. The mouth has thick lips. The colouration is bluish with 10-11 longitudinal golden stripes that are particularly evident in large specimens. When young this fish feeds on small crustaceans, while the adult is mainly herbivorous. Lives near rocky and sandy seabeds rich in vegetation from 2-3 to 20 metres. Measures up to 50 centimetres.

Gilt-head bream - *Sparus aurata*

The body is oval, tall and laterally compressed. The head is powerful and the mouth has large molar-formed teeth. The colouration is grey with golden and silvery reflexes. The eyes are united by a golden band. It can live in water with variable salinity and feeds on crustaceans and molluscs. Found on sandy and detrital seabeds from 2-3 to 40 metres. Measures up to 70 centimetres.

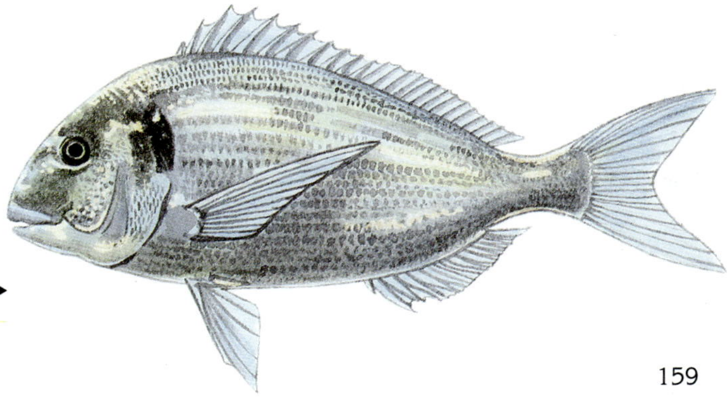

Black seabream - *Spondyliosoma cantharus*

Fish with oval, compressed body. The snout is pointed, but short. The mouth is slightly oblique and points upwards. The dorsal is very long, but can be completely bent along the back. The colouration is brownish grey with metallic reflections and golden, longitudinal streaks. It often forms large groups and feeds on alga and crustaceans. Lives on rocky or sandy seabeds or near neptune grass from 10-15 to 150 metres. Measures up to 60 centimetres.

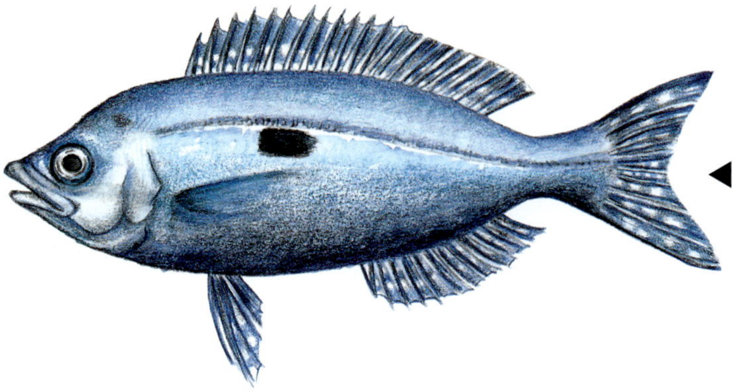

Centracanthidae
Blotched picarel - *Spicara maena*

The body is elongated and somewhat compressed. Slightly convex on the back of the head. The upper jaw is very protractile. The colouration is bluish or greenish grey on the back; the flanks are silvery with a rectangular, dark mark. Feeds both on small crustaceans and molluscs and algae. Lives on rocky seabeds or among neptune grass from 5-7 to 170 metres. Measures up to 25 centimetres.

Picarel - *Spicara flexuosa*

Fish with elongated, somewhat compressed body. The upper jaw is very protractile. The colouration is yellowish or bluish or greenish grey on the back; the edges of the dorsal fin is dark. A rectangular, black mark can be observed on the flanks. Feeds mainly on small crustaceans living on the seabed. Found on sandy and muddy seabeds from 5-7 to 130 metres. Measures up to 20 centimetres.

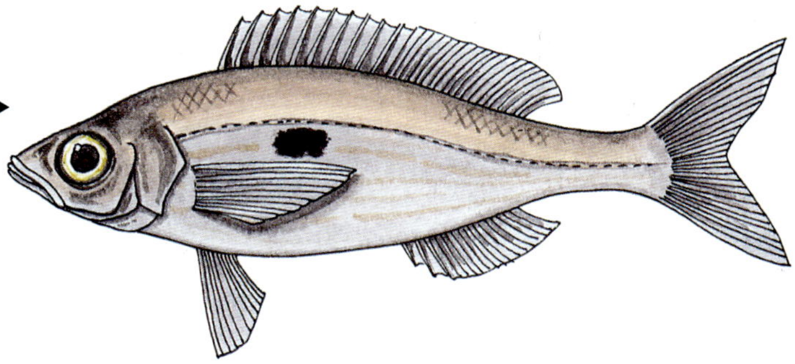

Sciaenidae family
Brown meagre - *Sciaena umbra*

The body is powerful with slightly arched back. The mouth points downwards and there are five pores on the front edge of the bottom jaw. The colouration is brownish with golden reflections. The ventral and anal fins have white front margins. Lives on rocky seabeds and near neptune grass from 5-7 to 180 metres. Measures up to 70 centimetres.

Shy drum - *Umbrina cirrosa*

Fish with tall, compressed body with straight ventral profile. The mouth is small and points downwards. Has a short barbel below the bottom jaw. The colouration is silvery grey with dark, oblique streaks on the flanks and back. This species is omnivorous and feeds on fish, invertebrates and algae. Lives on rocky, sandy and detrital seabeds from 10-15 to 100 metres. Measures up to 100 centimetres.

Mullidae family
Red mullet - *Mullus barbatus*

The body is slightly compressed. The head is short, with a pair of barbels under the lower jaw, which are as long as the pectoral fins. The front profile of the head is almost vertical. The colouration is pink or reddish. Lives on muddy or detrital seabed from 10 to 500 metres. Measures up to 30 centimetres.

Striped red mullet - *Mullus surmuletus*

Fish with somewhat compressed body. The head is short with a pair of barbels under the chin, that are longer than the pectoral fins. The front profile of the head is clearly oblique.
The colouration is reddish with a dark band that extends from the eyes to the tail. Lives on rocky or detrital seabeds from 10 to 500 metres. Measures up to 40 centimetres.

Pomacentridae family
Damselfish - *Chromis chromis*

Fish with oval, compressed body. The head is short, the mouth small. Adults are brownish, while the young are an almost fluorescent shade of blue. Forms dense schools above meadows or rocky projections. Lives near rocky seabeds and close to meadows from 4-5 to 50 metres. Measures up to 15 centimetres.

Sphyraenidae family
Barracuda - *Sphyraena sphyraena*

Tapering, compact body, laterally compressed. The head is long and the snout pointed; the lower jaw is prominent.
The two dorsal fins are quite separate. The colouration is bluish grey on the back with numerous dark vertical bands on the flanks. Feeds on fish and sometimes also on squid and deep-sea crustaceans. Lives in open waters from the surface to 100 metres. Measures up to 165 centimetres.

Labridae family
Rainbow wrasse - *Coris julis (male and female)*

Fish with slender, tapering body. Females have brown or dark red backs and a light band on the flanks. Males are bigger, and have bluish green backs and blue-edged red or orange bands on the flanks. The colour difference is associated with the sex inversion typical of the species. Lives on rocky seabeds and near neptune grass from 2-3 to 120 metres. Measures up to 25 centimetres.

♀

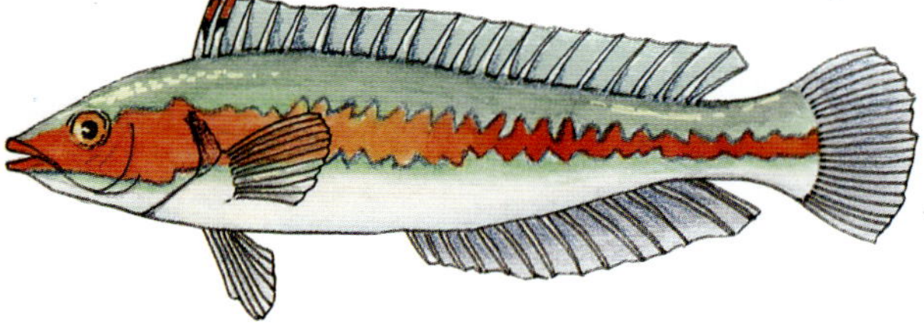

♂

Labridae family

Cuckoo wrasse - *Labrus bimaculatus*

Fish with elongated, somewhat compressed body. The head is longer than the body is tall. Young and female specimens are orange or red with three dark spots on the back. Males are brownish with greenish blue head and have bluish marks on back and flanks. In the reproduction period they build nests of algae in neptune grass meadows. Lives on rocky seabeds and near meadows from 3-5 to 200 metres. Measures up to 40 centimetres.

Green wrasse - *Labrus viridis*

Fish with elongated body and a long, pointed snout.
The colouration is usually greenish with a lighter belly. A white stripe often runs on the flanks from head to tail. Feeds on crustaceans, molluscs and small fish. Lives on rocky seabeds and near neptune grass from 4-5 to 50 metres. Measures up to 45 centimetres.

Five-spotted wrasse - *Symphodus roissali*

Fish with stout, oval body. The head is as long as the body is tall, the snout is short. Females are brownish or greenish-brown. Males are reddish brown or green with yellow and greenish spots and red lips. Both have a spot on the caudal peduncle and five spots on the dorsal. Feeds on invertebrates, including small sea-urchins. Lives on rocky seabeds and near neptune grass from 2-3 to 30 metres. Measures up to 20 centimetres.

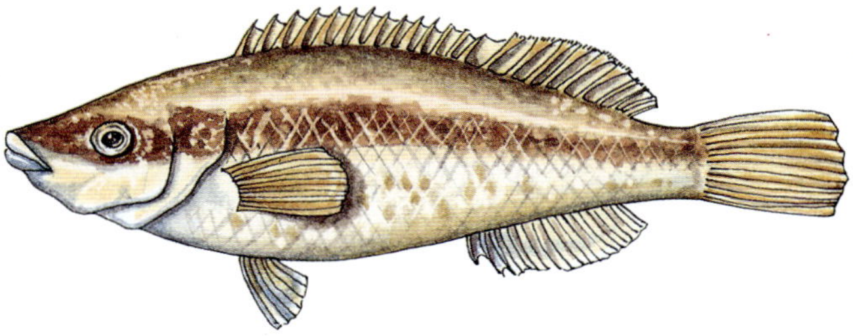

Peacock wrasse - *Symphodus (Crenilabrus) tinca*

The body is oval and somewhat compressed. The snout is elongated and pointed. Young and female specimens are greenish or brownish grey with white lips. Males are greenish, bluish or yellowish green with rows of small red spots, the upper part of the head is blue. The male builds nests with algae. Lives on rocky seabeds and near neptune grass from 2-3 to 80 metres. Measures up to 44 centimetres.

Ocellated wrasse - *Symphodus ocellatus*

Fish with oval, very compressed body. The head and snout are short. Females are yellowish brown with green or pink streaks on the flanks. Males are green, orange or brownish with two dark longitudinal streaks and bluish spots. Both sexes have a spot on the peduncle and one on the operculum. The male builds several nests in the centre of his territory. Lives on rocky seabeds rich in algae from 5 to 30 metres. Measures up to 15 centimetres.

Axillary wrasse - *Symphodus (Crenilabrus) mediterraneus*

Fish with oval, stout body. The head and snout are short. Young and female specimens are a yellowish, marbled brown. Males are bluish, brownish or greenish grey with longitudinal rows of small bright points. Both sexes have a spot on the peduncle and one on the operculum. Feeds mainly on molluscs. Lives mainly close to neptune grass meadows from 2-3 to 40-50 metres. Measures up to 18 centimetres.

Ornate wrasse - *Thalassoma pavo*

The body is elongated and compressed with oval, pointed head. The mouth is small with large lips. The lobes of the caudal are elongated. Females are greenish brown with a dark lateral band. Males have red heads with bluish streaks and a red vertical band behind the operculum. Usually forms small groups with one male and a few females. Lives on rocky seabeds and near neptune grass meadows from 2-3 to 150 metres in the southernmost regions of the Mediterranean. Measures up to 25 centimetres.

Pearly razor fish - *Xyrichthys novacula*

The body is very compressed; the head is very tall and the profile almost vertical in adult specimens. The dorsal fin extends along almost the whole body. Feeds on invertebrates and small fish. Curiously, if threatened, this fish buries itself. Lives on sandy and muddy seabeds and near neptune grass meadows from 4-5 to 50 metres. Measures up to 30 centimetres.

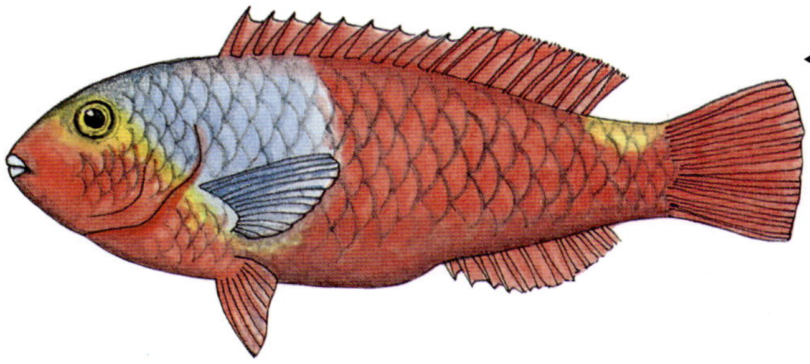

Scaridae family
Parrotfish - *Sparisoma cretense*

The body is ovoid, elongated and somewhat compressed. The mouth is terminal and has strong jaws and beak-like teeth. Females are reddish, males brownish or greenish. Feeds on molluscs, crustaceans and algae that it scrapes off the rocks. Lives on rocky seabeds and near neptune grass meadows from 3-4 to 40-50 metres. Measures up to 50 centimetres.

Uranoscopidae family
Star-gazer - *Uranoscopus scaber*

The body is solid and slightly compressed at the rear. The head is large and flat towards the back. Has a retractile tentacle inside the mouth, that serves as bait for small fish. The colouration is greyish brown. Lives on sandy and muddy seabeds from 15 to 250 metres, where it buries itself so only the eyes and bait tentacle emerge. Measures up to 35 centimetres.

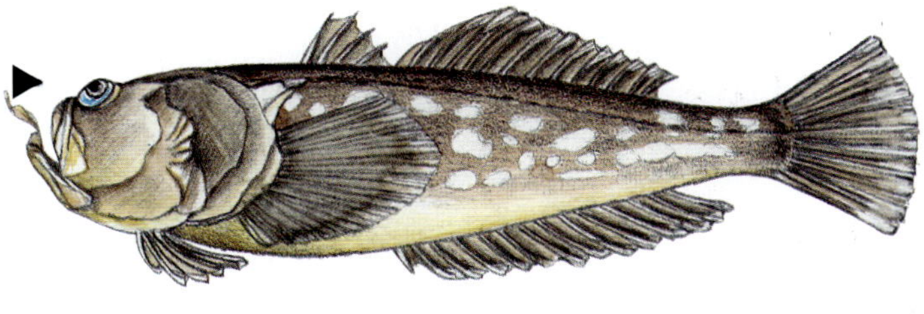

Trypterygiidae family
Black faced blenny - *Trypterigion tripteronotus*

The body is elongated and spindle-shaped and the snout pointed. The dorsal is divided in three parts. The colouration is greyish brown. During the mating season the males are red with black head. Territorial by habit, this fish is found on rocky, poorly-illuminated seabeds from 1-2 to 8-10 metres. Measures up to 8 centimetres.

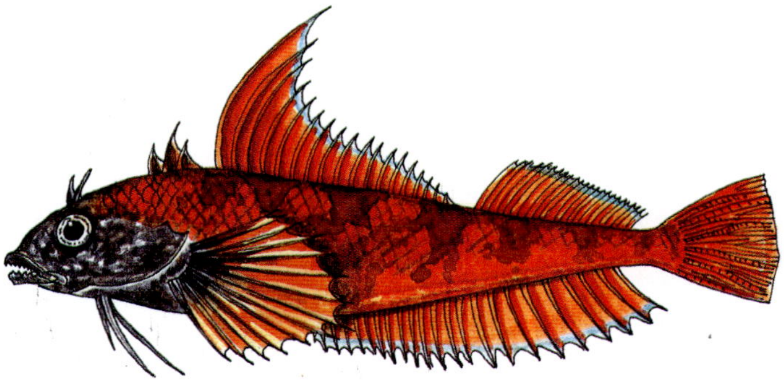

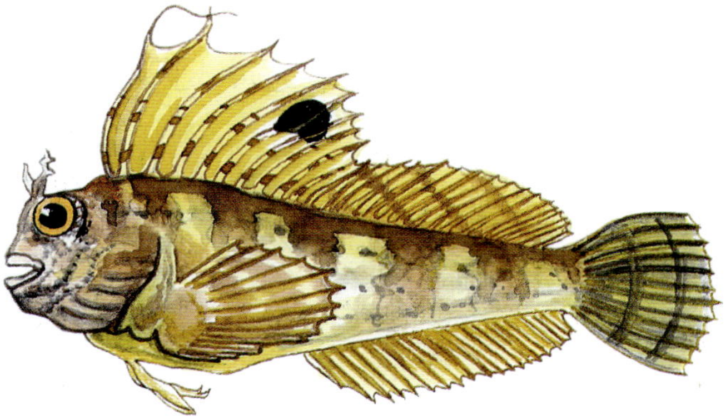

Blennidae family
Butterfly blenny - *Blennius ocellaris*

The body of this blenny is elongated. The head is stocky with rounded profile. Recognized by the large dorsal fin with a big ocellar mark. Feeds on small benthic invertebrates. Lives on rocky and detrital seabeds from 30 to 200 metres. Measures up to 20 centimetres.

Peacock blenny - *Lipophrys pavo*

This blenny has an elongated body, the snout is short and the front profile almost vertical. Adult males have a characteristic crest on the nape. The colouration is greenish with vertical dark blue-edged bands. Lives on rocky or sandy seabeds rich in algae from the surface to 5-7 metres. Measures up to 13 centimetres.

Tompot blenny - *Parablennius gattorugine*

This large blenny has a stocky head and oblique-profiled snout. Long frayed tentacles over the eyes. The colouration is brownish with dark vertical bands. The male is territorial and defends the eggs fiercely during the mating season. Lives on rocky seabeds and neptune grass meadows from 2-3 to 30-35 metres. Measures up to 30 centimetres.

Striped blenny - *Parablennius rouxi*

The body of this blenny is particularly tapering; the head is small and the front profile of the snout is almost vertical. Feathered tentacle over each eye. The colouration is whitish with a dark longitudinal band. Usually territorial, it lives in the cavities left by molluscs or in the tubes of encrusting worms. Lives on rocky seabeds from 2-3 to 40 metres. Measures up to 8 centimetres.

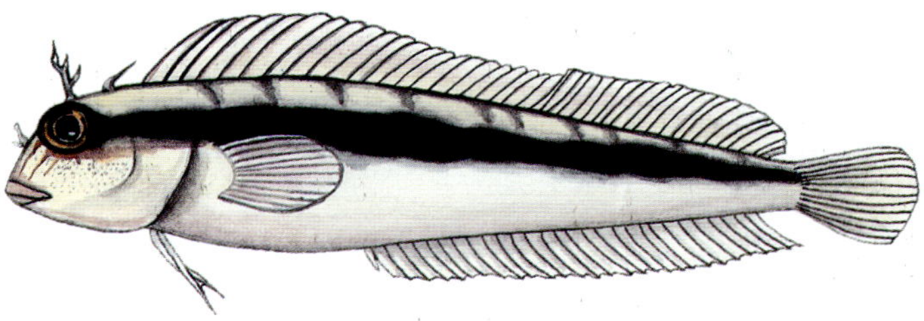

Ammodytidae family
Sand-eel - *Gymnammodites cicerellus*

The body is elongated and terminates in a long and pointed snout. The upper jaw is protractile. No ventral fins.
The colouration is brown with greenish reflections on the back, the head is dark blue and the belly silvery. During the night it hides in the sediments of the seabed. Lives on detrital seabeds from a few metres depth to 120 metres. Measures up to 17 centimetres.

Callionymidae family
Dragonet - *Callionymus lyra*

The body is elongated. The triangular head is wide and flattened. In male specimens the first dorsal is very tall. No scales on the body. The colouration is yellowish brown; females have greenish blotches and males bluish ones during the mating season. The males are very aggressive and territorial towards other specimens of their kind. Lives on sandy and muddy seabeds from 10-15 to 400 metres. Measures up to 30

Gobiidae family
Red-mouthed goby - *Gobius cruentatus*

Goby with elongated body; the head is large and the mouth wide. Lips and cheek are bright red. The colouration is reddish brown with irregular blotches. Feeds on small crustaceans and molluscs. Lives on rocky and sandy seabeds and near neptune grass from 10 to 40 metres. Measures up to 18 centimetres.

Buchicchi's goby - *Gobius bucchichi*

Elongated body covered in rough scales. The body is large with bulging cheek. The colouration is yellowish light grey with small dark spots, some on the eyes. Lives on sandy-muddy seabeds and near neptune grass meadows alongside *Anemonia sulcata*, among which tentacles it can seek refuge if threatened without being nettled. Measures up to 10 centimetres.

Black goby - *Gobius niger jozo*

Goby with subcylindrical body with a large, slightly flattened head and wide mouth with thick lips. The first dorsal of male specimens has long filamentous rays. The colouration is greyish black with a black mark on the dorsal. Feeds on various types of invertebrates, including insect larvae when it ventures into brackish waters. Lives on sandy, muddy and detrital seabeds from a few metres to 80. Measures up to 15 centimetres.

Scombridae family
Little tunny - *Euthynnus alletteratus*

The body is robust and spindle-shaped, without scales except for the front of the body and the lateral line. The colouration is bluish on the back, with an irregular pattern of streaks and blotches, and silvery white on flanks and belly. Feeds on small oceanic fish as anchovies and sardines. Lives in coastal waters from the surface to 50 metres. Measures up to 1metre.

Bonito - *Sarda sarda*

Small tuna with tapering body. The mouth is very wide and the two dorsal fins are set very close together. The colouration is metallic blue with dark streaks on the back and silvery on the flanks and belly. Forms large schools that mainly hunt shoals of oceanic fish. Lives in coastal waters from the surface to 200 metres. Measures up to 90 centimetres.

Chub mackerel - *Scomber japonicus*

The body is elongated and rounded, and terminates in a pointed snout. The eyes, of which front and rear is covered by a fatty eyelids, are distinctive. The colouration is greenish blue streaked with black on the back and silvery yellow on the lower part of the flanks and underneath, characterized by small dark spots. Feeds on anchovies and oceanic invertebrates. Lives in shoals in oceanic and coastal waters from the surface to 300 metres. Measures up to 50 centimetres.

Albacore - *Thunnus alalunga*

The body is tapering, with pointed head and large eyes. The first dorsal is taller and more developed than the second. The pectorals are very long; when extended they reach beyond the dorsals. The colouration is metallic blue on the back and white on the flanks and belly. The dorsals and anals are yellow. Feeds on oceanic fish and squid. Lives in oceanic waters; its diffusion is determined by the temperature. Measures up to 1 metre.

Xiphiidae family
Swordfish - *Xiphias gladius*

The body is robust and characterized by a snout that terminates in an elongated rostrum shaped like a sword. The colouration is brownish black on the back and flanks and light underneath. This fish migrates over long distances, moving from the feeding areas to the warmer waters where it mates. Lives in oceanic and coastal waters from the surface to more than 600 metres. Measures up to 4.5 metres.

Scophthalmidae family
Brill - *Scophthalmus rhombus*

Typical flatfish with eyes on the left side. The body is oval and wide; the mouth is terminal and very oblique. The first rays of the dorsal have characteristically frayed edges. The colouration is brown or greyish with numerous small dark spots and tiny white points. Feeds on small fish and invertebrates, which it also catches at some distance from the seabed. Lives on sandy seabeds from 10-15 to 120 metres. Measures up to 75 centimetres.

Bothidae family
Wide-eyed flounder - *Bothus podas*

Flatfish with eyes on the left side, set obliquely. The front profile of the head is almost rectilinear, especially in mature males. The colouration is brownish with numerous different coloured blotches, from white to bluish to yellow. Feeds on small fish and invertebrates. Lives on sandy-muddy and detrital seabeds from 10-15 to 400 metres. Measures up to 45 centimetres.

Soleidae
Sole - *Solea vulgaris*

Oval flatfish with eyes on the right side. The snout is rounded and forms a fleshy lobe. The mouth is small and slightly curved. The colouration varies from greyish to reddish brown with dark spots. The tip of the pectoral is dark. Feeds on worms, molluscs and crustaceans. Lives on sandy and muddy seabeds from 5-10 to 200 metres. Measures up to 70 centimetres.

Balistidae family
Triggerfish - *Balistes carolinensis*

Wide, oval body, highly compressed and covered in thick, rough scales. The snout is pointed, the mouth has strong incisors. The first dorsal fin has large spiny rays that can be blocked in erect position. The colouration is blue grey and marbled with spots on the fins. Lives near rocky seabeds from 4-5 to 100 metres. Measures up to 45 centimetres.

Molidae family
Sunfish - *Mola mola*

Unmistakable fish with oval, very compressed and tall body. The dorsal and anal fins are very developed and join in the rear in a kind of caudal fin. Brownish with light and silvery-grey blotches on the flanks. Feeds on jellyfish, coelenterates and fish larvae. Lives in oceanic waters between the surface and 360 metres. Measures up to 3 metres.

168 An encounter with a turtle (Caretta caretta) *in the Mediterranean is always a memorable event, even if it is not always easy to follow them in the water.*

In March 1995 my second book had just been published when, purely by chance, I met Diana Hampson (of St. Andrew's Divers Cove) in London. It was she who suggested I should write an Underwater Guide to the Maltese islands.
This book is the direct result of that conversation - and I only hope that it is worthy of the faith so many people have put in me.
Of course, it would not have been possible if it had not been for the assistance and patience of a great many people - not least the many, many divers who tolerated me, my cameras and my jokes during their own short stay in Malta.
I only wished there were sufficient room to include a photograph of all of them within these pages because theirs is the real credit - any errors and omissions are strictly down to me.
To Diana, and all those whose names appear below I offer a very big "thank you":

MALTA - Strand Diving Services: Jonathan Callus, Richard Lewis, Alex & Andrea Naplava, Simon & Hermi Sammut and Lawrence Spagnol. Sport Diving Ltd: Ray Ciancio, Brian Dollimore and Kenneth Bonnici.

GOZO - St Andrew's Divers Cove: Mark Busuttil, George & Maryanne Camilleri, Dino, Joe Gaffiero, German Rosjas, Christian Schay, Gary Squires and Toni Tatarski.

UNITED KINGDOM: Steven Greenaway - Greenaway Marine. David & Jennifer Knight - Cameras Underwater. And, of course, my son Daniel - for carrying my spare camera!

PHOTOGRAPHIC CREDITS

Kurt Arrigo: pages 20 C, 31 G, 63 I, 71 F, 94 B, 95 (D, F), 130 (C, D), 131 G, 134 F, 139 F; Massimo Borchi: pages 7 (E, F), 9 (E, H), 12 B; Stefano Cellai: page 9 G; Anne Conway: pages 12 D, 13 (G, E, F); Michael Darmanin: page 19 D; Andrea Ghisotti: pages 16 A, 20 (E, F, G), 22 F, 35 F, 43 F, 49 F, 63 E, 67 G, 70 D, 75 H, 78 D, 79 G, 82 D, 86 D, 87 G, 91 G, 95 E, 99 H, 103 E, 106 D, 111 (G, H), 114 C, 119 I, 123 E, 131 I; Gilles Martin/Ag. Speranza: pages 8 B, 12 A; M. Mastrorillo/Ag. Sie: pages 4 A, 11 D; Mario Micallef: pages 17 F, 20 A, 38 D, 39 (E, G), 46 D, 47, 62 B, 63 G, 71 G, 90 B, 91 E, 94 C, 110 A, 111 (E, F), 114 (B, D), 115 E; Ned Middleton: pages 5 (C, D), 16 B, 18 C, 20 D, 22 B, 22 E, 26-27, 30 (A, B, C), 31 (E, F), 34 (A, B, C, D), 35 (E, G), 38 (A, B, C), 39 H, 42 (A, B, E), 46 C, 48 A, 49 (G, H), 52 (B, C, D), 53 E, 62 (A, C, D), 63 H, 66 (A, B), 70 (A, B, C, E), 74 (A, B, C, D), 78 (A, B, C), 82 (A, B), 83 (E, G), 86 (A, B, C), 90 (A, C, D), 98 (A, B, C, E), 102 (A, C), 106 (A, B, C), 110 (B, C, D), 114 A, 118, 119 E, 122, 126, 127 (G, H, I), 130 (A, B, E), 134, 135 E, 138, 139 H; Mauro Panci/Ag. Sie: pages 6 C, 8 C, 9 F; Vincenzo Paolillo: pages 19 G, 20 B, 31 H, 35 H, 42 C, 43 G, 48 G, 49 E, 67 (E, F, H), 71 H, 75 G, 79 H, 83 F, 91 F, 95 (G, H), 98 D, 99 G, 102 B, 103 (F, G), 107 E, 115 F, 119 (F, H), 123 (F, G, H), 134 G, 139 (E, G); Roberto Rinaldi: pages 1, 2-3, 4 B, 6 (A, B), 7 G, 8 A, 10 (A, B, C), 11 F, 16 C, 17 (D, E), 18 (A, B), 19 (E, F), 22 A, 22 C, 168; P. G. Sclarandis/Ag. Sie: pages 8 D, 11 E; Angelo Tondini/Ag. Focus Team: pages 12 C; Vaisse/Ag. HOA QUI Speranza: page 11 G; C. Valentin/Ag. Speranza: page 6 D; Alberto Vanzo: pages 22 D, 30 D, 39 F, 42 D, 43 H, 48 (B, D), 53 F, 63 F, 66 (C, D), 71 I, 75 (E, F), 79 (E, F), 82 C, 83 G, 87 (E, F), 102 D, 103 H, 107 (F, G), 115 G, 119 G, 127 (E, F), 131 (E, H), 134 H; Imperial War Museum: pages 46 (A, B), 52 A.

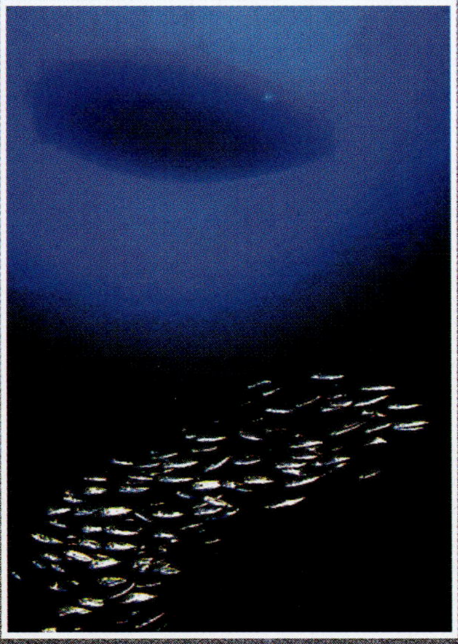

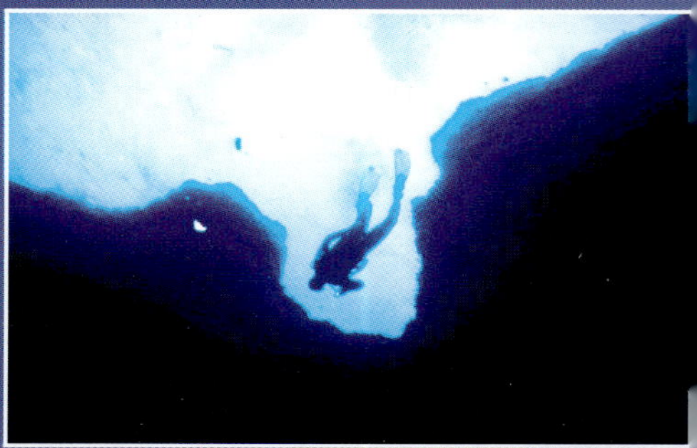

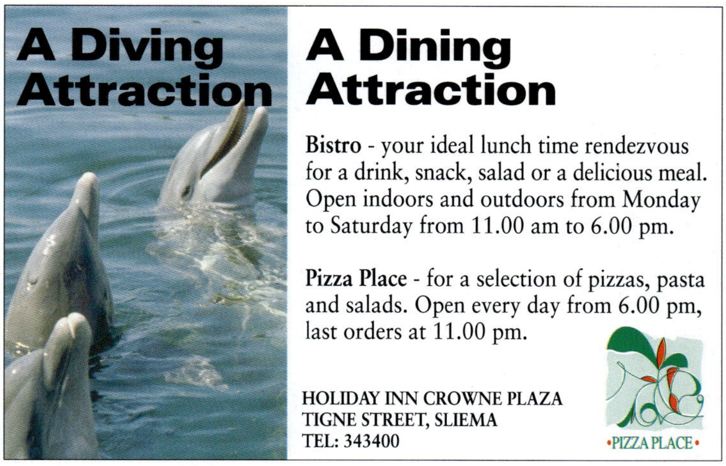

Comino – the diving experience!

Comino *is the smallest island of the Maltese archipelago. It is situated between the two main islands of Malta and Gozo. Both islands can be reached in approximately 20 minutes by our own boats. Comino is also known for its beautiful and interesting diving sites. In fact, a good eight diving sites can be found around this island. A startling sea scape of caves and grottos lies below the water level making it a favourite for scuba divers and snorklers.*

The Comino Hotel & Bungalows are the only inhabited buildings on the island . At the hotel one finds a very well equipped diving venture with professional instructors including PADI courses. But diving is not the only sport to be found at the hotel. In fact you can also find a water sports centre and ten sand tennis courts.

You may wish to spend the day relaxing at one of the small private sandy beaches or by the large swimming pool. There is also a pool for children. Or you may prefer to enjoy a country walk, exploring this island where traffic is unknown. Spend a perfect day in Comino.

COMINO HOTELS

tel: 529821 • fax: 529826 • e-mail address: comino@digigate.net

Internet address: http://www.digigate.net/cominohotel

GOZO the beautiful

GOZO Village HOLIDAYS

Villagg Tal-Fanal

Gozo, the smaller, sister island of Malta, has a history, beauty and charm unique in the Mediterranean.

Just nine miles by five and surrounded by a crystal clear sea, it is a haven of hospitality.

Gozo Village Holidays have lovingly restored a variety of centuries old farmhouses using the materials and skills of their ancestors. The mellow limestone walls and the flagstone floors are complemented by antique furniture, stone arches and wooden beams. Discreet but modern kitchens and bathrooms complete the comfort. Each window presents its own rural or sea views. A friendly maid keeps them spotlessly clean; and our staff are on call 24 hours a day for assistance and advice. Most farmhouses come with gardens and pools.

Gozo Village Holidays also offers"a Village within a Village" at Ghasri – a cluster of maisonettes built around a large landscaped swimming pool. Each unit is superbly finished with typical farmhouse style furniture, stone arches and discreet but modern kitchens. You can feel the atmosphere of the life of a typical Gozitan village on your doorstep.

We welcome you to a new concept in complete relaxation.

A few kilometers away is Ta' Frenc Restaurant, a converted farmhouse with a beautiful garden for al fresco dining, also under the same management.

11, Capuchin's Street, Victoria, VCT 10, Gozo — Malta.
Tel: (+356) 563520 Fax: (+356) 558397

YOU HAVE TO SEE IT TO BELIEVE IT!

Island of Joy

GOZO 360°

A spectacular sound and vision experience which brings the island to life!

in – ENGLISH, FRENCH, GERMAN, ITALIAN, DANISH, DUTCH, SPANISH and MALTESE.

MONDAY to SATURDAY 10.30, 11.30, 12.30, 13.30, 14.30, 15.30,16.30
SUNDAYS & PUBLIC HOLIDAYS: 10.30, 11.30, 12.30, 13.30

CITADEL THEATRE

Castle Hill, Rabat, Gozo Tel: 559955/6 Fax:559957

· OUR LAGER ·

The time is now - Kinetic energy.
SEIKO
AUTOMATIC
GENERATING SYSTEM
From the undisputed leaders in watch technology,
the world's first quartz watch to work without a battery.
SEIKO
AVAILABLE ONLY FROM AUTHORISED DEALERS